Modernizing Main Street

[Modernizing Main Street]

Architecture and Consumer Culture in the New Deal

Gabrielle Esperdy

The University of Chicago Press
Chicago and London

Gabrielle Esperdy is an architectural historian and associate professor of architecture at the New Jersey Institute of Technology.

Publisher's note: *Modernizing Main Street* is a volume in the series Center Books on American Places, created and directed by the Center for American Places.

The University of Chicago Press, Chicago 60637
The University of Chicago Press, Ltd., London
© 2008 by The University of Chicago
All rights reserved. Published 2008
Printed in the United States of America

17 16 15 14 13 12 11 10 09 08   1 2 3 4 5

ISBN-13: 978-0-226-21800-7 (cloth)
ISBN-10: 0-226-21800-7 (cloth)

Library of Congress Cataloging-in-Publication Data

Esperdy, Gabrielle M.
  Modernizing Main Street: architecture and consumer culture in the New Deal / Gabrielle Esperdy.
    p.   cm.
  Includes bibliographical references and index.
  ISBN-13: 978-0-226-21800-7 (cloth: alk. paper)
  ISBN-10: 0-226-21800-7 (cloth: alk. paper)   1. Storefronts—United States—History—20th century.   2. Commercial buildings—United States—History—20th century.   3. New Deal, 1933–1939.   4. Consumption (Economics)—United States—History—20th century.   I. Title.
  NA6225.E87   2008
  725′.2097309043—dc22
                                                                    2007023927

♾ The paper used in this publication meets the minimum requirements of the American National Standard for Information Sciences—Permanence of Paper for Printed Library Materials, ANSI Z39.48-1992.

This book is for Julie.

[**ACKNOWLEDGMENTS**]

This book began life in a seminar on the modern landscape at the Graduate Center of the City University of New York, which was then located on West Forty-second Street just east of Times Square. The "crossroads of the world" was an epicenter of building modernization in the 1930s, and in the 1990s, when I first started looking at storefronts, it was thrilling to walk along Broadway and Seventh Avenue and see bits and pieces of structural glass and extruded aluminum still visible beneath six decades worth of commercial accretion. I'm not sure if it is possible, or even necessary, to thank an entire city, but New York has my undying gratitude for being a source of constant inspiration and continual delight.

Less abstractly, my friends, family, and colleagues have helped in ways both large and small, both materially and emotionally. At the CUNY Graduate Center, where I began this research; at Pratt Institute, where I continued it; and at NJIT, where I finally finished the book, I received generous scholarly and professional counsel from Rosemarie Bletter, Kevin Murphy, Deborah Gans, and James Dart, among many others. I am especially grateful to NJIT University provost Priscilla Nelson for providing generous financial support for this publication.

Thanks are also due to those architectural historians who I am fortunate enough to count among my friends. Jesús Escobar, Jonathan Massey, Joanna Merwood, Andy Shanken, and David Smiley read pieces of the book and offered critical insights, usually at critical moments. I am also grateful to those anonymous reviewers whose feedback helped make this a better book.

Robert Devens at the University of Chicago Press and George Thompson at the Center for American Places, as well as their staffs, offered good-natured support and boundless patience as I labored to turn my draft manuscript into a final book. Their task was made a little easier, I hope, because I was able to rely as well on my friends in the book world: Anne Savarese and Louise Quayle provided sound advice about the travails of academic publishing and helped see me through all stages of the process.

Anita Cooney, my dear friend and architectural co-conspirator, deserves special thanks for keeping me sane and focused on more than one occasion when I was ready to toss the manuscript out a window. For so much listening and reading, I am grateful.

Finally, and most importantly, this book would never have happened without the steadfastness, succor, and support of my beloved partner, Julie Hertzog. Though she logged more miles on Main Street than any New Yorker should have to endure, from Maine to California her belief in me never wavered. As the poet said, "We have circled and circled till we have arrived home again, we two, we have voided all but freedom and all but our own joy." Thank you for everything, Miss Julie.

The Warner Brothers musical *Gold Diggers of 1933* opens with a close-up of Ginger Rogers draped in shimmering silver dollars. As she begins to sing, the camera pulls back to reveal coin-clad chorines and a stage filled with stacks and stacks of oversize coinage, both wittily reflecting the buoyant optimism of her lyrics:

> We're in the money, we're in the money;
> We've got a lot of what it takes to get along!
> We're in the money, the sky is sunny,
> Old Man Depression you are through, you done us wrong.
> We never see a headline about breadlines today.
> And when we see the landlord we can look that guy right in the eye
> We're in the money, come on, my honey,
> Let's lend it, spend it, send it rolling along![1]

"We're in the Money" must have seemed like the ultimate escapist fantasy when *Gold Diggers* was released in June 1933. With unemployment and economic stagnation at their height, Old Man Depression was far from through, and the movie audience knew it. Indeed, he soon comes crashing back into the film as the number ends abruptly with creditors shutting down the theater and seizing the costumes and sets for unpaid bills. Ginger, now stripped of her silver dollars, merely shrugs her shoulders and quips, "That's the Depression, dearie."

However much this climax reflects the cynical realism for which Warner Brothers was well-known in the early 1930s, it is possible that there was at least a modicum of sincerity in the song's sunny outlook. For only three months before the film's debut, Franklin Delano Roosevelt had assumed the presidency and there was anticipation across the United States that the much-heralded return to prosperity was finally on the horizon. Though Roosevelt had cautioned against placing too high a value on material wealth in his inaugural address, noting that "happiness lies not in the mere possession of money," Americans were surely hoping that the new president's New Deal would at least bring them a little closer to what Ginger Rogers was singing about.[2]

They were right, of course: much of the New Deal was intended to stimulate the lending and spending of money, to such a degree, in fact, that these transactions became potent symbols of social and economic recovery, and very nearly a patriotic duty. And that's what this book is about: how a New Deal program—one as deliberately popular in its appeal as a Ginger Rogers musical and just as sophisticated in its marshaling of financial, industrial, and artistic resources—devoted itself to lending and spending during the Great Depression. This book is also about what became of that money once the New Deal sent it rolling along.

As symbols, lending and spending are somewhat abstract and transitory: however much a bank loan, a car bought on credit, or a purchase from the local five-and-dime might have contributed to a return to prosperity in the 1930s, who really knew about it besides those involved in the transaction—banker, borrower, car dealer, car owner, salesclerk, and shopper? Certainly, the cumulative effect of all such loans and purchases registered in financial statements and sales receipts and, eventually, in local and national economic statistics, but how much confidence could a bunch of numbers inspire? National advertisers were insisting that "Wall Street may sell stocks, but Main Street is still buying goods."[3] But if Americans were to believe this, lending and spending were not enough. Though historians have recently revealed the value of local spending initiatives and "shopping for recovery" programs in the early 1930s, as the Depression wore on some sort of tangible evidence was required to serve as a physical manifestation of the return to prosperity.[4] That symbol emerged in the grimmest years of the Depression in an unlikely place: the Main Street storefront.

In 1934 the federal government estimated that there were 1.5 million stores operating in the United States. The majority were in the central business districts and principal commercial corridors of large cities and small towns, though increasingly they were also found on the rapidly developing roadsides of the urban periphery. Over the next ten years, financial institutions, merchants, and property owners lent and spent $5 billion to physically improve these stores. This represented an economic investment in not only individual buildings and businesses but, ultimately, in the country as a whole at a time when large-scale construction had almost ground to a halt and over 4 million building industry workers were unemployed.

Most of the money was spent on exterior renovations, especially new facades attached to the fronts of existing buildings. These "modernized" storefronts were usually fabricated of such machine-age materials as structural glass, enameled steel, glass blocks, and extruded aluminum. On Main Streets where breadlines and forgotten men were all too familiar, these storefronts offered a striking counterpoint, an image of modernity that was deliberately at odds with the dismal present because it symbolized a hopeful future. But while these storefronts appeared new and different, they quickly became commonplace and familiar, produced by a nationwide, government-sponsored modernization movement that was active in over eight thousand communities at its height. By the end of the decade, the effort to "modernize Main Street" was an unqualified success: the storefronts were on Fifth Avenue in New York, on Wilshire Boulevard in Los Angeles, and on virtually every Main Street in between.

In many cities and towns, storefronts modernized in the 1930s are still standing on Main Street to this day (fig. 0.1). And while most Americans recognize them, few realize the role they played in ameliorating the effects of the Great Depression. In fact, the significance of these storefronts has been almost entirely forgotten in the intervening decades, except by a handful of scholars and critics whose purview is broad enough to include an artifact as quotidian and commercial as the storefront. But these storefronts, and the movement that spawned them, deserve to be better known, for they have much to tell us about American culture in the Depression decade, when urbanism, consumerism, and modernism all converged on Main Street and thousands of storefronts embodied the vital concerns of the day.

Figure 0.1 West Main Street, Newark, Ohio, including the Brutalist-inspired Newark City Building, the modernized storefronts of the Sparta Restaurant and the Newark Coin Exchange, and Louis Sullivan's Home Building & Loan. (Photographs by the author, 1999.)

While discrete aspects of the modernized storefront are well documented, this book is a synthetic study that ties together their social, political, economic, and architectural dimensions. In the current literature, it is the modernized storefront's architectural dimensions that are best known. Because of their striking visual qualities, storefronts appear in books and articles about art deco and streamlined moderne design and in place-based studies of the 1930s.[5] When they are the work of well-known architects and industrial designers, the analysis is often detailed and related to the larger concerns of the Depression.[6] Preservation studies have also examined modernized storefronts, paying particular attention to the glass, metal, and other materials used in their construction. While most of these studies have looked at the challenges these materials present for contemporary conservation, several have also considered their relationship to the Depression-era building industry.[7] Bringing these formal and material considerations together, this book treats the storefronts as a cohesive group and places them in the context of the organized modernization movement that shaped their built reality.

The past several decades have also seen the emergence of several bodies of scholarship that, while not dealing with building modernization directly, provide an important starting point for understanding the influences that informed the movement. These include studies of interior decorating and design, commercial architecture, retail building typologies, and the American roadside, as well as sociological and historical examinations of the spaces and practices of shopping and consumerism. This work considers how marketing and advertising, gender and class, and the proliferation of corporate chains and automobiles have marked the constructed landscape, both social and physical, in the United States in the twentieth century.[8] As a unique intersection of consumer culture and building, the modernized storefront begs to be examined in relation to these issues.

The storefront's urban context is equally important to understanding its significance, especially since Main Street was the center of the nation's commercial life in the 1930s. A number of historical and geographic studies provide insight into the spatial patterns, urban images, civic values, and cycles of stasis and change that characterized the Main Street morphology before it modernized.[9] As these studies have shown, Main Street *was* downtown. It existed not only as a particular place, but as a social and economic phenomenon understood to have similar characteristics regardless of the size or scale of the community.

While today the term "Main Street" tends to refer exclusively to small-town America, in the 1930s it included the business and shopping districts of large cities as well. This is an important distinction, and one that is necessary to comprehend the development and scope of building modernization during the Depression. Though there is a prevailing contemporary view that Main Street was a backward-looking archetype that was nostalgic and tradition-bound, the historical record shows that the opposite was true.

In this respect, the work of historians who have utilized Joseph Schumpeter's idea of "creative destruction" to explain urban transformation in the early part of the twentieth century is especially useful when examining the modernization of Main Street in the 1930s.[10] Though the scale of transformation was smaller and the destruction wrought upon the physical landscape was much less intensive than that which cleared slums and built skyscrapers, the same dynamic interplay of economic and cultural forces was at work on Main Street. The impact of these forces are evident in Alison Isenberg's *Downtown America*, which charts the evolution of urban centers—small and large—over the course of the twentieth century and discusses, albeit briefly, the movement to modernize Main Street in the 1930s.[11] Isenberg recounts how real estate interests and members of the building industry deployed modernization to maintain property values and to stimulate building activity and material sales during the Depression, and she accurately identifies storefront modernization's preoccupations with consumer psychology and architectural style.[12]

To truly understand modernization in the 1930s, it is also necessary to situate the practice within the specific historical context that transformed it from a cyclical trend into an organized movement—Franklin Roosevelt's New Deal. On the surface, any connection between the federal government and the modernized storefront is obscure at best: storefronts are obviously commercial, as opposed to civic, and tied to the demands of the market and private enterprise, as opposed to public need. In addition, no federal agency actually modernized storefronts in the 1930s the way the Public Works Administration built courthouses and schools or the Treasury Department built post offices. Most studies examining the New Deal's impact on the constructed environment have focused on projects like these, in which the government was the direct builder, whether of urban housing projects and suburban subdivisions, bridges and highways, or playgrounds and parks.[13] But a broader notion of federal sponsorship reveals that even though the federal government did not build modernized storefronts, it was nonetheless directly responsible for them. In fact, given their widespread occurrence, they constitute a materially significant and highly symbolic portion of all New Deal building activity.

Though building modernization as a strategy to combat the building industry depression had been around for several years, the New Deal took the lead in 1934, following passage of the National Housing Act. As authorized in the legislation's Title I, the Federal Housing Administration (FHA) began insuring private lenders against losses on low-interest loans made for the modernization of existing residential and nonresidential buildings. At the same time, the FHA embarked on an ambitious public relations campaign intended to promote building modernization as a curative to the woes of the Depression: modernization would stimulate the building activity that would put money back into circulation and put people back to work; the modernized store would stimulate the shopping activity that put even more money back into circulation, especially from those who had previously been unemployed. Scholars have long recognized the importance of the 1934 National Housing Act, but most have overlooked the operations of this Modernization Credit Plan. Instead, they have examined Title II, which provided mortgage insurance for new residential construction and is considered by many as the prelude to the FHA's postwar mortgage guarantee program (the one that essentially underwrote the nation's suburban expansion). Even those who have examined the impact of Title I have tended to consider only the modernization of residential buildings, rather than the FHA's "Modernize Main Street" initiative.[14]

Relying on previously unexamined records at the National Archives, this book investigates that initiative and the widespread modernization movement it stimulated, revealing how and why it focused on the Main Street storefront. It begins by exploring how Main Street emerged in the popular imagination in the early part of the twentieth century as an embodiment of an urbanistic and cultural ideal, an iconic locale that was frequently at odds with its local reality by the 1930s. By then Main Street had been forced to confront decentralization and shifting retail patterns, including the development of the shopping strip and the rise of corporate chains. Though Main Street cherished its self-image as a bastion of community-minded, small-scale enterprise—the little merchant—its dominant booster culture insisted this image be redefined for the twentieth century. At a moment when the cultural lag between the nation's largest cities and its smallest towns was collapsing, Main Street viewed itself in the same league as New York or Chicago, and embraced an image that was progressive, future-oriented, and modern. Modernizing Main Street was a means to this end.

The federal government deftly exploited this situation after modernization became public policy. Its massive campaign to encourage modernization tapped into Main Street's conflation of business and community values and transformed a state-sponsored effort to prop up large-scale capitalism into what seemed to be a populist mass movement far beyond the reach of Washington and Wall Street. This movement was successful at local and national levels because it relied on the sophisticated apparatus of modern advertising and public relations to stimulate consumption, even in the midst of the Depression. At the government's instigation, the building industry did the same thing. Corporate manufacturers of building materials commenced a wide variety of promotional activities—including extensive advertising, private consumer financing, and architectural competitions—to "sell" modernization simultaneously to architects and retailers. The goal was to increase sales despite the contraction in large-scale building activity. Manufacturers achieved this principally through retooling and remarketing their product lines to meet the needs of storefront modernization via the architect's design specifications and the retailer's merchandising requirements.

Here building material manufacturers were following the model of consumer-goods manufacturers who had restyled their products for visual appeal to increase sales in the Depression. What was effective in selling cars and refrigerators was also effective in selling storefronts. Mass-produced (or at least composed of standardized parts), widely marketed, easily purchased on credit, and featuring instantly recognizable, up-to-date stylings, the modernized storefront had an awful lot in common with the Chrysler Airflow and the Coldspot Super Six. Ultimately, this consumer-goods model became a paradigm for building modernization, eventually influencing every aspect of the movement, from financing to design. At a moment when ideas about obsolescence, fashion, gender, and social anxiety were entering American culture to a greater extent than ever before, it is not surprising that they also entered American *building* culture. These ideas were as effective in the modernized storefront as they were in other consumer goods because they responded to, and drew strength from, something that was understood as a defining feature of American culture in the 1930s—the experience of modernity.

This modernity ranged far and wide across the modernization movement, but it expressed itself most dramatically in the storefront's formal and symbolic attributes. These relied, in part, on the architecture of the

International Style, or at least its surface motifs of asymmetry, unornamented facades, planar and curving forms, ribbonlike windows, and bold graphics. As such forms appeared on Main Street, usually in combination with stylistic motifs derived from streamlining and art deco as well, they heralded the arrival and popular assimilation of European modernism, producing a distinctly American hybrid. But they also heralded the New Deal's vaunted return to prosperity as the forms quickly became identified with progress, optimism, and an all-consuming national quest "to be modern." Within the culture of the Great Depression, form and symbol were so potent that they produced thousands of storefronts that had significance far beyond their status as discrete objects.

Economically, each individual storefront was inconsequential since the cost of design, fabrication, and installation could be as low as $1,000. Architecturally, the impact was more visual than spatial, since design was confined primarily to the *front*. Socially and politically, modernization reflected the baser instincts of the free market since it was principally motivated by profitability, self-interest, and competitive consumption. But taken together, their meaning changed. Socially, modernized storefronts served as a visual harbinger of imminent prosperity to inspire public confidence, stimulate consumption, and provide a focus for the redirection of civic self-representation. Politically, they extended the New Deal's sphere of influence as the government attempted to effect change at a most basic level of the capitalist free market and to transform the impulse to spend into an act of national importance. Economically, storefronts accounted for a substantial portion of building activity in the 1930s, reviving an industry that had spiraled downward since 1929 and providing work for designers, contractors, and manufacturers. Architecturally, they provided an opportunity for the widespread introduction of modernist design to the everyday landscape, while simultaneously applying aspects of American product design to the scale of a building.

Ultimately, whether considering storefronts individually or as a group, it is futile to separate these diverse dimensions. In reality they were woven together by the major cultural forces of the 1930s—the crisis of the Depression and the pressures of burgeoning consumerism. The storefront emerged as a product of consumer culture, satisfying transient merchandising programs, reflecting fleeting aesthetic values, and moving swiftly from design to installation and from utility to disuse. These were precisely the qualities that enabled the storefront to respond so quickly to the critical imperatives of the Depression. Because it is subject to the exigencies of the marketplace—and the imperatives of supply and demand and production and consumption that this implies—the store-front registers cultural developments with an immediacy and directness denied more permanent or monumental forms of building. What the characteristic storefronts of the 1930s registered was the disruptive impact of the Depression, quickly transformed into a material and rhetorical staging of recovery and progress.

As it responded to the Depression, as it was shaped by the consumer culture, the modernized storefront produced something that, ironically, transcended its historical moment. It became a modern vernacular, a form of architecture that, for better or worse, authentically reflected the culture of the United States in the 1930s. *Modern* because it emerged from the twentieth century. *Vernacular* because it was emerged from the American landscape—the commercial corridors of Main Street.

In *Delirious New York*, Rem Koolhaas audaciously declared that he was Manhattan's ghost writer, recovering the lost history of its prewar skyscrapers and the culture they produced. In that same spirit, I am Main Street's ghost writer on the pages that follow. This book recovers the history of the modern vernacular as manifest in the prewar storefronts and the culture they produced. The words are mine; the story is theirs.

CHAPTER 1

Main Street, U.S.A.

On the morning of April 6, 1936, a tornado struck Gainesville, Georgia, with devastating force. By the end of the day, two hundred people were dead and over $13 million worth of property was damaged or destroyed. This small town, fifty miles northeast of Atlanta, had seen its share of troubles since 1929, from the boll weevil to factory closings. These, in turn, had a dramatic impact on other businesses in town, especially retail enterprises, as the unemployed of Gainesville and surrounding Hall County cut back their spending to the absolute, bare minimum. Thus, even before the tornado hit, Gainesville's economic and social situation was all too typical in 1930s America. So, too, was the downtown that bore the brunt of this decline, over fourteen square blocks encompassing Main Street and Courthouse Square.

This district had emerged haphazardly in the nineteenth century, with the majority of its buildings dating to the railroad boom between 1870 and 1900. Though Gainesville tried to keep its infrastructure up-to-date—in 1902 it became the first city south of Baltimore to have streetlights—by the 1930s it was ill prepared to deal with the crush of cars that now jammed Main Street and its secondary thoroughfares. As a further result of the town's growth, commercial uses had infiltrated the residential

Figure 1.1 Courthouse Square in Gainesville, Georgia, after the April 1936 tornado. The tornado produced an estimated $13 million in property damage, with nearly every business building in the commercial blocks of Main Street and the square either destroyed or severely wrecked. Despite the devastation, Gainesville's citizens saw this as an unprecedented opportunity to improve the community. (National Archives and Records Administration, photo no. 69-N-12413c.)

areas surrounding the historic center, leading to concerns about excessive business frontage and creeping blight. By the mid-1930s such concerns extended even to Courthouse Square, which business leaders now regarded as in need of extensive improvement and repair if it was to retain its prestige.

And now a storm had leveled downtown, leaving the buildings on Main Street and the Square in ruins (fig. 1.1). When the debris was finally cleared away, Gainesville's citizens decided to transform the disaster into an opportunity and were "determined to rebuild along better and finer lines than ever before." Such was the opinion of President Franklin Delano Roosevelt, who toured the devastation three days after the tornado hit and declared his intention to return to the town in the near future to see what had been accomplished. In the president's mind, Gainesville possessed a cooperative and progressive spirit that exemplified the best of America. Thus, despite the extent of the damage and the persistence of the Depression, Roosevelt was confident that when he returned he would find "a better and greater Gainesville," one whose commercial and civic heart had not merely recovered but had significantly improved.[1] However heartfelt his sentiments, when Roosevelt lauded Gainesville's spirit and heralded the small town's imminent rebirth, he embraced, with keen political acumen, a culture and a place whose social and economic consequence to the nation as a whole had become increasingly apparent as the Depression wore on.

❖

> Did you ever sit at the window of the Commercial House in some forlorn town and look down on its Main Street, the treeless stretch lined with buildings of every shape and description (but not one of them by any happy accident either attractive in itself or as part of the ensemble) and imagine what you would do if you were God, or even a first class architect with a bankroll like Rockefeller's?

New York advertising executive Earnest Elmo Calkins posed this question to readers of the *Rotarian*, the Rotary Club International's monthly magazine, in March 1935. He then related the story of an architect who redesigned the facades along a small town's commercial block so successfully that "a miracle was wrought," concluding optimistically that this sort of commercial property improvement would occur frequently once businessmen learned "that beauty pays." In the middle of the Great Depression, Calkins hoped to convince civic-minded Rotarians to embrace a program of "town betterment," with building modernization as its basis and economic advantage as its goal. Calkins's program was also part of a long-term architectural remedy for what he perceived as the ugliness of the everyday American environment, especially the "heterogeneous hodgepodge" of commercial centers lacking both aesthetic merit and visual order. Calkins was unequivocal that these were the districts most in need of improvement: "the place to begin is Main Street."[2]

Main Street Morphology

It was not by chance that Calkins selected this specific locale. By the 1930s "Main Street" had long been a recognizable urban morphology, with most American cities and towns possessing a principal commercial corridor or district identified figuratively, and often literally, by the term (fig. 1.2). By the 1930s it had also acquired a deeper significance. As journalist John Gunther noted in his 1946 continental travel log *Inside U.S.A.*, "Main

Street had embedded itself into the language" following the publication of Sinclair Lewis's best-selling novel of 1920, becoming an iconic locale that referred as much to a cultural outlook as a physical place.[3] Though Lewis painstakingly detailed a commercial landscape of brick buildings and pressed-tin cornices, iron-and-glass storefronts, and temple-fronted banks, his Main Street was "not only the heart of a place called Gopher Prairie, but ten thousand towns from Albany to San Diego." In his 1922 novel *Babbitt*, Lewis observed that "a stranger suddenly dropped into the business-center of Zenith could not have told whether he was in a city of Oregon or Georgia, Ohio or Maine, Oklahoma or Manitoba."[4] There was a "universal similarity" to Main Street that encompassed its buildings, its institutions, its people and their habits: "The shops show the same standardized, nationally advertised wares; the newspapers of sections three thousand miles apart have the same 'syndicated features'; the boy in Arkansas displays just such a flamboyant ready-made suit as is found on just such a boy in Delaware." Beyond identifying Main Street's ubiquity, Lewis's novels underscored two other characteristics: its self-improving tendencies and its progressive self-image. In *Main Street* the leading citizens of Gopher Prairie are determined to make it a "model town," and even the novel's disgruntled heroine hopes to beautify it.[5] In *Babbitt* the town of Zenith celebrated its "modern ideas" and believed it represented the vanguard of "a new type of civilization," one that sought to distinguish itself from larger cities, like New York and Chicago, which it disparaged even as it emulated them in matters of culture and civicism.[6] Though Lewis's assessment of Main Street's cultural dimensions was ultimately pejorative, his portrayal would resonate throughout the era, notably in popular and sociological studies that analyzed what Lewis disdained.

Frederick Lewis Allen's informal histories, *Only Yesterday* and *Since Yesterday*, and Robert and Helen Lynd's data-laden field works, *Middletown* and *Middletown in Transition*, generally supported Lewis's observations while avoiding his condescension and negativity. In particular, they offered evidence of what Lewis had sarcastically described as "Main Street's extraordinary, growing, and sane standardization of stores, offices, streets, hotels, clothes and newspapers."[7] The cause of this standardization was the burgeoning consumerism of post–World War I prosperity; the effect was the gradual erosion of the psychic distance and cultural lag between big city and small town. In 1931 Frederick Lewis Allen observed "the conquest of the whole country by urban tastes and urban dress and urban ways of living." By 1934 Robert Lynd had statistical evidence to support this claim. He concluded that a movement of

Figure 1.2 Main Street in Franklin, New Hampshire, in a postcard view circa 1920. This typical Main Street featured two- and three-story buildings executed in various popular commercial styles, plate-glass and cast-iron storefronts, wide sidewalks, parking for automobiles, and more than a few chain stores. (Collection of the author.)

"style progression" was under way, speeding up "the geographical spread of fashion from New York," and effecting "a closer binding of Main Street to Fifth Avenue."[8] Advertising and the popular press made similar claims. Jesse Rainsford Sprague, a frequent contributor to *Harper's*, noted how residents of small towns invariably got "the big-city urge" and looked to see how "Fifth Avenue corresponds to Main Street back home."[9] What they found, according to advertising executive Paul Bonner, was that "everyone [in Oklahoma] is just as much alive as the man who stands at the corner of Fifth Avenue and 42nd Street."[10] That same corner, representing the nation's über–Main Street, served as the cover illustration for a special report that appeared in *Architectural Forum* in 1939.

In this examination of Main Street as "a real estate phenomenon, a customer of building, and as a design problem," the national standardization Lewis decried was celebrated as "Main Street, U.S.A." (fig. 1.3). Across the country, Main Streets possessed an "essential homogeneity" regardless of size and location: "Breakfast Number Three is likely to consist of the same orange juice, toast, and coffee in New York, N.Y. as in New Albany, Ind., and the drug store in which it is served is sure to be as nearly like its big-city prototype as the proprietor can make it."[11] Even outside observers like Ilya Ilf and Evgeny Petrov, Soviet writers

Figure 1.3 "MAIN ST . . . a design problem." Here, storefront architectural details overlay a photograph of a typical commercial corridor in need of design intervention. According to the editors of *Architectural Forum*, Main Street was more than mere real estate; it was also a potential customer of building services. (*Architectural Forum* 70 [February 1939]: 86. Courtesy of the Avery Architectural and Fine Arts Library, Columbia University.)

who toured the country by car in 1935, were struck by these similarities. Not only did they, too, note the sameness of the American breakfast, but they also observed that "between the biggest town and the smallest town in America there are more similarities than differences."[12] Strung out along arterial highways from Maine to Florida (U.S. 1), from the District of Columbia to San Francisco (U.S. 40), and from Chicago to Los Angeles (U.S. 66), this Main Street—whether praised, condemned, or objectively analyzed—was a signifying landscape both physically and culturally constructed. Since at least the late nineteenth century, Main Street was defined by the buildings and establishments that lined it and by the image of community or individual it projected. Together, building and image created a collective identity that traversed local or regional domains to reach a destination of national consequence. This was especially true during the Great Depression when Main Street became a crossroads for social and economic recovery and, as these intersected, for a modern American culture.

By the mid-1930s this Main Street was at a critical juncture in its morphological evolution due to pressures brought to bear not only by the Depression but by preexistent social and economic conditions that the Depression merely exacerbated. These were cultural agents powerful enough to transform the physical pattern and spatial matrix that was fixed by 1900—a linearly developed, densely built strip in which commercial establishments clustered together to form a business and retail zone occupying contiguous, intersecting, or parallel blocks. In larger cities and towns, several such zones or multiple strips might exist, depending on the population and the concentration of real estate development. Not every commercial corridor was known as Main Street, but their structures and functions were the same regardless of their geographically specific names.[13] A typical strip consisted of two- or three-story buildings arranged in continuous rows, punctuated by additional structures whose heights varied from four to ten stories depending on the size of the town and the value of the land. Much of Main Street's built fabric dated to the era of rapid economic expansion in the late nineteenth century and possessed a formal organization largely determined by commercial and speculative real estate exigencies.[14]

Programmatically, Main Street's buildings were bipartite with principal street-level retail space of standardized frontage (larger concerns occupied two or more standard lots) and secondary upper stories leased for office, light manufacturing, or residential purposes. In configuration, these buildings were usually narrow, since excessive street frontage added to the cost of the land, and deep, to make up for square footage lost in store width. Stylistically, the buildings were tripartite with a range of Victorian decorative motifs disposed across cast-iron and plate-glass storefronts, intermediary stories of flat brick or stone accented with picturesque window surrounds, and finally a terminating, often outsize, ornamental cornice. As historians of commercial architecture have noted, this standard two-part/three-part building format was a roadside constant, always discernible beneath the shifting fashions of the Italianate, Romanesque, or Beaux-Arts classicism to which it was continually subjected.[15] By the turn of the century, this building type provided a small degree of formal coherence to a Main Street assemblage all but overwhelmed by the visual cacophony of market-driven architectural eclecticism. By the eve of World War I, any semblance of organizational order that Main Street possessed was further obscured by an advertising superstructure of painted windows, hanging signs, and scaffolded billboards, all of which proliferated with increasing intensity well into the 1920s.

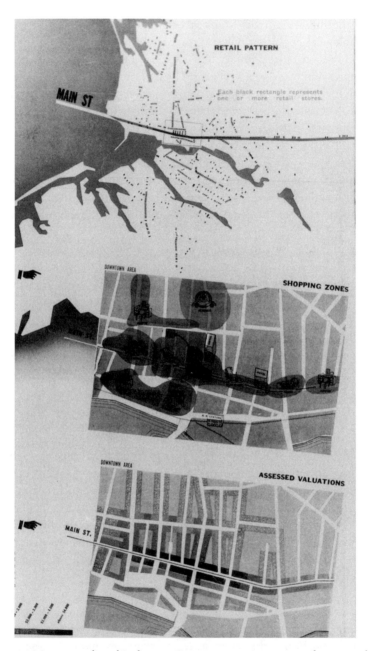

Figure 1.4 Mapping studies of Bridgeport, Connecticut, representing retail patterns, shopping zones, and assessed valuations of a typical Main Street. The analysis was especially concerned with the number and location of stores. (*Architectural Forum* 70 [February 1939]: 77. Courtesy of the Avery Architectural and Fine Arts Library, Columbia University.)

By that decade a wide range of commercial establishments occupied Main Street's characteristic buildings, almost always including a grocery store, a drugstore, a clothing store, and a gas station. These four retail types represented a large portion of the 1.5 million stores that the U.S. Commerce Department estimated were operating on Main Street in 1929. Of this number, the majority (89%) were small, independently owned shops with annual sales of less than $12,000—a figure that would drop to less than $10,000 by 1933.[16] Though economically inconsequential individually, when taken together these stores formed a powerful center for a community's commercial activity—the retail zone with the highest concentration of businesses, pedestrians, customers, and, most crucially, profits. The economic efficacy of these autonomous establishments remained constant through more than a half century of boom-and-bust cycles from the Civil War to World War I, but this situation changed during the extended economic expansion of the 1920s.

Though local chambers of commerce and merchant associations worked hard to promote Main Street's collective business interests throughout the prosperity decade, these trade groups were unable to regulate the opening of too many rival stores that continually drove each other out of business. Even more significantly, they were unable to forestall the precipitous rise of two new forms of retailing that offered serious competition for independent Main Street establishments. As the chain store and the neighborhood shopping area became familiar fixtures of the commercial landscape, they influenced Main Street with their distinctive economic and architectural presence—both on and off the older business strip. Often the chain store and shopping area operated in tandem, since chains frequently occupied key anchoring positions. By the 1920s Main Street faced increasing competition from retailers, chain and independent, operating out of these new and expanded buildings. If the actual economic impact of this competition was still somewhat diffuse, the threat was perceived to be grave enough as to warrant a serious response.

Competing Retail Forms

To Main Street observers, there was little question as to how the shift to chain and outlying shopping area retailing had occurred. In the period after World War I, real estate developers began to successfully lure retail tenants and their customers away from older shopping districts to new centers located outside the downtown core, on the urban periphery or in the suburbs, where land values were lower and rents were cheaper.

The size and quality of these areas varied greatly, from carefully planned plazas and centers to cheap commercial strips.[17] The latter were usually single-story, rapidly built blocks located along major roads leading out of town and away from Main Street. Intended primarily as stopgap buildings to generate modest income from land to be more profitably developed in the future, such "taxpayers" had been around since the turn of the century, when their construction was precipitated by new streetcar and railway lines.[18]

It was the rise of the automobile in conjunction with the freewheeling real estate speculation of the 1920s that truly stimulated construction of mile after mile of these exurban taxpayers. Offering convenience retailing, taxpayer strips served newly developed residential neighborhoods sprawling out from downtown cores and Main Street districts. Long and low, they responded to the horizontal spread of the highway and to the imperatives of the automobile, especially as builders set them back from the road to provide perpendicular or diagonal parking for passing vehicles. When traffic threatened to overwhelm curbside parking, adjacent vacant lots, usually to the rear of the strip, were paved over to accommodate the growing number of customers arriving by car. Eventually, taxpayer developers even provided direct access from parking lots to stores through rear entrances. This represented a crucial break with the established Main Street pattern that had always privileged the street facade. Despite these concessions to the car, the taxpayers were still linear commercial corridors that served, effectively, as secondary Main Streets—what Chester Liebs has called "Main Street by extension."[19] They would thrive in prosperity and suffer in depression as much as their older downtown counterparts, and, as a result, discussions of commercial corridors in the 1930s would frequently fail to distinguish between them.

Also located on the urban periphery, but distinct from speculatively built taxpayer strips, were the so-called community or neighborhood "shopping centers," which, as Richard Longstreth has shown, represented a new commercial paradigm consciously planned (and owned and managed) in opposition to Main Street's strictly linear pattern. Though their true impact would not be felt until after WWII, throughout the 1920s and 1930s the shopping center—including such notable examples as Country Club Plaza in Kansas City (begun 1922), Westwood Village in Los Angeles (begun 1928), Suburban Square outside Philadelphia (1929–30), and the Park and Shop in Washington, D.C. (1930)—was promoted as a workable commercial model offering retailers and their customers an enticing alternative, or at least a complementary adjunct, to older Main Streets and downtown districts.[20] Advocates of the planned shopping center, who were often proponents of urban decentralization as well, criticized Main Street as haphazard, chaotic, and poorly planned. Indeed, Main Street was all of these things, and such conditions were worsened by the presence of cars. Since these densely built corridors were conceived before the age of the automobile, they were ill-equipped to deal with its onset. In 1946, when *House Beautiful* called for the construction of decentralized shopping areas and planned shopping centers across the country, it looked back on the old Main Street form and concluded that it represented "a chronic shopping problem that [had] been with us long before the war." Not surprisingly, the magazine pinpointed the car as the source of Main Street's historic and contemporary troubles: "Most of us do our shopping by automobiles on Main Streets designed for the horse and buggy."[21]

As automobile usage increased exponentially after World War I, Main Street's traffic congestion reached dangerous densities: gridlock, lack of parking, and pedestrian/auto collisions became serious, widespread problems. In Connecticut as early as 1923, the Highway Department took steps to relieve the congestion of the most car-clogged Main Streets in the state, those of Fairfield County towns running north along U.S. Route 1 from Greenwich to Bridgeport. Numerous improvements were tried: installing stoplights, widening roadways, providing shopper parking, and constructing through-traffic bypasses. According to the New England Regional Planning Commission, none of these projects was effective and Fairfield County's Main Streets were deemed nearly obsolete as traffic arteries and commercial corridors.[22]

Theorists and designers Catherine Bauer and Clarence Stein reached similar conclusions in their 1934 study "Store Buildings and Neighborhood Shopping Centers," which used market and formal analyses as a basis for economic and architectural planning of local retail facilities. Using Huntington, Long Island, as their illustrative example, the authors held up the traditional commercial corridor as a consummate failure, arguing that Main Streets were "hang-overs from the past" that failed to recognize that the car had been a "dominating feature" of American life for over two decades.[23] It was toward this supposed disregard for the needs and conveniences of car-driving customers—as well as pedestrians forced to confront the car—that Bauer and Stein directed much of their criticism of Main Street. Not only did the typical Main Street environment lack adequate provisions for parking or a smooth flow of traffic, but the buildings themselves were wholly unsatisfactory in their strict frontality and flat displays. "Show windows," noted the authors, "are of little use to people driving by in automobiles." Of course, Bauer and Stein were also quick to condemn the more recent phenomenon of taxpayers, "strung out in miserable rows, unrelated to the needs or the form of the community which they pretend to serve." With Stein's Radburn model (designed with Henry Wright) and Clarence Perry's neighborhood-unit as their ideals, the authors argued that these problems could be easily overcome when retail services were accommodated in shopping areas properly designed "for the Motor Age." These were cohesive building assemblages with stylistic unity, regulated signage, covered pedestrian walkways, off-street parking, planned traffic patterns, and a diverse complement of retail services. All of these were lacking in the typical Main Street, an uncoordinated series of individual stores that Bauer and Stein characterized dismissively as "a monotonous eyesore."[24]

Too Many Stores

Bauer and Stein had reasons for criticizing Main Street's physical form that went beyond its incompatibility with modern shoppers and their cars. They also believed Main Street was an egregious example of unregulated zoning and laissez-faire planning policies. In particular, they found fault with a distinctly American approach to real estate development, at work in small towns and large cities alike: property fronting main thoroughfares was automatically zoned for business or commercial use regardless of existing economic and demographic factors, producing an excess of business frontage. As an illustration of the land-use condition this created, the authors cited the situation in Los Angeles, where over-zoning resulting from a 1921 ordinance created a quantity of business property so excessive that Bauer and Stein claimed, erroneously, that it would have served the needs of the entire population of the United States.[25] Though its impact was less dramatic elsewhere, this long-standing zoning practice not only dictated Main Street's original form, but remained an active agent in Main Street's speculative development during prosperity and depression.

This practice also informed Main Street's guiding real estate and retail principles, founded on a correlation between concentrations of businesses and people: "the more stores the more profit; the more passers-by the more business, therefore the higher property values." As a result of this equation, the authors believed that Main Street's store buildings were "turned out like sausages, long strips of them, all alike, no matter how different might be the requirements of site, special use, or of grouping."[26] The average Main Street, they concluded, was oversupplied with commercial buildings and commercial establishments. In other words, there were simply too many food stores, drugstores, clothing stores, and gas stations to serve the needs of any one community as defined by its population and purchasing power. Bauer and Stein's identification of ineffectual zoning practice as the root cause of this surplus of stores clarified a difficult situation that the retail industry had already recognized. As the editor of one retail trade journal put it: "We have too many stores now, and we shall continue to have too many until the common hazards of retailing are more widely understood."[27]

The most hazardous aspect of American retailing was a direct consequence of the retail surplus: the intense competition that, even in a healthy economy, threatened to put many merchants out of business. Simply put, store closure was the ultimate risk the retailer faced when entering the profitable but dog-eat-dog Main Street marketplace. As Bauer and Stein noted, even during the 1920s, "those good old days of so-called 'normalcy,'" the majority of smaller independent stores managed only a marginal business performance, with average annual sales of $5,500. This was barely enough to net proprietors a living wage once salaries, rent, and other overhead were paid out.[28] Adding to that bleak picture were government statistics culled from the Commerce Department's Census of Distribution for the supposedly prosperous years 1926–29. These indicated that as a national average between 10 and 15 percent of all Main Street businesses failed each year, and between 30 and 60 percent of all *new* Main Street businesses failed during their first year of operation due to adverse competition.[29] With the onset of the Depression, the situation worsened: competition for scarce consumer dollars became exceptionally fierce since the amount the public was willing or able to spend dropped 50 percent between 1929 and 1933.[30] This had a direct bearing on Main Street's store mortality rate. Though the actual number of stores forced out of business by increased competition and decreased spending during the first four years of the Depression was difficult to calculate because the Commerce Department had incomplete statistics for independent retailers, estimates put the annual mortality rate at 25 percent.[31] Other industry observers suggested that this percentage was too small, and that the "deathroll" itself was probably much higher than the estimated 375,000 stores, especially if it was adjusted to include not just the *dead* but the *mortally wounded* as well—those thousands of other retailers whom jurist Clarence Darrow, reporting on the progress of the National

Recovery Administration, identified as "struggling desperately for bare existence."[32]

Complicating the situation and rendering the numbers even less meaningful was a concomitant store "birthrate." For every store that shut down, another opened up to take its place, as in the archetypal Main Street community of Middletown, where Robert and Helen Lynd observed "a considerable shuffling of retail stores into and out of business." The Lynds concluded that this was a natural condition of "the free-for-all merchandising system of a laissez-faire economy," one that worsened during the Depression as competition intensified.[33] Retail analysts concurred, recognizing this condition as endemic to Main Street's unregulated economic planning and regarding it as a factor in Main Street's oversupply of commercial establishments (fig. 1.5). Even during the first four years of the Depression, store openings almost kept pace with store closings, so that by 1933 the aggregate number of independent retailers had declined only 2 percent. In the context of declining sales brought on by the economic crisis—in Middletown net retail sales fell 57 percent on average—this meant that in 1933 just as many stores were competing for half as much business as in 1929. This further raised the stakes of competition and, in all probability, placed the majority of these newest stores into that growing retail category of minimal profitability and marginal existence. Yet, in that same cycle of retail mortality and store turnover on Main Street, one could discern, as the Lynds did in Middletown, another trend equally reflective of national commercial developments—a trend with the potential to transform the economic structure and the architectural appearance of the traditional commercial core.

Chain Store Age

What the Lynds observed in *Middletown* was that Main Street had become extremely vulnerable to the incursion of chain retailers. This was not a new phenomenon in 1933, but rather one that possessed renewed vigor after a brief caesura following the Crash of 1929. The decade that preceded the Depression had already witnessed the escalating presence of chain stores on and off Main Streets across the country, affecting nearly every aspect of American retail: there were chain candy stores (Loft's), tobacco stores (United Cigar), shoe stores (Regal), drugstores (Walgreen), bookstores (Doubleday), clothing stores (Mangel's), and movie theaters (Loew's), among many other types. The most famous and ubiquitous were the chain variety stores, the success of which laid the foundation

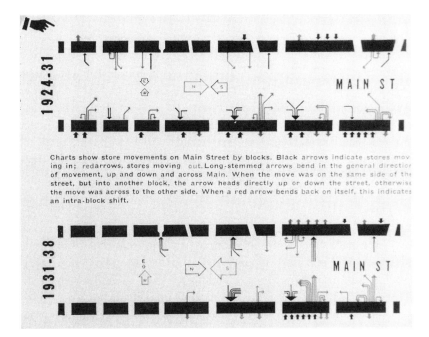

Figure 1.5 Chart showing store turnover rate for Main Street in Bridgeport, Connecticut, 1924–38. The arrows indicate the frequency of stores moving into and out of each location and the direction of movement. (*Architectural Forum* 70 [February 1939]: 78. Courtesy of the Avery Architectural and Fine Arts Library, Columbia University.)

for the expansion of other multiple unit retailers. Variety chains, both the general merchandise type and the limited-price five-and-dimes, had multiplied gradually since before the turn of the century when Woolworth's (founded 1879), Kress (1896), and J.C. Penney (1902) developed almost in tandem with Main Street itself.[34] These chains usually occupied two commercial lots joined behind a single standardized facade with standardized signage and displays. They quickly became "All-American institutions"—community fixtures recognizable from coast to coast but especially in small towns.[35] More than half of all J.C. Penney stores, for example, were in towns of under five thousand people. Once five-and-dime chains like Kresge's, McCrory's, J.J. Newberry's, and W.T. Grant's joined the field, often competing with each other on the same Main Streets, it was inevitable that chains would dominate the variety segment of the retail market.

By the early 1920s, the chains had proliferated sufficiently for writers and critics to refer to them offhandedly, using familiar chain names as descriptive literary shorthand. In Lewis's *Main Street* after Carol Kennicott and her husband splurge on an expensive dinner in a Minneapolis/St. Paul hotel, the next morning they "sneaked round the corner to economize at a Childs' Restaurant."[36] It was unnecessary for Lewis to explain to his readers that Childs was a self-service chain, founded in 1889, with fifty restaurants nationwide by 1920, or that Childs had an established reputation for offering affordable, home-style fare in clean, white-tiled interiors. In *Manhattan Transfer* (1925), it was similarly unnecessary for John Dos Passos to explain that Childs outlets in New York City were equally well-known as late-night hangouts for slumming denizens and tourists alike: "The pancakes were comfortably furry against his gin-bitten tongue. Jimmy Herf sat in Child's in the middle of a noisy drunken company. . . . The clock over the cashier's desk said three o'clock."[37]

The United States had entered the "chain store age," at least according to the publishers of an eponymous trade journal that commenced publication in 1925. With separate druggist, grocery, and general merchandise editions, *Chain Store Age* indicated the degree to which chains had increased their share of these respective markets through the multiplication of retail units. While chain expansion hardly rivaled the merger mania that characterized other industries during the prosperity decade, it was a notable enough development for economist John Kenneth Galbraith to observe that "the chains were at least as symbolic of the era."[38] Even chains well established prior to the 1920s experienced a tremendous spurt of growth during the boom years: by 1927 there were nearly 1,600 Woolworth stores, and J.C. Penney outlets had grown from 371 to more than 1,000 between 1923 and 1927 alone.

By 1930 chains were so pervasive that a reporter for the *Nation* observed that "in a comparatively short time—within the past five or six years to be exact—the chain store has completely altered the economic life of the American community." This amounted to a virtual economic revolution pitting the small independent merchant against the large corporate chain. By the early 1930s, it seemed inevitable that the chains would win the battle for Main Street, so indomitable did they appear to many observers. Citing figures for Louisville, Kentucky, but claiming them to be representative of "every fair-sized city or town," the *Nation* noted that chains controlled nearly 90 percent of all retail business conducted on the local Main Street. In 1925 the situation had been nearly the reverse, with most retail business going to locally owned independent establishments.[39] In actuality, Louisville's ratio of chains to independents was much higher than the nation as a whole, but the conclusion was the same: the volume of business conducted in chain stores *did* increase markedly during the 1920s, doubling, tripling, and in some cases quadrupling what it had been in 1919. This increase was achieved through rapid chain expansion—both the opening of new stores and the acquisition of existing ones.

By 1929 chain sales accounted for only 22 percent of the country's $50 billion retail business, but the fact that the chains gained this market share so quickly caused genuine concern among their independent competitors and the federal government as well. In 1928, at the request of the U.S. Senate, the Federal Trade Commission (FTC) launched a six-year investigation of the nation's estimated twenty thousand retail chains to uncover potentially monopolistic practices and unfair methods of competition in relation to independent retailers. The FTC was especially concerned about the expansion of chains in the grocery field, which was not only the largest of the four major retail groups, but was also the field where the chains had made their greatest progress.[40] The largest grocery chain in the country, the Great Atlantic and Pacific Tea Company (A&P), grew from fewer than 400 stores in 1920 to over 15,100 in 1929.[41] Many of these new A&Ps—along with the chains Kroger, American Store, and Piggly Wiggly—were self-service combination food stores selling produce, meats, breads and cakes, and canned and packaged goods under one roof. These were *super*markets whose spatial requirements would have a dramatic urban and architectural impact on the American landscape. Because they required large selling floors, between four to six thousand square feet, supermarkets were difficult to accommodate in typically narrow Main Street buildings. Hence, some grocery chains opted for combined frontage. A&P Unit No. 820, for example, opened in a double storefront on Main Street in Fairfield, Connecticut, in 1914. In 1927, when the store wanted to expand its premises, it annexed an adjacent site, buying out the lease of the butcher who occupied it and knocking down the party wall to create a triple-width combination store.[42] Such expansions were not always practical in terms of cost, size, or the availability of adjacent space. Thus, the new combination supermarkets were more often housed in taxpayer strips, where cheap retail space and large commercial buildings were easier to obtain than on Main Street proper.

So many of these chain supermarkets opened *off* Main Street that by 1931 Frederick Lewis Allen wryly commented that "Mrs. Smith no longer patronized her 'naborhood' store; she climbed into her $2000 car to drive to the red-fronted chain grocery and save twenty-seven cents on her daily purchases."[43] As a chain store customer, this Mrs. Smith was like an increasing number of American consumers across the nation's socioeconomic spectrum: as *Fortune* put it, "The chains are capitalizing on Main Street, not only from the extremely rich and the extremely poor, but from middle incomes of $5,000 or so."[44] Consumers put their faith in a recognizable chain store brand name at the expense of independent Main Street retailers because of the chains' growing reputation for dependability (of merchandise), efficiency (of operations), and especially economy (of volume buying). These were the consumer-friendly store attributes that analysts inside and outside the retail industry identified as most responsible for the expanding volume of chain business, not only in the grocery trade, but in all sectors of American retail.[45] When the full force of the Depression hit in 1932–33 and retail sales plummeted 50 percent overall, chain sales declined only 15 percent, a retention of business that could only be explained by an increase in unit sales, meaning that more customers were making more purchases at the chains at the expense of the country's 1.3 million independent traders.

Even before the Depression, single stores on Main Street had suffered the ill effects of burgeoning chain loyalty. The individual butcher, baker, mom-and-pop grocer, clothier, or druggist was simply unable to match the chains' ready capital, marketing data, and economies of scale, all of which were deployed strategically to attract customers. Chain managers viewed these factors as the constructive benefits of large-scale trade, rather than as unfair advantages. In fact, they claimed they were raising business standards in the communities in which they operated, compelling independent merchants to follow their lead in lowering costs, improving service and quality, and passing savings on to the consumer. The independents could try to keep up, but they could not really compete—not when chains could make as little as 2.5 cents per dollar of sales and still stay in the black.[46] By the late 1920s, the nation's independent merchants were growing restive in the face of this expanding chain competition. Those merchants who remained on Main Street—because they owned their buildings, had long-term leases, or were simply committed to their communities—watched helplessly as their sales and profits dropped while those of chain stores in taxpayers and new shopping areas, or even on Main Street itself, rose precipitously. Once the decampment to the chains intensified as the Depression set in, the erosion of the independents' customer base steadily worsened and many merchants struggled to keep their doors open amid drastic consumer belt-tightening. The chains, however, were able to exploit the economic situation to further establish themselves on Main Streets across the country.[47]

Though the chains were initially buffeted by the stock market crash, the event did not herald a business catastrophe; rather, the Depression presented a singular opportunity for business expansion. By the fall of 1932, conserving cash outlays, closing marginally profitable stores, and consolidating operations had enabled the chains to recover sufficiently to undertake new expansion campaigns. The monthly real estate postings in *Chain Store Age* during 1932 and 1933 indicate that five-and-dimes, supermarkets, drugstores, and shoe and clothing retailers were aggressively establishing new outlets after a twenty-four-month period of near inactivity.[48] Published announcements of store openings, signed leases, new construction, and store modernization also reveal how the chains were targeting Main Street, which, despite its current travails, was still regarded as the prime business location in small towns and large cities alike. During the economic prosperity of the 1920s, chain operators had often found themselves in bidding wars with other chains over the most desirable Main Street locations. While such bidding tended to inflate property values, as the president of one drugstore group recalled, most chains were willing to sign "long-term leases at prohibitive rentals" because of the concentrated customer base a Main Street location assured. With the Depression, however, the real estate situation on Main Street reversed itself: "Now the most desirable locations can be had almost on the lessee's own terms."[49]

The chains seized this opportunity and eagerly leased empty Main Street storefronts for bargain rents: "We've profited by the times," the director of the National Tea Company proudly declared in November 1932, explaining his chain's continued expansion into traditional commercial centers. This Chicago-based grocery chain, with over three hundred stores in the Midwest, had taken advantage of depressed rates to lease "the most desirable locations," a move that would not be as easy after business conditions returned to normal. While expanding chains encouraged other multi-unit retailers to adopt a similar carpe diem attitude—"we repeat, now is the time to expand"—they were at least mildly anxious, in the midst of the ongoing FTC investigation, at appearing too opportunistic in taking advantage of the depressed real estate market. Hence, expansionist zeal was often tempered with declarations of concern for Main Street's economic recovery. National Tea, for example, intimated that renting store space at hugely discounted rates almost qualified as a public service since they were coming to the aid of "tax burdened landlords" who would otherwise have faced foreclosure or receivership.[50]

Chain Store Modernization

In the midst of the national crisis, the chains also claimed that their store improvement and modernization efforts were further proof of a community-minded, public-spirited attitude because of the building activity and economic stimulation that these programs generated. Of course, the fact that low interest rates and reduced material and labor costs induced by the stagnant economy "offered an advantage too great to be ignored" was not to be underestimated as the chains planned their modernization programs.[51] These were under way as early as 1932, a year recognized at the time as the worst in the history of American retailing. That November, when *Chain Store Age* conducted its first store modernization survey, the trade publication found that the nation's largest chains, encompassing over fifty thousand stores and six major retail groups (grocery, five-and-dime, restaurant, drug, shoe, and clothing), had adopted "almost without exception" active modernization programs designed to "stimulate sales" during the current period of "reduced public buying-power."[52]

These programs included the installation of updated storefronts, the enlargement of premises, and the complete interior and exterior renovation of buildings for the opening of new stores. Though the scale of modernization varied from chain to chain and from unit to unit, from as little as $500 for signage or lighting improvements to as much as $5,000 for a gut renovation, total expenditures were impressive. In November 1933 *Chain Store Age* estimated that American chains had spent $33 million to modernize stores in the past twelve months, a figure representing nearly 15 percent of the year's total commercial construction. In 1934 the annual chain modernization expenditure was estimated at $37 million; in 1935 it nearly doubled to $70 million. *Chain Store Age* editor Godfrey Lebhar confidently declared that chain store modernization was playing an important part in the building industry recovery and contributing favorably to the nation as a whole. Here he accurately characterized the growing prevalence of chain store modernization in the early 1930s, noting that the closer the nation came to turning the long-sought "corner" of the Depression, "the more certain it becomes that we shall find [the corner] occupied by a modernized chain store"[53] (fig. 1.6).

The chains undertook these multimillion-dollar modernization programs for a variety of reasons, but most basically they were carrying out a declared "prime objective" to keep their stores up-to-date. For many chains, store modernization in the early 1930s was simply a continuation

How Chains Modernized in 1935

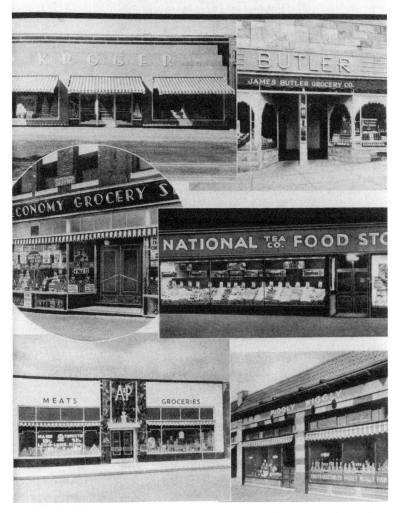

Figure 1.6 "How Chains Modernized in 1935." Photo spread showing modernized storefronts of grocery chains including A&P and Piggly Wiggly. By the middle of the decade, chains were claiming that their frequent store modernizations were assisting in the national economic recovery. (Photo permission from *Chain Store Age*, November 1935, 91. Copyright Lebhar-Friedman, Inc., 425 Park Avenue, NY, NY 10022.)

of a standard practice of design "evolution," which accepted regular change in store appearance as necessary for an establishment to remain viable in the marketplace. The Melville Corporation, which owned several shoe store chains, developed a dozen different storefronts during its first decade in existence (1922–32), installing them successively throughout the years with a goal of "converting all existing stores to the latest type as rapidly as possible." Melville's out-of-date Rival Shoes storefront had a vaguely classicized art deco styling, with a recessed, centrally placed arched entrance and a non-illuminated sign flanked by faceted display windows. The new Rival storefront was decidedly jazzier, with an off-center entrance and primary display window articulated as a single expanse of plate glass topped by a neon sign inscribed in a zigzag frame. The new front also had a taller bulkhead to raise the display platform and give the shoes more visual prominence (fig. 1.7).

The company implemented these conversions not because it considered the extant fronts "obsolete," but because it considered them "passé" and believed that changing them would bring increased business. Though Melville failed to specify the semantic distinctions it perceived between "obsolete" and "passé," it is clear that neither term referred to physical disrepair. Instead, deploying what would prove to be one of building modernization's most important rhetorical devices, they referred to a formal quality of *out-of-dateness* and an implicit desire to modernize, as the chain articulated it, "for the sake of change itself."[54] Change was necessary, according to chain executives, because storefronts began losing aesthetic and fiscal value from the moment they were installed. After a certain period of time, the duration depending on market conditions, the front no longer possessed "the ability to win attention from pedestrians" It was this enervation of the storefront's so-called pulling power that modernization was intended to counteract by creating a new image for an existing store, adding the "up-to-the-minute appeal" that the chains believed had a direct bearing on additional sales.[55]

In retailing, a simple axiom was always in effect, regardless of the state of the market or the status of the merchant: "A store which looks best usually fares best"—attracting the most customers, transacting the greatest volume of business, and generating the highest profits.[56] If most chains engaged in some level of modernization activity even in prosperous times, budgeting at least modest capital appropriations to improve store appearance, when overall sales and profits were down they felt the obligation to modernize even more keenly, since such declines were usually accompanied by intensified competition for limited consumer spending.

Figure 1.7 Rival Shoes in Newark, New Jersey, before and after modernization, 1932. Chains modernized regularly in the early 1930s in order to keep their stores up-to-date in terms of architectural style and merchandise display. Here Rival Shoes retained only its signature typeface when it modernized an existing unit. (Photo permission from *Chain Store Age*, November 1932, 654. Copyright Lebhar-Friedman, Inc., 425 Park Avenue, NY, NY 10022.)

A.S. Beck Shoes on Fulton Street in downtown Brooklyn demonstrates this type of competitive chain modernization. Prior to its remodeling, the Fulton Street store was a typical "conservative" Beck's unit from the early 1920s. A standard type with an arched opening and classical molding, the chain deemed the front "satisfactory" because it was similar in size and appearance to the other stores on the block, none of which sold competing merchandise. In 1932, however, a rival shoe chain moved into an adjoining storefront, precipitating a decline in Beck's business. The chain determined that "resuscitation" was necessary and hired architect Vahan Hagopian to design a new front that would "present something different"[57] (fig. 1.8).

For the Fulton Street modernization, Hagopian modified the exuberant modernistic design he had recently executed (1929) for Beck's flagship store on Fifth Avenue at Forty-fifth Street in Manhattan. Using less expensive materials, he created a downscale version that was still highly effective and eventually received a "best store" award from a Brooklyn merchants association.[58] Extending the vestibule of the existing store by four feet, Hagopian created a deep arcade with the show windows arranged in angled setbacks flanking the door and focusing sight lines on the entrance. Hagopian heightened this directional pull by tiling the arcade's ceiling with arrows and chevrons. Extending the storefront's facade a full story above the street and deploying a bold color scheme of ocher, silver, gold, black, and purple augmented the attention-getting devices of the modernization. Purposefully designed to "totally dominate the competitor," Hagopian's scheme did its job: the competing shoe store was forced out of business within months of the modernization's completion. Because of its success at drawing business away from the competition, Beck executives regarded Hagopian's design as "functional" rather than "decorative," implying a use value that translated directly into dollars, the increased business credited to the modernization.[59]

While modernizing existing units to maximize sales volume was cheaper than opening new stores, most chains usually implemented an improvement policy of "better stores" in conjunction with an expansion policy of "more stores."[60] Adding another dimension to the concept of better stores in the early 1930s was the recognition of a "psychological effect" that modernization had upon the buying public. The storefront was always intended as an expression of the personality of the chain housed within, impressing upon passersby some essential aspect of the chain's reputation, be it a commitment to service or the quality of its merchandise. Prior to the Depression, this expression was largely autonomous

Figure 1.8 A.S. Beck Shoes in Brooklyn, New York, before and after modernization, 1932. Vahan Hagopian's eye-catching modernistic design was intended to draw customers away from the competing chain next door. According to Beck executives, Forsythe Shoe was out of business within several months of the modernization's completion. (Photo permission from *Chain Store Age*, October 1932, 600. Copyright Lebhar-Friedman, Inc., 425 Park Avenue, NY, NY 10022.)

and hermetic, externalized in form but internalized in meaning, as it concerned only a narrow retail sphere. But after 1929 this expression engaged the larger world and the social realities of contemporary America. As chain executives and managers interpreted it, a modernized storefront struck "a keynote of confidence," sending out a "strong" and "constructive" message that the chain was "getting ahead in spite of conditions" and was too busy "to have time to worry about the Depression." This was a message that would become increasingly significant as the decade wore on, especially after the federal government turned its attention to building modernization as a way to mitigate the effects of the Depression. For the chains themselves, if the message of modernization was to achieve "maximum effectiveness," eliciting a positive response regarding business optimism from the general public, the design of the storefront was crucial.[61]

As early as 1932, the chains dedicated themselves to storefront improvement policies with a single focus: to "make our stores modern."[62] While the chains and their designers liberally interpreted what modern was, producing storefronts of considerable stylistic variety, the goal of modernization was always the same: to render in built form an institutional self-conception of the corporate chain as a "modern business" run by a "progressive merchant." Since the chains were already regarded as "exponents of modernism," both in store design and retail practice this was, perhaps, not an unrealistic desire.[63] But, in emphasizing their own modernity, the chains sought to further distinguish themselves from those traditional independent retailers who had "worried themselves out of existence by standing still and shivering in their boots," rather than embracing modernization.[64] In stark contrast, the chains claimed they had been "raising the standards of store appearance and store maintenance throughout the entire retail world." Not only did they believe they were improving commercial architecture; they also believed they were making a larger social contribution as well in the "beautification of Main Street."[65]

In his 1996 autobiography, architect Morris Lapidus, who was a prolific store re/designer in the 1930s and 1940s, looked back on this wave of store modernization as "a new era on Main Street" brought about by chain expansion. Lapidus recalled how the chains, who were then his principal clients, took advantage of Depression conditions by scouting new store locations in states slated to receive large allocations of federal funds for work relief projects, anticipating the employment and the consumer spending such projects would create. Mangel Clothing Stores, for example, bought out independent dry goods establishments across Tennessee following congressional authorization of the Tennessee Valley Authority in 1933.[66] This sort of takeover was a common practice at the time, as chains took advantage of bargain or bankruptcy prices to buy out struggling independent merchants. Out of concern for public perception of this apparent exploitation of the depressed independent retail market, the chains downplayed their acquisitions of existing independents and minimized the role these buyouts played in chain expansion strategies. Nonetheless, the Federal Trade Commission found that in many retail groups—especially limited-price varieties, shoes, dry goods, and apparel—such acquisitions represented a significant percentage of all chain store openings in the first three years after the Crash, as high as 40 percent, according to government estimates. Though the FTC stopped short of accusing the chains of predatory practices in buyouts, it did ask Congress to grant it the authority to block chain store monopolies before they developed.[67]

As far as the chains were concerned, the FTC findings amounted to a complete exoneration, and they dismissed the "plight of the small retailer" as the sour grapes of business rivals. Further, the chains claimed that Main Street's independents were simply ill-equipped to handle the fair, market-driven competition presented by multi-unit retailers.[68] *Chain Store Age*'s Godfrey Lebhar, a leading chain lobbyist and apologist, took this dismissal of independent retail practices a step further. In a 1933 editorial, he asserted the chains' implicit modernity by criticizing as *retardataire*, anachronistic, and even unsanitary the mantle of nostalgia in which the independents cloaked themselves:

> I have an affectionate memory of the old time merchant and his place in the community. . . . I have fond recollections, too, of the horse and buggy, but I think I would prefer a 1933 automobile or one of our air-conditioned de luxe trains. I don't believe many of us yearn for the days of the cat-in-the-cracker-barrel, the flies-in-the-molasses-barrel, and the sawdust floors. Retailing has changed. The old time store is as much out of date as the first movie theater, the kerosene lamp, the mustache cup, Congress gaiters, and the flint firing musket. . . . If the independent couldn't hold on to his business against honest competition he would not deserve to hold it, from the point of view of consumer economics.[69]

In disparaging the independents, Lebhar was responding defensively to certain negative sentiments that gained in popularity in the late 1920s and were likely to return as the current economic crisis worsened. Further intensifying these sentiments was the fact that independent store failure and chain store success were inextricably linked not only in the minds of the independents, but in popular conception as well. Resentment toward the chains finally reached a public breaking point in 1929, coalescing into an anti-chain backlash. Though short-lived, this backlash would prove significant to Main Street's subsequent evolution as it attempted to recover from the dual onslaught of the Depression and the chain retailer.

Main Street vs. Wall Street

The reaction against the chains was fomented late in 1929 by a Louisiana businessman and part-time radio announcer named William Kennon Henderson, who declared war on the chain store as a personal crusade. From a radio station he owned and operated (KWKH), Henderson began an evening program in which he attacked chain stores as "damnable thieves from Wall Street" whose only community interests were stealing local money and destroying local livelihoods.[70] These broadcasts—which included vituperative, frequently anti-Semitic, and obscenity-laced tirades—were heard across the South and eventually nationwide, since Henderson regularly usurped frequencies and exceeded his licensed power. By the spring of 1930, his program had attracted so much public attention, from supporters and detractors alike, that *Fortune* declared "the Chain Store Issue" the mostly hotly debated topic in the nation after Prohibition.[71] To sustain this public interest, Henderson organized a retail "militia" known as the Merchants' Minute Men, a group that was little more than an anti-chain propaganda machine. By 1931 Henderson claimed that the Minute Men were thirty-five thousand strong and active in four thousand towns nationwide organizing store boycotts (this often involved harassing women who shopped at chains) and lobbying state lawmakers to pass anti-chain legislation. Both activities were successful. A grocery chain in Birmingham, Alabama, claimed it lost one-third of its business as a result of a Minute Men boycott. Several southern states, including Kentucky and West Virginia, passed bills instituting a graduated sales tax based on store volume, a policy that specifically targeted the chains. Over the next few years, the Merchants' Minute Men spawned a number of similar campaigns to help independent merchants "to fight the menacing octopus of the chain store system."[72]

Given the social and economic climate of the United States in the early years of the Depression, it is not surprising that these anti-chain campaigns sustained a degree of public interest, not the least because William Henderson, beneath his blustering profanities, clearly understood the terms of rhetorical debate appropriate to a country in crisis. At a time when middle-class Americans were casting about for someone to blame, Henderson fixed upon recognizable protagonists whose sympathies and loyalties were unmistakable and whose local features were easily sketched by Main Street consumers across the country. This made it simple for the general public to distinguish the victims from the perpetrators, while ignoring the fact that the consuming public itself was complicit in the perceived victimization of the independents. In valorizing independent merchants and demonizing corporate chains, Henderson created tangible personifications of a cultural opposition often viewed as a fundamental conflict of twentieth-century America. Though the battle between the independents and the chains was obviously a confrontation of old and new forms of retailing, it represented something more significant than profit margins and sales volumes. It represented a conflict between old-fashioned American individualism and the collective imperatives of modernity, between the archetype of small business and the stereotype of Big Business, between Main Street and Wall Street.

Even before the Depression, these iconic thoroughfares were recognized as symbolically antithetical, representing oppositional social and economic positions. In 1929 Harvard political economist William Z. Ripley argued that since the end of World War I, the United States had witnessed a shift from "personal businesses" to "corporate enterprises," each exemplified by the extremes of Main Street and Wall Street, which was also the title of his book. For Ripley this shift indicated "the constructive forces" at work throughout the country transforming the American producer culture into an American consumer culture, "a land of milk and honey, of material well-being where plumbing, radio sets and Ford cars abound." Ripley hoped that by increasing popular comprehension of the current business situation, Wall Street might be made to better serve "the common good" historically centered in Main Street.[73] A few years later, no such rapprochement was possible.

By the mid-1930s distinguishing Main Street and Wall Street as differing moral orders helped the middle class make sense of the Depression and offered a psychological salve for the social and economic wounds it had inflicted. Robert and Helen Lynd observed that Middletown regarded itself as a community of "small businessmen," though it counted several prominent industrialists among its leading citizens. Further, Middletown carefully distinguished "Wall Street gamblers," who were blamed for the Depression, from hometown "little fellows," who represented "the purest strain of our American democratic economy." In Middletown's own battle between the independents and the chains, local merchants exploited these distinct identities in their accusations that the chains were "unneighborly," financed by "outside capital," and responsible for "taking money out of the community."[74] In Main Street America, where business values and social values were routinely conflated, this was the worst kind of censure.

Such allegations were leveled against the chains so routinely that *Chain Store Age* was compelled to publish a series of articles to refute the charges. These articles reveal prevailing Depression-era attitudes toward the chains as "absentee-owned big business" and the independents as "locally-owned small business." While the chains were seen as anonymous retail "machines" and "giant enterprises . . . ruling over thousands of stores scattered over a widespread area from remote headquarters located invariably in Wall Street," the independent was viewed as a "good citizen . . . doing his part for the common good."[75] The implications were clear: since the chains lacked established ties to the communities in which they operated and had no long-term material stake in their welfare, they lacked the hometown sentiment, civic spirit, and social obligation that the independents presumably possessed as a natural result of their local orientation. *Chain Store Age*, obviously, considered these assessments unfair and untrue, but understood that they constituted very nearly an article of faith among the general public: "The independent merchant is an important part of our business setup and it would be a national calamity if he were eliminated."[76]

Such a calamity must have seemed a distinct possibility to the merchants themselves, and even to some retail analysts, since independent retailers were so regularly folding on the country's Main Streets. As the Bureau of Foreign and Domestic Commerce (BFDC) reported, "Small stores are believed by some to be on the road to extinction." But exactly what would happen if they became extinct was unclear. From a retail standpoint, their loss would mean "inconvenience to the public," according to the BFDC.[77] But from an economic standpoint, even the elimination of all 1.3 million independent stores in the United States would not have been catastrophic. Though the U.S. business structure would have been altered, it would not have been destroyed, as other retail classes absorbed the independents' merchandise, sales, and at least a portion of their workforce. Nonetheless, the apparent trend toward the elimination of the independents elicited increasing expressions of concern and alarm from many Americans.

That such a development had implications for local and national business conditions is made clear by Middletown's reaction to the closing of the town's leading department store, its largest independent retailer. When the store finally succumbed to chain competition and declared bankruptcy in April 1934, community leaders and residents alike viewed the event as an ominous portend of a "general collapse" to come.[78] By that time, especially in smaller cities and towns, the closing of important retail establishments had become a routine misfortune of the Depression, as is evident in "Main Street Ten Years After," a 1933 *New Republic* article describing the collapse of a third-generation furniture store in a quintessential small town. As important a community landmark as the county courthouse, the furniture store had occupied one of the most prominent buildings on Main Street even before the road was paved. Like the local bank, it was regarded as "a Gibraltar of stability" in the economic and social life of the town; like the bank, the store inevitably failed.[79] Then, in what the author saw as a final insult to the town's remaining independent retailers and a final affront to the town's collective self-esteem, the furniture store's landmark building was taken over by a chain—an event greeted on Main Street with a mixture of resentment and resignation.

Missing from the public sentiment in both cases was any sense of culpability on the part of the buying public concerning the store's demise, even though local consumers had abandoned the old stores for the chains. This reflects the characteristic ambivalence of Main Street's customers, who, though giving lip service to the national importance of independent retailers, were unwilling to alter the buying habits—patronizing the chains—that were the most damaging to those merchants.[80] It is perhaps understandable that during the Depression civic concerns were subordinated to the exigencies of consumers' pocketbooks more than during times of prosperity. In the 1930s the potential savings offered by the chains went beyond normal economizing, becoming a virtual necessity for maintaining one's standard of living, even among those "to whom thrift was formerly little more than a Sunday-school word," as a *Chain Store Age* editorial accurately observed in 1933.[81] But if public purchasing forsook the independents for economic expediency, why did public opinion remain steadfast to them?

Business historian Mansel Blackford provides a partial answer: "Twentieth-century Americans have frequently differentiated between small businesses, which they have seen as inefficient and backward, and small business people, whom they have come to admire . . . as bastions of political as well as of economic democracy."[82] Since at least the era of Thomas Jefferson, the small businessperson symbolized the self-reliant entrepreneurship and "pull yourself up by your bootstraps" individualism on which the American way of life was mythically founded. This symbolism grew more powerful as capitalism and democracy, business values and community values became inextricably linked. As small businesses faced the takeovers, mergers, and bankruptcies marking the hegemony of the modern corporation in the early decades of the twentieth century, the small businessperson became a cherished icon of dogged perseverance and hardscrabble determination. In the 1930s the independent Main Street retailer was one of the most familiar personifications of that iconic figure. Though the chains, the Depression, and consumer disregard brought the independent store to the brink of extinction, the independent store owner endured: first, as an embodiment of America's increasingly erroneous, and thus ever more desirable, self-conception as a nation of small, autonomous, privately owned businesses; and second, as a repository of the admirable cultural values of democracy and individualism associated with that deluded self-conception.

Even the routinely cynical Sinclair Lewis discerned these values in the figure of the independent retailer in It Can't Happen Here, his 1935 dystopian novel chronicling a fascist takeover of the United States beginning in a small New England town. In Fort Beulah, Vermont, an independent grocer named Clarence Little defends democracy against the ruling political elite, the National Council of Corporations (Corpos), long after the town's banker, doctor, and other members of the professional middle class (Lewis's standard Rotarian/booster targets) have capitulated. Rejecting a Corpos plan to take control of his store and make it part of a centralized business conglomerate, Little pays the ultimate price for his defiant independence: he is beaten to death by paramilitary thugs.[83] Though Lewis intended It Can't Happen Here as a warning against American complacency in the face of growing German and Italian dictatorships, the novel also stands as a commentary on the contemporary domestic situation. And as in the novel, to many observers this situation was about more than competing retail forms; it was about competing political and economic philosophies. Nowhere was this more apparent than in the administration of Franklin D. Roosevelt and the policy struggles of the New Deal.

Among New Deal policy makers, there were two distinct theoretical positions concerning the economic structures manifest in the independents and chains. Though these positions were not wholly antithetical in practice, they were based on dynamically oppositional concepts of a *traditional* American economy and a *modern* American economy. On one side were the New Dealers who embraced a progressive tradition stemming from Louis Brandeis's Supreme Court trust-busting and the anti-monopoly policies of Woodrow Wilson's New Freedom. These Brandeisians denounced big business as "economically inefficient and socially dangerous." They called, in the words of Brandeis himself, for "a return to the little unit" and the classical society of small competitors participating in a market regulated only enough to prevent profiteering and monopoly.[84] On the other side was the Brain Trust, which rejected this view as unrealistic and out-of-date. According to New Dealer Raymond Moley, they disagreed with the "traditional Wilson-Brandeis philosophy that if America could once more become a nation of small proprietors, of corner grocers and smithies under spreading chestnut trees, we should have solved the problems of American life."[85] To the members of the Brain Trust, it was Brandeis's little unit that was economically inefficient. Big business was not only ruthlessly efficient; it was an unavoidable fact of life. Since the monopolies and oligopolies that large corporations engendered were the rule, not the exception of the modern American economy, any attempt to eliminate big business was both naive and impractical. Instead, the Brain Trust sought to bring about government cooperation with big business, regulating it only through mutually beneficial prescriptions such as the economic planning of the National Recovery Administration.

Despite their differences, these two opposing camps came together to work on policies that protected small retailers (satisfying the Brandeisians) without punishing corporations or corporate chains (satisfying the Brain Trust), especially after the invalidation of the NRA in 1935 and the shift toward the Second New Deal. The best known of these compromise policies emerged from the Robinson-Patman Act of 1936, which forbade wholesalers and manufacturers from giving preferential discounts or rebates to chain stores and other large buyers and also established the now-familiar "suggested retail price."[86] While it was a step toward leveling the retail playing field, enabling the independents to compete more effectively with the chains, the legislation did nothing directly to help the independents regain customers they had already lost to the chains. Thus, by mid-decade store failures, turnovers, and takeovers continued in an ever-intensifying cycle.

Main Street in Crisis

On Main Street itself, as an actual place and not merely a symbol, the combined impact of increased retail competition and decreased consumer spending was swift and deleterious, not only on individual businesses but on the commercial district as a whole. Economically, it was a vicious cycle: the storekeeper went bankrupt; his employees were thrown out of work; his wholesaler or distributor took a loss on unpaid merchandise; his landlord had to write off back rent. Physically, the impact was no less significant—and perhaps more obvious (fig. 1.9). Failed stores created empty storefronts; empty storefronts created what Bauer and Stein termed "unsightly vacancies"; and vacancies created "blight." The opening of new stores in those spaces was not necessarily a corrective since they were often fly-by-night, low-rent operations that, in themselves, constituted a blighting presence. For planners in the 1930s, blight was an infectious urban pathogen, the first symptom of that full-blown disease known as the slum. If it continued unchecked, this blight would drive down rents and property values and would eventually destroy the commercial viability of the historic Main Street corridor—especially when accompanied by the continued development of peripherally located shopping areas.[87] Making the situation worse was the fact that, in addition to empty storefronts, it was not uncommon to find Main Street's typical mixed-use buildings vacant and shuttered above the first floor. For those buildings still occupied at street level, it was a battle to stave off total dereliction.[88] Often once a struggling merchant finally shut his doors, the landlord abandoned the building, with arson sometimes following on the nation's most stricken commercial corridors.

Anecdotal evidence suggests that in their blighting presence, empty Main Street storefronts were regarded, almost like breadlines, as one of the more conspicuous signs of the Depression. In *Since Yesterday*, Frederick Lewis Allen observed how "walking through an American city . . . you might notice that a great many shops were untenanted, with dusty plate glass windows and signs indicating that they were ready to lease."[89] In Middletown the situation was the same, but there the Chamber of Commerce worked to persuade landlords not to board up their vacant buildings because of the debilitating effect it would have on "local business morale"—a recognition of a direct correspondence between Main Street's

Figure 1.9 Abandoned storefronts circa 1935. By the middle of the decade, such vacancies were considered harbingers of blight that would drive down rents and property values and had the potential to generate commercial slums. (*Architectural Forum* 65 [September 1936]: 242. Courtesy of the Avery Architectural and Fine Arts Library, Columbia University.)

physical appearance and its psychological outlook.[90] The empty storefronts of those first Depression years were an unavoidable confrontation with the national trauma that was otherwise being denied by national advertisers whose products were normally displayed in those now-vacant storefronts. Advertisers in the pages of popular magazines may have been keeping alive a spectacle of consumption and a mythology of prosperity, but Main Street's independent merchants knew the reality.[91] They were eking out a marginal retail existence, reducing overhead as much as possible, and cutting back even on routine maintenance and repair.

As the breadlines got longer and consumers' belts got tighter, and neglect and abandonment continued to spread across Main Street, the independents suffered the added indignity of watching the chains continue their retail entrenchment through methodical modernization programs. The average Main Street independent had enough market savvy to know that he, too, had to keep up appearances to continue to attract customers. But keeping up appearances required cash the merchant did not have because his shabby store, along with his higher prices, was not attracting customers anyway. The more the customers stayed away, the more run-down the store became. Thus, despite the vital presence of the chains, Main Street appeared to be in unmistakable decline. According to the 1935 description by architect and planner Arthur C. Holden, Main Street had become "a frazzled district" filled with "tawdry business streets." Suffering from "blight, depreciation, congestion and obsolescence," these streets had degenerated into "economic and social liabilities." Main Street, Holden argued, required immediate physical and fiscal intervention lest it become a "vicious plague spot" in cities and towns across the country.[92]

Government statistics offered evidence corroborating Holden's dramatic picture of Main Street's decline. Many of these came from the 1934 Real Property Inventory (RPI), carried out as a work relief project under the auspices of the Bureau of Foreign and Domestic Commerce (BFDC) of the U.S. Department of Agriculture. The overarching purpose of the sixty-four-city inventory was to obtain an accurate picture of national real estate conditions by assembling comprehensive data on the physical and financial state of the country's building stock. While the survey's focus was housing, it included commercial buildings as well, partly because these were deemed crucial to accurately determine land use and property values, and partly because commercial buildings, including the standard Main Street type, often included one or more dwelling units.[93] In addition, as the RPI revealed, during the Depression economic necessity drove many small retailers to take up residence in the back of their stores, resulting in a category of "partially converted structures" with a mix of business and residential units that varied from the original configuration.[94] Among the gathered data was information on materials and methods of construction and building condition, categorized as good, in need of minor or major repairs, or unfit for use. A follow-up survey of retail buildings in twenty-three RPI cities examined store location (central shopping district, business subcenters, or neighborhoods) and evaluated buildings according to exterior and interior appearance on a good, fair, or poor basis.[95]

Government agencies, notably the Federal Housing Administration's (FHA) Research and Statistics Division, began utilizing RPI data as soon as it became available.[96] FHA reports examining the impact of changes to business and residential districts in urban centers and analyzing retail trade in relation to a community's economic stability determined that the spread of peripherally located residential areas, the increase in automobile usage, and the growth of the chain store had all led to the rise of outlying commercial centers. This was paralleled by the deterioration of the central business district to such an extent that by 1934 the volume of retail sales made by stores *outside* the core exceeded those *inside* it by 25 percent. There was every indication that this gap would continue to widen.[97]

FHA analysis also revealed the physical consequences of this outward movement of people and retail, especially the infiltration of peripheral residential areas by commercial uses that had "an unstabilizing effect upon property values," leading to neighborhood blight. Since the FHA found that "as the distance from the commercial uses increases, the average value of the residential property and the average rents have a tendency to increase," to preserve the new residential areas it was crucial to simultaneously preserve the "traditional retail nucleus" of Main Street itself.[98]

When attempting to draw a retail/real estate profile of Main Street's buildings, the FHA coordinated its analysis of RPI data with statistics taken from the Commerce Department's Census of Distribution and Survey of Current Business and from a random store survey conducted by the FHA's own Industrial Division. These combined data revealed a great deal about the correspondence between a store's physical state and its sales volume, location, and the income level of its customer base. In particular, the FHA found that "the decline in both the number and purchasing power of people living near the main business center" was a crucial factor in Main Street's overall depression.[99] More specifically, the data also revealed the extent of that decline, illustrated by the physical condition of Main Street's buildings. Though the nature of disrepair varied widely, most stores suffered from "a generally unsatisfactory appearance" of exterior elements, including storefronts, signage, display windows, and entrances, and interior elements, including layout, lighting, and merchandising and mechanical equipment—in other words, nearly every aspect of a store building's physical condition was deemed in need of improvement.[100] FHA analysts also ranked physical condition according to need, determining that 62.5 percent of Main Street's 1.5 million retail buildings needed "immediate" repairs and improvements, and that in 80 percent of these cases, meaning half of the nation's retailers, the repairs were "urgent."[101]

The government's figures were more conservative than those of the retail and the building industries. The National Retail Dry Goods Association estimated that 75 percent of all stores needed improvement and repairs. *Architectural Forum* reported that 90 percent of all stores needed "surface or structural improvements."[102] Significantly, these percentages represented the number of independent stores operating on Main Street in the middle of the Depression decade. By then the retail and building industries were already actively cooperating with the federal government to assist these merchants in forestalling Main Street's decline. While this assistance was intended to help the independents compete with their chain rivals, it was also intended to help a depressed national economy and a depressed national psyche. Main Street, U.S.A., as a place and a symbol, was about to become the road to recovery.

CHAPTER 2

The New Deal on Main Street

In March 1938 Franklin Roosevelt returned to Gainesville, Georgia. It was nearly two years since a devastating tornado destroyed most of downtown. Now, however, instead of the destruction and debris that greeted him in 1936, Roosevelt toured a town almost entirely rebuilt, with a new civic center and courthouse, new schools, and new utilities. "You were not content with rebuilding along the lines of the old community," Roosevelt observed. Rather, Gainesville had determined "to eliminate old conditions [and] to build a better city."[1] Nowhere was this more obvious than in the business district surrounding Courthouse Square: the park was landscaped and improved; the streets were repaved and widened; ample automobile parking was provided in angled spaces and an adjacent municipal parking lot. Most impressive, however, were the buildings themselves, which were not merely repaired but modernized with updated designs and materials. In place of the eclectic jumble of commercial structures that typified the district before the tornado were uniform building lines and harmonized facades and signage (fig. 2.1). In repairing the damaged structures on Main Street and the square, planners convinced merchants and property owners to coordinate their buildings across the district, successfully asserting a degree of architectural control

Figure 2.1 Courthouse Square in Gainesville, Georgia, as rebuilt with New Deal assistance after the 1936 tornado. The blocks fronting the square were now characterized by uniform building lines and simplified, harmonized facades. (*Architectural Forum* 66 [February 1937]: 157. Courtesy of the Avery Architectural and Fine Arts Library, Columbia University.)

that was unusual within such a free-for-all market-driven environment. Storefronts still displayed sufficient individuality to distinguish one shop from the next—thus satisfying the merchandising needs of Main Street—but for the first time they were now part of a coherent ensemble. So successful was this effort that the editors of *Architectural Forum*—who described pre-tornado Gainesville as "any and every old town in the U.S., haphazard, out-at-elbows, gray, disjointed"—made the startling observation that Gainesville could now "look down its nose at those unfortunate towns which were not wrecked by tornado."[2]

At first glance it seems remarkable that a small southern town with dwindling municipal resources was able to rebuild itself so quickly in the midst of the Great Depression. But Roosevelt had decided to make the reconstruction effort a showcase of New Deal programs, including those of the Public Works Administration, the Works Progress Administration, the Reconstruction Finance Corporation, and the National Emergency Council. Among the alphabet soup of agencies whose representatives turned up in Gainesville was one whose involvement was especially notable, not because the Federal Housing Administration helped the town with the construction of its new residential subdivisions, but because the FHA also helped Gainesville rebuild its "businesses houses."[3] Roosevelt had singled out the tenants of those *houses* in his address, noting the importance of "small storekeepers" to what he called "the continuation of the American system," that is, the persistence of capitalist democracy. It was essential to secure their "participation in prosperity," and a variety of Roosevelt's initiatives were intended to do just this. But among New Deal efforts to assist small business, the FHA's program was unique. While its ends were the same as price regulation and market intervention—to stimulate the economy and encourage consumer spending—its means were far more tangible in a real and physical way as it promoted the modernization of Main Street storefronts.

The merchant who is committed to his location through ownership or long-term lease is particularly affected by changes in the public's buying habits. He realizes that such changes occur because other and modernized stores are drawing his trade away from him. He, too, must modernize to hold his trade.

Federal Housing Administrator Stewart McDonald offered this frank assessment of a familiar retail situation in July 1935. Though he did not state it explicitly, McDonald was reminding independent merchants of the ramifications of increased competition from chain retailers who had been opening new stores and modernizing existing ones at their expense. The independents needn't have despaired, however, because McDonald was offering them the opportunity to "compete on an even basis" with their rivals. The time had come to "Modernize Main Street for Profit!"[4] McDonald's admonition to the nation's merchants appeared in a government booklet published to coincide with the New Deal's latest initiative to combat the Depression: low-interest, federally insured loans to repair and improve business properties. The focus on Main Street was both obvious and timely, given its significance as a locus of commerce and community and its steady decline since 1929. This was reflected in the government's statistical data, which showed that nearly three-fourths of the nation's commercial buildings were in a state of genuine physical disrepair due to nearly five years of deferred maintenance, rapid turnover, and even abandonment. Left unchecked, this decline represented a serious threat not only to the nation's real property, but to its tax base and, by extension, its national wealth. But in urging the modernization of Main Street, the government's concern was not only to forestall the physical and fiscal erosion of the commercial core; it sought to forestall its social erosion as well. Understanding the importance of Main Street in American life,

Figure 2.2 Modernize Main Street logo, 1935. This logo appeared in March 1935, after the loan limit for the Modernization Credit Plan was raised to $50,000. The slogan "Better Housing for American Business" indicates that the campaign to modernize Main Street was an offshoot of the Better Housing Program. (FHA, *Modernize for Profit*, 1935, inside back cover. National Archives and Records Administration, Record Group 31.)

the government viewed its modernization as a public symbol of recovery during the continued trauma of the Depression—one necessary "for the stability of the nation"[5] (fig. 2.2).

Main Street and Its Workers

That stability was imperiled by an economic spiral that began with a vast group of workers whose standard of living prior to the Depression was considered relatively high. Labor Secretary Frances Perkins called these workers the nation's "ready spenders," dispersing large portions of their incomes on goods and services in their local communities, on their local Main Streets. As the purchasing power of these workers declined after 1929, the stores and establishments in which they did business began to suffer as well, leading first to local economic depression, manifest in Main Street's run-down stores, and then to a broader retail decline that created a so-called "lack of market" for manufacturers of consumer goods. This, in turn, had a negative impact on those industries, their workers, and then *their* local communities as the devastation spread.[6] Modernizing Main Street was intended to reverse this trend by providing immediate reemployment for the workers with whom the decline began—those of the building industry.

In the United States in the 1930s, no sector of the economy was more severely depressed than the building industry. Building activity—including new construction and additions, alterations, and repairs—declined gradually in the second half of the 1920s, from a high of $4 billion in 1925. In the first years of the Depression, building activity dropped precipitously: to $3 billion in 1929, to $1.5 billion in 1930, and to a nadir of $400 million in 1933.[7] Accompanying this decline in activity was an unprecedented increase in unemployment well beyond the industry's traditional seasonal layoffs. As a result, the building trades and allied professions experienced higher unemployment in the 1930s than any other American industry, placing among the jobless such highly skilled, highly paid workers as carpenters, bricklayers, plasterers, electricians, and plumbers, as well as engineers and architects.[8] While the exact number of total unemployed workers in the building industry was difficult to determine, Secretary Perkins estimated it to be approximately 2 million people, nearly 80 percent of all workers attached to the building industry. By one count, this was nearly 30 percent of all unemployed Americans in the worst years of the Depression.[9]

As discouraging as these figures were, their significance was far graver. Because the building industry was one of the basic components of the national economy, its depressed state had a far-reaching effect. Industries directly related to building or supplying building needs—especially manufacturers of durable and producer goods such as glass, steel, cement, lumber, and electrical parts—suffered a proportional decline in production and rise in layoffs. Between 1929 and 1933, employment in these areas fell over 50 percent, leaving an estimated 2.5 million workers jobless. Though consumer goods manufacturers and federal work relief would absorb nearly 1 million of the unemployed, over 3.5 million workers in the building trades and related industries stood idle by mid-1934, according to the most conservative figures. With work relief to be phased out in the coming months, labor experts predicted this figure would climb to over 5 million in the winter of 1934–35.[10]

It was in anticipation of this staggering count of jobless Americans in the spring of 1934 that New Dealers proposed a new legislative packaged intended to stimulate the building industry and gainfully reemploy its workers. At that moment, however, there was little indication that Main Street was about to be transformed by federal mandate, for the legislation that Congress was then considering was unequivocally a housing bill. Only the most careful readers of the proposed National Housing Act would have noticed that its program of "real property conservation" was intended to bring all American buildings—commercial and industrial, as well as residential—"up to the standards of the times" through "repairing and modernizing."[11]

As a federally sponsored effort to generate productive employment while preserving the built environment, Roosevelt's newest program was akin to the natural conservation efforts of the Tennessee Valley Authority and the Civilian Conservation Corps. But unlike those initiatives, products of the legislative fervor and fiscal largesse of the Hundred Days of the first New Deal, this program reflected the more cautious and restrained political climate of 1934 when Roosevelt was forced to address growing conservative discontent with relief expenditures and market regulation.[12] To this end, when explaining the new bill as it was under congressional consideration, Roosevelt distinguished its potential for real job creation from boondoggle work relief. He also deferred strategically to business interests and the free market, noting that the program offered "support for" and "cooperation with private capital and industry" rather than intervention and controls. Instead of direct government funds for property conservation, Roosevelt proposed government insurance of loans made for property conservation. This loan insurance mechanism would, in the president's words, "produce tangible, useful wealth in a form for which there is great social and economic need." For partisans across the political spectrum, such "wealth" would come only from recovery and not from relief—from private sector paychecks and not from government handouts.[13] This shift from relief to recovery reflected the Keynesian ideology of the so-called second New Deal, which favored expanded employment, cheap and accessible credit, and large-scale, coordinated government action to achieve economic prosperity. Each of these steps had a prominent place in the real property conservation program that President Roosevelt outlined for Congress in May 1934.

Building Modernization as Public Policy

This program was largely the work of the National Emergency Council (NEC), a committee created by executive order late in 1933 and charged with coordinating the field activities of the New Deal's alphabet agencies and relief programs.[14] At one of the NEC's first meetings in January 1934, at which the president himself was in attendance, John H. Fahey, chairman of the Home Owners' Loan Corporation (HOLC), requested a $2 billion appropriation to enable the HOLC to expand its money-lending operations beyond the prevention of mortgage foreclosures to include loans for the improvement and modernization of houses. According to Fahey, this expansion would not only help stabilize and improve residential property values; it would also "create healthy activity in the building trades." While Roosevelt generally approved of this modernization scheme, he was concerned about the use of direct government funds: "Was there any way to get the government out of the lending business?"[15] Within a few months, the NEC had devised a modernization plan that satisfied the president's request. Dubbed the Modernization Credit Plan (MCP), this proposal would shortly be drafted into Title I of the National Housing Act. The MCP's structure was similar to several pre-Roosevelt property improvement finance schemes that encouraged privately funded building modernization as an economic stimulant.[16] But as it delicately balanced between the interests of business and the interests of workers, it was also a product of the second New Deal.

In this sense, the New Deal's deployment of modernization reflected a distinct shift in attitude toward the practice. Prior to the Depression, especially in the 1920s, modernization was regarded as a real estate strategy concerned with ends and not means since the modernized building was more important than the act of modernization. As architecture and real estate writers noted at the time, it was only after a building was modernized that it would generate the increased property values, rents, and profits that were the primary economic motivations for undertaking facade changes, interior renovations, or equipment updating.[17] That this realty orientation disconnected modernization from those who produced it— from architects, engineers, contractors, tradesmen, and manufacturers— was both symptomatic of the boom-time marketplace of the prosperity decade and largely inconsequential. Not only were those same producers sharing in the profits of prosperity, channeled into the building industry through the construction boom, but the industry as a whole minimized the importance of modernization practice, regarding it as a sideline of building, worth only $300 million annually versus $3 billion in new construction.[18] After 1929 this situation gradually reversed itself as modernization was repositioned as a central building industry activity capable of producing jobs, increasing demand for materials, and generating economic revival.

The principal authors of the Modernization Credit Plan were Marriner S. Eccles, a Utah banker and special assistant to Treasury Secretary Henry Morgenthau, and Albert L. Deane, president of the General Motors Holding Corporation, one of the automaker's consumer finance divisions.[19] Eccles was a Keynesian and a staunch supporter of deficit spending by the government as long as it increased purchasing power, expanded credit, and stimulated the circulation of private funds. For Eccles, the goal was "generating a maximum degree of private spending through a minimum amount of public spending."[20] Deane, a consumer credit expert who pioneered installment buying in the auto industry, favored any plan to support aggregate worker income, since this could be finessed through careful marketing into potential car sales. Largely unconcerned with federal deficits, Deane was anxious to maximize consumer credit in order to bolster shrinking purchasing power.

Their distinct fiscal agendas merged in the MCP, which proposed federal loan insurance for funds extended by private lenders rather than direct government funding through relief and loans. The federal insurance would cover 20 percent of all modernization loans made by a single financial institution, a high-enough coverage to stand as a complete guarantee.[21] By guaranteeing these loans rather than making them, the government hoped, as the *New York Times* put it, to "coax reluctant capital out of hiding" without interfering in the operations of private business.[22] The government would absorb up to $200 million on loan losses, plus the operating costs of a new agency to administer a nationwide campaign to promote modernization. Unlike a comparable relief appropriation, which would allow the government to expend only the stated amount, this subsidy had the potential to generate $1 billion of private lending activity. This activity would take the form of individual loans that required no collateral, only the local lender's positive assessment of the borrower's "strength of character," a bold move in the 1930s. Initially, borrowers were restricted to property owners, and individual loans were capped at $2,000, but the MCP was liberalized in 1935 to permit lending to long-term tenants and lessees and to allow loans up to $50,000 for business properties. Both of these changes were directed at Main Street merchants, who were seen as an untapped modernization market.[23]

Since the goal of the MCP was to generate as much building and lending activity as possible, Eccles and Deane proposed that all types of real property, and not just residences, should be eligible for the government-insured credit offered in the housing bill.[24] As Eccles explained it to the House and Senate Banking Committees, "If a man with a small store building or a garage or an apartment house was willing to make repairs . . . that money loaned and spent would serve just as useful a purpose as the money spent on a home." Beyond this, he predicted that "a very substantial amount" of insured credit would be used for nonresidential modernization.[25] Similarly, since the goal of the MCP was to put as much capital into circulation as possible, Eccles and Deane proposed that all types of legitimate credit agencies should be eligible for the new government insurance. This was significant because in 1934 only 1 percent of American commercial and savings banks were authorized to make, or were interested in making, small character loans of the type the MCP proposed.[26] Installment lending companies and the finance corporations run by manufacturers and retailers like General Electric and Sears, Roebuck did make such loans, but these were generally limited to the purchase of consumer products like cars and refrigerators. Only building and loan associations, as small community lenders with personal knowledge of their customers, routinely made renovation and construction loans based on character, rather than collateral. With the federal government acting as virtual cosigner and guarantor, the MCP would drastically change this situation for lenders and borrowers alike.[27]

The architects of the plan envisioned the three basic lending scenarios that would be possible through the MCP. In the first scenario, a borrower went directly to a bank, filled out a credit statement and application, signed a promissory note upon approval, and received the proceeds of the loan in cash.[28] The second scenario was the same, but the proceeds of the loan were dispersed as a cashier's check made out to a specific contractor or dealer already engaged by the borrower and accepted by that person as cash. In the third scenario, a building industry middleman transacted the modernization loan. This could be either a building contractor partnering with a local lender or a supply or an appliance dealer working with a finance company operated by the manufacturer whose products he represented.[29]

To the MCP's supporters, these scenarios represented a vast "democratization of credit" to be made available not only to "gilt-edged individual borrowers" but to "the man in the street" as well.[30] To its detractors, this democratization was of questionable value, even if the objective was noble and necessary, because it seemed to encourage consumer debt through installment buying. What particularly concerned the plan's fiscally cautious congressional critics was that for the MCP to function properly as a stimulus plan, hundreds of thousands of property owners and tenants would be encouraged to take out loans for building improvements they could not necessarily afford.[31] The high-profile presence of a consumer debt advocate like Albert Deane did nothing to calm conservatives' fears that the program would stimulate industry and get tradesmen off relief squarely on the back of the middle-class consumer.[32] In this respect, the critics were correct, but in the wave of enthusiastic promotion that accompanied the launch of the MCP, any friction between modernization sellers out to make a profit and modernization buyers being asked to take on debt would be largely ignored.

Ultimately, the MCP's potential to generate accumulated consumer debt was considered irrelevant since the plan was envisioned as a temporary measure designed to bring relief through employment with minimum delay. It would be phased out once the permanent mortgage program stipulated in the National Housing Act's Title II was operational, sustaining employment stimulation through new residential construction. This coupling of short-term and long-term employment measures was a typical New Deal contrivance: immediate relief, sustained recovery, and permanent reform in a single piece of legislation. As it turned out, however, the MCP's success at economic pump-priming combined with the building industry's resistance to sustained reemployment prolonged the life of the emergency provision until 1943, when wartime construction and manufacturing made its continuance unnecessary.[33]

A National Campaign

After the MCP was signed into law following the passage of the National Housing Act in the spring of 1934, it was necessary, as Frank Walker put it, "to persuade people to take advantage of this plan."[34] This persuasion was the heart of a national campaign launched in the summer of 1934 to aggressively promote the MCP. Known as the Better Housing Program (BHP), this campaign was the responsibility of the Federal Housing Administration, which sprang into feverish activity shortly after its official establishment in June. Though the BHP began as a public-awareness campaign, it shortly became something more significant: a populist mass movement seemingly grassroots, yet sponsored and controlled by the federal government itself. Purposefully conceived as a civic-oriented appeal, the BHP appeared to be as far removed from federal legislation and credit markets as Washington's lawmakers and lobbyists were from Main Street America. But it was on those same Main Streets beginning in July that the emblems and slogans of this latest New Deal program gradually appeared, on lapel pins, on window posters, and on billboards, as the FHA secured BHP participation at the local level.[35]

By mid-September over one thousand communities—"from New York with its population of 7,000,000 people to the small hamlet of Sholes, Nebraska, population 90"—had opened BHP offices and organized local campaigns, enlisting individuals, businesses, and governments in the campaign to convince property owners to modernize. The latter were especially eager to cooperate with the BHP, hoping that modernization, in addition to economic and employment stimulation, might restore financial health to a real estate tax base that had been eroding since 1929.[36] With FHA encouragement, elected officials issued modernization proclamations and declared special "civic spirit" and "celebration" days to inaugurate the local BHPs. In Detroit a mayoral proclamation in October 1934 opened the inaugural meeting of the Motor City's BHP, an event held in the General Motors Auditorium with a keynote address by the FHA's public relations director Ward Canaday. In New York Mayor Fiorello La Guardia proclaimed "Better Housing Month" in November 1934 and requested that every eligible New Yorker act "as promptly as possible to modernize and improve his real estate."[37] Such public gestures, as Robert and Helen Lynd observed, served as rallying points for expressions of group solidarity and loyalty, especially in times of crisis.[38] This certainly seemed to be the case with the BHP. By the end of 1934, the number of organized local campaigns had nearly quadrupled to 3,822, a figure that included most American towns with populations over 5,000, as well as the ten largest cities in every state. In October, when the FHA confidently proclaimed: "Modernization Drive Sweeps Nation," it hardly seemed an exaggeration.[39]

As a national campaign, the BHP was modeled on the Liberty Loan Drives of World War I, but it also resembled the massive publicity effort of the National Recovery Administration (NRA).[40] As orchestrated by Hugh Johnson in the summer of 1933, the NRA generated an unprecedented amount of national hoopla and organizational frenzy. In the spring of 1934, there was talk in the Capitol that President Roosevelt would name Johnson himself to head the FHA, since his proficiency at stirring public sentiment and marshaling public support from a demoralized populace would have benefited this new promotional campaign.[41] When army general Johnson was passed over in favor of oil executive James Moffett as the FHA chief, the tenor of incipient BHP was decisively altered. Instead of "rouse the troops" exhortation, the BHP would utilize methods of persuasion borrowed from sales and marketing. Instead of relying solely on the motivation of "We Do Our Part" commonality, incentives of self-interest and individual profit often eclipsed collective national interest. Though the FHA would sometimes resort to unabashed patriotic rhetoric in promoting modernization, the BHP itself resembled less a mobilization of troops than an entrepreneurial business expansion. This was not entirely inappropriate since the FHA described itself as "first of all, a business organization."[42] But it meant that the local campaigns appeared to resemble in no small degree a nationwide chain of offices, bureaus, or showrooms whose managers used chummy social appeals to win the approval of the local business fraternity. Frequently set up in abandoned Main Street storefronts, these BHP offices existed solely for the purpose of "selling modernization," not merely as an antidote to the Depression, but as a slick business proposition that knowingly blended civic boosterism and political populism.

Though a private sector business and sales ethic pervaded the Better Housing Program, this does not imply that the BHP was unregulated or lacking in federally administered controls. In fact, the opposite was true, as the FHA carefully orchestrated the BHP from its regional, state, and district offices with a deft combination of laissez-faire and micromanagement. This permitted individual latitude in program promotion, even as it rigorously enforced procedural implementation. In other words, even as the FHA closely administered the BHP, it gave the program the public appearance of a freewheeling, free-market enterprise existing apart from government intervention or emotional appeals: "It is not charity—it is not patriotism—it is good business." Agency officials repeatedly emphasized that the BHP/MCP program was neither "a government drive" nor "an ordinary sales campaign," though it was actually an amalgam of both. Rather, they claimed it was "a business instrumentality" that would allow banking, building, and manufacturing to resume normal activity and growth.[43] These claims were the work of the FHA's Public Relations Division, which described itself as responsible for "the selling end of the business." Under the direction of Ward Canaday, an advertising and car company executive as well as a time-payment/credit-finance pioneer, the PR Division devised a publicity program that, in Canaday's words, created a "ground swell of public opinion" to increase demand for modernization while carefully avoiding any semblance of promotional "ballyhoo." This was accomplished through the nationwide distribution of publications that provided a stream of modernization information flowing from Washington to the states, to the local BHPs, and then to the individual property owner.[44]

Already by the fall of 1934, the FHA had released a vast amount of these publications to communities participating in the BHP: over five dozen bulletins, booklets, brochures, checklists, application forms, posters, and printer's mats, as well as buttons, transparencies, metal signs, and billboards (fig. 2.3). These materials were available free of charge and in quantities both large and small. For the basic explanatory publication *How Owners of Home and Business Property Can Secure the Benefits of the National Housing Act* (FHA-101, twenty-three pages), the FHA advised that towns with populations under 2,500 order between 100 and 250 copies, and that cities with populations over 1 million order between 30,000 and 75,000 copies. In New York, the New York Central Railroad alone ordered 60,000 copies of FHA-101 for distribution to its employees and passengers on its commuter lines running into and out of Grand Central Terminal. By October 1934 the FHA claimed that it was sending out 30,000 booklets a day to those who would buy building modernization and those who would sell it.[45]

The publications aimed at buyers included a sophisticated array of promotional materials designed to generate maximum publicity for modernization. One of the most successful was the *Modernization Clip Sheet*, an eight-column broadside sent regularly to 14,000 daily and weekly newspapers.[46] It functioned as a sort of FHA wire service, providing dispatches of unrestricted editorial copy and camera-ready illustrations appropriate for real estate, building, home, and opinion pages, as well as local or metro news coverage. Predictably, *Clip Sheet* articles supported the work of the MCP by examining the state of the building and retail industries and real estate and financial conditions, and including statistics on reemployment, construction, lending volume, and industrial production. Invariably, they also had an optimistic slant intended to show that economic conditions were improving. The *Clip Sheet* also provided extensive coverage of the technical, practical, and aesthetic aspects of building modernization. Written as if they were reports on national trends— "Public Now Demands Up-to-Date Stores"—these articles were often accompanied by illustrated modernization case studies with the specifics of a project's location, cost, and the extent of modernization work. "Modernized on Main Street" is a typical example, explaining how the owners of the Block & Kuhl department store in Moline, Illinois, spent $2,800 to install a seventy-foot-long glass-and-metal storefront (fig. 2.4).[47]

By October 1934 the PR Division reported that material from the *Clip Sheet* was being used by the *New York Times*, the *Washington Post*, and the *Los Angeles Examiner*, as well as dozens of small local papers. During

NEW STORE FRONTS ATTRACT CUSTOMERS

(Mat No. FHA 310)

Money Spent on Modernizing Under New Liberal Terms May Prove to Be Wise Investment

Modernizing may prove to be the way to take "For Rent" signs off vacant store and shop buildings. No progressive tenant wants an old, dilapidated structure. Buildings in a good location and in good condition, however, usually rent without delay.

You can get loans now from your local bank or other financial institution to modernize stores, shops, and other types of business property. The National Housing Act has made money available to property owners for this purpose on the most reasonable terms ever offered.

You can borrow as much as $2,000 and pay it back monthly over a period up to 5 years (at the discretion of the financial institution).

Modernizing a store front is not expensive if you use some of the new surfacing materials. They can be easily applied and add greatly to the outward appearance. Money wisely spent in this way frequently means the difference between no income at all and a substantial profit.

Here are some pointers to remember in modernizing stores or shops: Provide maximum window display space flush with the building line; a wide entrance door, preferably opening in; simple exterior lines; space above the entrance for a large sign; and adequate lighting and ventilation for show windows.

Before-and-after view of a bakery shop modernized with some of the new surfacing material. An investment such as this will frequently pay for itself.

Figure 2.3 Printer's mat prepared by the FHA Public Relations Division to promote building modernization. The mat was available free of charge and featured a generic article about the benefits of storefront improvements alongside before-and-after photographs of a typically modernized front. (FHA, *Portfolio of Publicity*, 1934, 77. National Archives and Records Administration, Record Group 31.)

Modernized On Main Street

Figure 2.4 "Modernized on Main Street," Block & Kuhl store in Moline, Illinois. This article was typical of those featured in the *Clip Sheet*, a broadside the FHA sent to newspapers across the country with ready-made editorial content. These articles were generally celebratory in their coverage of the modernization movement and the building industry. (*FHA Clip Sheet* 8, no. 7, 1936. National Archives and Records Administration, Record Group 31.)

the first eighteen months of the program, newspaper coverage relating to modernization and the BHP amounted to 17,300 printed pages and included special Better Housing sections and daily and weekly Better Housing features. In addition, FHA figures indicated that during those same eighteen months, this coverage generated nearly 67 million agate lines of modernization advertising, representing revenues of over $33 million.[48] Since these figures included only direct tie-ins (ads mentioning the FHA by name or displaying its emblem), the agency predicted that the actual linage and revenues were even greater.

Less profitable than newspaper coverage but equally important in generating widespread publicity were the FHA's nonprint media promotions. In 1935 the agency launched the *Better Housing News Flashes,* a series of newsreels produced jointly with Pathé and Movietone. Distributed free of charge to the nation's movie theaters, the *News Flashes* were intended to "carry the message of modernization, repair, and new construction in graphic terms." Each *News Flash* was a talking short feature, five to six minutes in length; "A Come-Back for Key West," documenting efforts to modernize the city's business district, was a typical title. By the summer of 1935, the *News Flashes* had been booked in over 10,000 movie theaters, including premier houses like Grauman's Egyptian in Hollywood and the Paramount in New York. At the conclusion of their cinematic runs, the FHA screened the *News Flashes* for trade groups, civic organizations, and schools. By 1936 the FHA estimated that over 40 million Americans had viewed the *News Flashes* during 150,000 scheduled showings.[49]

Paralleling the newsreels was a drive to place modernization coverage on the radio. Eventually numbering 18,000 broadcasts, this coverage included FHA-prepared public service announcements, special interest features, and "human interest playlets"—ten-minute dramas designed to personalize the need for modernization. There were also multiweek programs broadcast on the major networks: *The Women's Hour* and *Your Home and Mine* were aimed at a predominantly female daytime audience; *The Master Builder* and *The Story of $1,000* were aimed at both female and male evening listeners.[50] Though produced in-house by the FHA, these series were sponsored by major corporations including General Electric, Johns-Manville, General Motors, and others who stood to gain materially from the national success of the modernization drive. The FHA's embrace of modern media like film and radio was well in keeping with the up-to-date, progressive tenor of the New Deal. In content, however, the FHA's newsreels and radio programs were in ideological opposition to the social critique and reformist agendas of many other government-sponsored entertainments of the period. Unlike the "Living Newspapers" produced by the Federal Theater under the auspices of the WPA, for example, the modernization productions would never be accused of creeping socialism. Rather, in their underlying consumerism and valorization of middle-class ideals and aspirations, they seemed intent on maintaining the civic and business orientation of Main Street itself.[51]

A Local Campaign

Nowhere in the modernization effort was this orientation more explicit than in the promotional materials aimed at the local BHP and pitched toward the sellers of modernization. For these men and women, the FHA supplied a series of technical bulletins and training manuals addressing every aspect of the modernization program in step-by-step procedures, rules, and regulations, all of which emphasized the benefits of community participation. First, by bringing money "out of hiding" and "back into the channels of retail trade," a local campaign stimulated all types of business and was "not simply a builder's program."[52] Second, by putting people back to work, it reduced relief expenditures. Third, by encouraging long-deferred repairs, a campaign improved the "usefulness and value" of real property, adding to "the beauty and appearance of a city." Here the FHA was adding a civic incentive to its primary business-creating inducements, a motivational coupling designed to appeal to the endemic community spirit so well documented in *Middletown*.[53]

Program procedures were spelled out explicitly in *Community Campaign*, issued in the summer of 1934 and serving as a guide for recruiting volunteers to its executive and advisory committees, beginning with a community's most prominent citizens and businesspeople. In New York, Manhattan Borough president Samuel Levy and real estate attorney Peter Grimm were appointed co-chairs of the Manhattan BHP while the presidents of RCA, American Radiator, Johns-Manville, and the Manufacturers Trust Bank, as well as Broadway's George M. Cohan and parade organizer Grover Whalen served on an advisory committee responsible for campaign oversight.[54] In Los Angeles the BHP formed a Committee of One Hundred "important Californians," including Hollywood notables Louis B. Mayer, Jack Warner, and Harold Lloyd, publishers William Randolph Hearst and Harry Chandler, airplane magnate Donald Douglas, Bullock's President P. G. Winnett, and U.S. Senator William Gibbs McAdoo.[55] In Chicago the advisory committee counted among its members the scions of such prominent Midwest families as

Armour, Cummings, and Pirie.[56] In smaller cities and towns, BHP advisory committees drew their members from those businesses that stood to gain most immediately from the modernization program, principally banking and building, but also from real estate boards and civic, fraternal, and veterans organizations with long traditions of community involvement. These included the Rotary, Lions, and Kiwanis clubs as well as the American Legion and the U.S. Chamber of Commerce, both of which passed national resolutions urging their affiliates to support their local campaigns.[57] For these organizations, the promotional work of the BHP was a logical extension of the community-boosting, business-building, and civic-pride agendas that were their organizational mainstay.

Other committees carried out the day-to-day operations of the local campaigns. The finance committee underwrote the cost of the campaign through contributions solicited especially from those who stood to profit directly from the campaign's success.[58] A campaign contribution, in cash or in-kind, enabled a business to display a BHP logo in its window, to use the BHP logo in advertising, and to tie its promotional activities with those of the local campaign. It also gave the contributor a place on the list of participating firms prepared by the local BHP and distributed to property owners considering modernization. The women's committee encouraged female participation as modernization boosters to staff information booths at fairs and expositions, conduct door-to-door canvassing, plan informational luncheons, run educational classes, and cultivate women as customers of modernization, both in the home and on Main Street, where they were taught how to use their influence as consumers to encourage the modernization of the stores they patronized.[59] The women's committee also worked with the local chapters of national organizations like the League of Women Voters, the Junior League, the DAR, the Federated Garden Clubs of America, and various ladies' auxiliaries. Eventually, the FHA reported the participation of 26,000 local chapters of 700 such organizations.[60]

The loan committee secured the participation of local financial institutions, which numbered 11,000 across the nation by the end of 1935.[61] This participation ranged from simply extending modernization credit to actively soliciting modernization business. In northern New Jersey, for example, a bank with branches throughout Essex County sent direct-mail letters and made follow-up phone calls to nearly 1,700 licensed building contractors offering to collaborate in modernization promotion.[62] The loan committee provided participating financial institutions with varying amounts of technical support, from direct assistance in credit investigations and loan closures to prescreening loan applicants through BHP financial bureaus in order to expedite the loan procedure. To assist the loan committee, the FHA provided a barrage of promotional information designed to convince banks to cooperate with the BHP, including blank credit statement forms, window and lobby displays, explanatory brochures, advertising mats, and a series of banking testimonials (fig. 2.5). In these, bank presidents, managers, and cashiers in cities and towns varying in size from 2,000 (East Islip, Long Island) to 780,000 (Boston, Massachusetts) recounted their firsthand experiences with MCP lending. As was typical of the FHA's approach to promotion, the testimonials supplied no-nonsense lending procedures and policies in the guise of Rotarian conviviality: "Any such knockers [refused loan applicants] would undo the work of a dozen boosters."[63]

This booster spirit was also evident in the work of the industry committees charged with cultivating broad-based BHP support among building and non-building-related businesses alike. These committees strove to swell public opinion in favor of modernization by convincing local firms that they would benefit from the BHP as soon as building tradesmen were back at work, drawing paychecks and purchasing goods and services.[64] They organized modernization exhibitions featuring small displays by local firms, be they plumbers, roofers, material suppliers, or the local chapter of the American Institute of Architects. These exhibitions were usually set up in the local BHP office, but occasionally they took place in more prominent locations: hotel lobbies, civic center auditoriums, armories, and public plazas.[65] At their best, these exhibitions functioned as a kind of multi-firm showroom, transforming the BHP headquarters or another rented space into a complete selling environment, a one-stop shopping center to simplify the purchase of modernization products and building improvements.

The industry committees also encouraged businesses to distribute home modernization information to their employees, to place modernization exhibits in their lobbies, and to modernize their own physical plants, be they stores, offices, or other commercial establishments. The *Philadelphia Evening Bulletin*, for example, not only launched a special modernization supplement in its daily newspaper; it launched plans to modernize its 1908 office building. In 1937 the newspaper installed new lighting and ventilation systems and a new black granite and glass-block facade designed by George Howe, architect of the PSFS Building.[66] The FHA provided additional support for these committees via a national direct-mail campaign with a number of industry-specific letters that were coordinated

Figure 2.5 Advertisement "blanks" prepared by the FHA Public Relations Division. These sample advertisements were supplied to local banks to secure their cooperation with the Modernization Credit Plan and to guide how they promoted the plan to the public. (FHA, *Sample Better Housing Program Advertisements*, 1936. National Archives and Records Administration, Record Group 31.)

with locally conducted telephone or in-person follow-up contact. In October 1934, for example, fifteen thousand letters were sent from Washington to every movie theater owner and operator in the country, asking them to permit lobby displays for literature distribution, to screen FHA films, and to modernize their facilities by installing new marquees, air-conditioning, and anything else deemed necessary for an up-to-date theater.[67]

The publicity committee promoted the campaign as widely as possible throughout its community to stimulate local media coverage and to generate its own. For the latter, it often utilized the FHA's *Portfolio of Publicity*. This *Portfolio* contained a tear sheet of "Facts and Figures for Editorial Writers," as well as twenty-two dummies for "suggested" feature news stories about modernization and the BHP that the committee would "feed" to newspapers, localizing them wherever possible.[68] Publicity committees also staged contests, gimmicks, and stunts to attract attention to the campaign. The BHP in Middletown, Ohio, organized a contest to select the property that would "benefit the most through modernization." While this was hardly a title of distinction, since the prize was $1,000 worth of free modernization work, over three hundred entries were received.[69] Promotional gimmicks advertising modernization often appeared in unexpected contexts: in Fulton, New York, the BHP logo appeared on milk bottle caps; in Lansing, Michigan, it appeared with the word "modernize" stenciled in red paint on every downtown street corner.[70] Many of these local activities were reported in *Better Housing*, a weekly newsletter produced in Washington and distributed to local BHPs for their internal use. According to the FHA, *Better Housing* was "designed to serve as a medium of exchange of helpful ideas" and, like any house organ, to boost morale and enthusiasm.[71] The local activities documented in *Better Housing* demonstrate a remarkable degree of marketing acumen in their simultaneous appeal to property owners and service to the modernization drive, often in the guise of hometown civic boosting. This was fully evident in the parades staged as "an effective opening gun" for the local campaigns (fig. 2.6).[72]

These parades had the expected trappings of a typical small-town cavalcade in the 1930s. Assembled with one part earnest enthusiasm and one part calculated hokum, they included Uncle Sam, marching bands, a fife and drum corps, Boy and Girl Scouts, waving politicians, and parade marshals. The heart of the parade followed these groups: the bandwagons, floats, and vehicles decorated with flags, bunting, and BHP signs and representing the local business community, especially its contractors, building suppliers, architects, and retailers. Businesses sent trucks mounted

Lewiston, Idaho, Welcomes Better Housing Program with Mile-Long Parade

Figure 2.6 Better Housing parade in Lewiston, Idaho. These parades, held across the country to kick off local campaigns, featured marching bands and floats supplied by the local real estate and building industries. They frequently included a "shabby shack" or small-scale run-down building in need of drastic modernization. (*Better Housing*, October 22, 1934. National Archives and Records Administration, Record Group 31.)

with multiple loudspeakers blaring patriotic messages: "Let's Americanize. Let's modernize." The parading motor vehicles were a kind of capitalist agitprop made all the more emphatic by the absence in the parade lineup of precisely those people who were to benefit most directly from the modernization drive: the ranks of unemployed building tradesmen. In the 1930s demonstrating workers—even benevolent, community-spirited ones—might have given a parade the aspect of a labor rally and perhaps an attendant whiff of communism, something local boosters would have wished to avoid at all costs.[73]

Instead, the Better Housing parades that took place on Main Streets across the country in the fall of 1934 were a hybrid pageant form reflecting the amalgamative nature of the BHP. Elements of patriotism, civicism, and commercialism were all present. As kickoffs to local modernization drives, they functioned in much the same manner, though on a greatly reduced scale, as commercial parades of the 1920s that were staged by groups of merchants with the cooperation of city officials and the police. Though often promoted as celebrations of some civic advance or improvement, such parades were really just merchandising opportunities for the local retailers.[74] The BHP parades offered building industry merchants a similar opportunity but with the perquisite of official U.S. government approval.

Often the attention-getting climax to the parade was the final float, a large flatbed truck decorated with signs and banners advertising local contractors and suppliers. Upon the truck, sitting like Santa Claus in the Macy's Parade, was a dilapidated building that had been jacked up and moved—every joist, window frame, and nail. The parade carried the "shabby shack" to its final destination on the town square or a vacant Main Street lot. There the building was unloaded and a "modernization miracle" commenced, as local building tradesmen began feverish work to transform the shack into a modern dwelling.[75] Such demonstrations were often a key event of the BHP, especially when carried out on a high-profile site—the courthouse lawn or a vacant lot in the business district. One of the most attention-getting demonstrations shared the limelight with a national exposition during "Modernization Day" at the Chicago Century of Progress International Exposition in October 1934. The focus of the demonstration was two identical nineteenth-century clapboard shacks. One was to be completely modernized; the other was to be left in its run-down state, with the pair presenting a "'before and after' perspective" for comparison. At 9:00 a.m. on October 24, Federal Housing administrator James Moffett stepped up to the house slated for modernization and, with crowbar in hand, ripped a rotting piece of siding off the front facade, signaling the commencement of the renovation. Over 125 tradesman and laborers then set to work in a model of orchestrated Tayloristic efficiency. Carpenters, bricklayers, plumbers, electricians, painters, and others moved in rapid succession to complete the transformation of "the eyesore" into the "house of marvel" by three o'clock that afternoon—in a mere six hours.[76]

The modernization demonstration was an unabashed publicity stunt, a novelty as worthy of a *Tribune* headline as the Century of Progress air show with which it shared column space.[77] It was "an extraordinary performance" celebrating the manual skill of building workers and not, as was usually the case in lauded BHP events, the managerial or promotional skills of businessmen. The spectacularization of this performance was heightened by the camera crew filming it for the newsreels and by the live radio hookup on NBC reporting on the modernization work in progress. If this play-by-play of hammers, saws, and paintbrushes was hardly as exciting as those publicity-worthy events and stunts of the previous decade—Floyd Collins trapped in a cave or Alvin Kelly sitting on a flagpole—it was an acceptable Depression-era version in which standard ballyhoo was overlaid with a veneer of respectable interest in national recovery.

Main Street Boosters

When submitting its second annual report to Congress in 1936, the FHA noted that its programs had been implemented and conducted by volunteers and proclaimed that "too much credit cannot be given to the public spirited citizens who have thus contributed their time, energy, and money in the interest of recovery."[78] That the FHA was able to secure widespread national cooperation without the use of coercive tactics or legal compulsion was one of the remarkable achievements of the BHP. By January 1936 nearly eight thousand local campaigns were under way and an additional fifteen hundred were in the planning stages. Certainly, this level of cooperation had not been achieved without incurring at least some expense on the part of the government: during the first eighteen months of the program, FHA headquarters in Washington spent over $1 million on what it called "the educational program" necessary to implement the Modernization Credit Plan.[79] This federal expenditure notwithstanding, the FHA's assessment of the voluntary and public-spirited character of BHP participation was largely accurate, but it fails to acknowledge the incentives that real estate historian Marc Weiss has identified as the "carrot on the stick" intrinsic to every successful FHA program. Weiss notes how carefully the FHA cultivated "an image of voluntarism" by dangling irresistible "carrots" before the depressed building and banking industries.[80] Loan insurance may have been the legal bait held out to obtain voluntary participation in the BHP and the modernization drive, but the irresistible lure was the promise of profits:

> You may cooperate with the Better Housing Program sponsored by the United States Government with profit to yourself and to your

country. . . . [It] is *your* program. No matter what your business, it will put money in your pocket if you accept the opportunity it presents you.[81]

If the BHP was promulgated and received as a sound business venture, this does not diminish the public-spiritedness of BHP participation. In the United States in the 1930s, and indeed during the whole period between the wars, business self-interest and community spirit were not antithetical propositions, especially in the Main Street communities where the BHP thrived. Rather, as diverse observers recognized at the time, the two had been conflated into the middlebrow culture of the booster, who sincerely believed that what was good for business was, without exception, good for the community. This fusion of business values and civic virtues into the phenomenon of boosterism may have been disparaged as Babbittry, but it was also condoned as local pride and understood as something that represented a quantifiable social trend.[82]

In *Middletown* the Lynds documented the astounding rise during the 1920s of clubs, associations, and movements that attracted legions of middle-class Americans to such all-encompassing causes as "civic betterment" and "civic progress." Working through chambers of commerce and Rotary clubs, boosters participated in a range of activities that included improving the physical appearance of local buildings, generating local publicity to attract new businesses and residents, and holding local pep rallies as ends in themselves.[83] Born of the war effort and nurtured during the prosperity decade, these community activities were expressions of "group solidarity." As the Lynds demonstrated in *Middletown in Transition*, they continued to flourish even in the economic crisis of the Depression. If anything, such activities may have actually gained in popularity during the 1930s as the middle class, reeling from "the shock of sudden and sharp institutional breakdown," found increasing comfort in optimistic slogans, campaigns, and "the paraphernalia of social organizations searching for things to boost" to revive that civic spirit that the Depression had dampened.[84]

Within the FHA, boosterism was deftly, but empathetically, exploited to create in the BHP a genuine popular movement, akin to the Townsendites or the Share-Our-Wealthers—a movement as earnest in its particular aspirations toward recovery through consumption as any of the other nonreligious, social evangelist crusades of the decade.[85] But among these other movements, the BHP occupied a unique position. So clearly part of what the Brain Trust's Gardiner Means called the "élan, optimism, evangelism, and adventure" of the New Deal, and enjoying full federal sponsorship, the BHP managed to attract precisely those middle-class Americans who distrusted both liberal thinkers and big government.[86] This the BHP accomplished through its use of knowing booster appeals, complete with appropriate lingo, exclamation points, and italics: "What an opportunity the Better Housing Program opens to Business! What a challenge to the initiative and energy of American genius for *doing*."[87] From its lapel pins to its inspirational meetings to its parades, the BHP cultivated and extended that preexistent enthusiasm for community co-operation and organization in which the businessman/citizen was not merely a volunteer, but a joiner, "a booster, not a knocker."[88] Like Sinclair Lewis's fictitious but all too real George Babbitt, the BHP participant would have recognized the local modernization campaign as "a force for optimism, manly pleasantry, and good business." A selling campaign that required persuasion and commitment, the BHP was what Babbitt heralded as "an opportunity for real he-hustling, getting out and drumming up customers." A combination of civic improvement, business development, and patriotism, it embodied what Babbitt celebrated as "that famous Zenith [read: Anytown] spirit."[89] In its adroit but irony-free deployment of the rhetoric, impulses, and habits of Main Street, U.S.A., the BHP and the modernization drive it promoted did not simply reflect booster culture; they *were* booster culture.

Canvassing Main Street

After the initial boosting frenzy of the local campaigns, after the parades, exhibitions, and banquets, came the hard work of selling modernization to property owners and qualified lessees, a responsibility that fell to the field campaign. Indeed, the field campaign was so critical to a successful community campaign that the FHA asserted that the work of the BHP committees were merely preparatory, "paving the way and facilitating the work of the field force."[90] Federal officials reinforced this attitude. The FHA's Title I administrator Albert Deane and its PR director Ward Canaday both explained to local civic groups and trade associations that the BHP was "essentially a sales effort" and that each community campaign should be considered "as aggressive a sales drive as possible," so that the potential modernization market might be adequately tapped in the interest of economic recovery.[91] This market, "so vast as to seem fantastic," was to be stimulated by local building-to-building canvasses to encourage, cajole, and persuade property owners and qualified renters to modernize.

For a campaign of this scale and significance to be effective, it would require a sales force both exceptionally organized and singularly motivated. For this reason the FHA recommended as director of the field campaign—the BHP's only full-time, paid position—the appointment of "a man of the sales manager type who has had wide experience in organizing and directing large groups of workers."[92] As a recognizable business type, the sales manager proliferated after WWI with the increased specialization of production and distribution in American manufacturing. Though in the 1920s Thorstein Veblen, H. L. Mencken, and others derided the sales manager as an egregious manifestation of the economy of "absentee ownership" and the culture of the "booboisie," to the U.S. government in the 1930s he possessed certain skills and enthusiasms that qualified him for the local BHP's "most important position."[93] In fact, the same qualities that made the sales manager an object of highbrow scorn recommended him to the FHA as a figure of middlebrow empathy. What Sinclair Lewis ridiculed, the BHP would laud:

> The Romantic Hero was no longer the knight, the wandering poet, the cowpuncher, the aviator, nor the brave young district attorney, but the great sales-manager, who had an Analysis of Merchandizing Problems on his glass-topped desk, whose title of nobility was "Go-Getter," and who devoted himself and all his young samurai to the cosmic purpose of Selling.[94]

Such a single-minded devotion to selling, coupled with the ability to inspire such devotion in others, was a highly desirable skill in the context of the modernization drive. In the 1930s Lewis's sneering "cosmic purpose" was transformed into a national aspiration toward economic recovery. If this did not imbue selling with a truly higher purpose, it at least provided ennobling pretensions for the sales managers motivating those volunteers and relief workers sent out into the local community to promote modernization.

The modernization field campaign that these managers supervised began with a mapping effort to divide the sales territory into geographical districts and sections to create manageable canvass units determined by the physical extent, density, type, and condition of buildings in the community.[95] This involved plotting the properties within sections using data from local real estate boards and tax assessors or CWA Real Property Inventories and was often accomplished with direct assistance from local municipalities. In Rhode Island, for example, the office of the city

Figure 2.7 Modernization billboard in Morristown, New Jersey, fall 1934. While it was erected specifically to announce a property canvass to be held in September and October, the billboard also promoted the local campaign in general, making a direct connection between modernization and local employment. (*Better Housing*, October 22, 1934. National Archives and Records Administration, Record Group 31.)

engineer in the state capitol at Providence supplied detailed district maps for the entire state, drawn up especially for the BHP field campaign.[96] Mapping was followed immediately by canvassing, which was typically was well publicized through newspaper advertisements, radio announcements, and even full-size billboards (fig. 2.7).[97] The purpose of the canvass was to contact every property owner and qualified lessee in the community and "urge" them to undertake modernization work. This included actively soliciting pledges to modernize as well as simply gathering information on potential modernization prospects. The intensity and duration of canvasses varied from community to community. In Atlanta, 2,500 canvassers covered the local field in a single day in October 1934, making 20,768 calls on property owners and tenants and producing $3.1 million in modernization pledges. In San Diego, by contrast, 50 field-workers took two months to conduct an initial canvass of residential properties followed by a second canvass of commercial properties. In Kansas, 300 field-workers conducted a short-term canvass in Kansas City, a town then comparable in population and area to San Diego, covering all home and business properties in ten days.[98]

The workers conducting these canvasses included civic-minded volunteers as well as salesmen representing building material and equipment suppliers on temporary "loan" to the BHP. The FHA considered these on-loan salesmen/canvassers "volunteers" since they participated in the campaign at no cost to the local BHP or the federal government. Their employers regarded them similarly, considering their BHP work as a sort of in-kind donation, as in Georgia, where a roofing supply company with branches throughout the state furnished a crew of fifty sales representatives committed to selling $1 million worth of building improvements through the MCP. To the company's president, the field campaign offered the opportunity to put private resources to public use: "We feel that we are rendering a public service as well as discharging a legitimate function of business."[99] Of course, it also offered the opportunity to increase demand for roofing supplies as a result of contact between property owners and credit machinery, facilitated by his company salesmen. While BHP critics saw this as a kind of collusion between private interest and a government agency, the FHA dismissed such concerns, frankly acknowledging that self-interest was necessary for the program's success.

Perhaps the most self-interested of all participants in the field campaign were the independent subcontractors, jobbers, and laborers who made up the majority of the field force, those building tradesmen who were unemployed or underemployed as a result of the depressed state of the building industry. A number of these plumbers, bricklayers, and painters were actually workers receiving federal or state relief, who were canvassing as part of their work assignments. Putting these tradesmen to work in the field campaign made sense since canvassing carried the possibility of job creation, stimulating modernization work that might get building tradesmen off the dole. Throughout the first six months of the BHP, the FHA offered anecdotal evidence to this effect, citing numerous communities, from Baltimore to San Antonio to Oakland, in which building tradesman/canvassers were removed from the relief rolls after finding work through the BHP.[100] In the FHA's view, "It was assumed that a project under which unemployed persons rang doorbells in an effort to create employment was a wholly meritorious project"—one appropriately funded by the Federal Emergency Relief Administration (FERA) and, beginning in 1935, by the Works Progress Administration (WPA) as well. It is difficult to ascertain how many of the approximately ten thousand local BHPs utilized FERA and WPA relief workers in their field canvasses, but evidence suggests that it was a high percentage that included campaigns in all forty-eight states. In New Jersey alone, each of the state's nearly three hundred local BHPs received an allotment of WPA workers, and some campaigns were funded entirely by the WPA as work relief projects. Such extensive use of relief workers enraged congressional opponents, who accused the BHPs of ethical violations amounting to "an army of 3,000 WPA workers employed to ring doorbells and drum up trade for contractors."[101] This may have been true, but the BHP canvass must also have had a certain appeal for self-respecting, independent building tradesmen as an honorable means of avoiding the humiliation of the dole, a factor that should not be underestimated as an incentive to unpaid participation in the modernization drive. As anecdotal evidence suggested at the time, and period recollections have continued to testify, American workers in the Depression were willing to try anything and exhaust all possibilities for finding employment before giving up and seeking relief.[102]

Furthermore, the opportunity the BHP presented for tradesmen to pitch their products had no small appeal in an era when the door-to-door salesman was a vaunted professional, an enterprising individualist whose success or failure was measured, in the popular imagination, by his own hard work and determination and not by the vagaries of an industrialized economic system beyond his control. This must have been particularly true in a moment when the system appeared to have abandoned nearly one-third of the country's building tradesmen. The FHA actively cultivated this ethos of door-to-door selling by continually reinforcing the notion that the modernization effort was a competitive sales drive, complete with quota systems and contests to improve field performance in securing prospects, pledges, and increased modernization business. The agency established quotas for the number of modernization jobs, dollar volume, and notes insured in each of the forty-eight states, as determined by population, purchasing power, building age, and other "business enterprise" or marketing factors.[103] It then tracked quota percentages attained and ranked participating communities and states accordingly in a competitive "race between regional divisions."[104] Quotas and rankings that served as inducements to field-force rivalry were all typical sales strategies of the 1920s and 1930s, advocated in popular salesmanship manuals and promoted by sales services and sales management publications, all of which underscored the "ask 'em to buy" basis of the BHP.[105]

Modernization Salesmen

This insistent sales message was essential to the success of the "follow-up" portion of the field campaign, described as "an aggressive sales effort" dedicated to "securing the final signature on the dotted line," that is, to turning prospects cultivated in the canvass into committed modernizers.[106] The primary activity of the follow-up section was the orchestration of contact between cultivated prospects and those the FHA dubbed "sales representatives," the architects, contractors, and material and equipment dealers whose job it was to confirm canvass pledges, provide firm estimates for property improvements, and finalize contracts for modernization work. Administrator James Moffett underscored their significance to the modernization drive in a speech to the Los Angeles BHP in January 1935 in which he declared that the best follow-up force consisted of "the men and women who stand to profit from a modernization campaign," not only because of their knowledge but because their vested interest made them uniquely persuasive salesmen: "People become very eloquent and strangely moving when they recommend something by which they will profit financially."[107] These follow-up representatives were apparently more than willing to participate in the modernization drive, hoping that it might, as the FHA promised, generate work weeks and months after the original canvass.

Architects prepared modernization plans and estimates for their assigned prospects, often in cooperation with contractors and dealers, and they consulted with property owners to consider style and structural changes requiring architectural services. General contractors hired salesmen to solicit extra modernization work and canvassed property owners and tenants in the vicinity of modernization jobs under way, effectively turning those jobs into ongoing demonstrations of the work they were doing. They also prepared unsolicited estimates for additional improvements at active job sites, demonstrating to the property owner the supposed economy of doing extra work while the current modernization was under way.[108] Dealers inventoried products and maintained adequate stocks in preparation for increased business once the prospects placed their orders. They also developed "vigorous merchandising ideas" for products that had been "growing dusty on the shelves for the last four or five years," hoping to sell them to the public in the context of modernization, something that building material manufacturers were doing simultaneously on the national level.[109]

The FHA stressed the importance of members of the building industry working as "a close-knit organization" in the field campaign, as demonstrated in New Jersey's statewide BHP. There the follow-up became a detailed "survey-sales system" that allowed field teams of specially trained architects, contractors, and realtors to finalize modernization deals by providing interested merchants or property owners with complete store or building improvement plans. Included were designs and working drawings, specifications, and cost-profit analyses to demonstrate how modernization might be amortized through increased sales—all of this provided free of charge and with no obligation. The field teams also presented outlays and payment schedules, but by promoting the MCP instead of cash payment, they placed the cost of a modernization project in a more favorable light, as a small monthly payment, rather than one lump sum. In a culture increasingly dependent on consumer credit, this payment option may have contributed to the success of the New Jersey plan and explain why it produced "a flood of applications" for store modernization work.[110]

So obvious were the FHA's declared benefits of participation in the follow-up—"it will put money in your pocket"—that during the first six months of the BHP, the agency did little to encourage architects, contractors, and dealers to pursue the sales leads that would turn modernization prospects into modernization clients.[111] By January 1935, though, the FHA was unsatisfied with the participation of local follow-up firms, as reports came in from the field that they were negligent in cultivating the prospects assigned to them by the local BHPs. The FHA now determined that these all-important sales representatives required some sort of programming or indoctrination to persuade them to dedicate themselves wholeheartedly to selling modernization. Early in 1935 the FHA announced a plan designed to educate all those involved in "the sale of the merchandise, material, and service" to be used in modernization.[112]

Through this educational program, the FHA attempted a thorough transformation of members of the American building industry, to convert architects, contractors, and dealers from passive participants into "active salesmen and active cooperators in the Better Housing Program." This was accomplished through a series of evening sales meetings that took place in nearly six hundred cities in the spring and summer of 1935.[113] Meetings focused on all of the programs of the National Housing Act—residential modernization and repair, commercial modernization, and new residential construction—but regardless of content, they always included speeches, sales clinics, and round-table discussions with a single goal: "The fundamental message given in the sales schools was 'Go out and ring door bells, and ask prospects to buy.'"[114] This message was conveyed in the sales-methods training that attendees received and in the speeches on "modern salesmanship" and "imagination in selling" that were the keynote of every meeting. Delivered by professional salesmen using texts prepared by the FHA, those speeches contained sensationally boosteristic palaver that at least partially substantiated charges that the FHA encouraged high-pressure selling. Even oblique references to Depression privations were translated into punchy sales lingo:

> I don't known how you men feel about it, but I think we have received a plate full of meat—a plate full of the food we have been hungry for. We have been told how we can do a selling job, and I know that we can do it. I'm asking you men now; will we ask them to buy?[115]

Architects in particular were thought to need this encouragement since their relationship to the expanding modernization business was somewhat different from that of other members of the building industry. Most contractors, subcontractors, and tradesmen had already been actively involved in building repair and improvement prior to the Depression, and for some firms and sole practitioners small, individually contracted jobs were an occupational and financial mainstay—the plumber fixing leaking sinks; the roofer fixing leaking roofs; the carpenter fixing the front porch. The door-to-door pitch and the self-merchandising that the FHA advocated were largely new, but the necessity of hustling for even a modest job was not. For contractors and tradesmen, the changes in business practice wrought by the Depression, and subsequently fostered by the modernization drive, were largely a matter of degree. For architects, however, as the FHA recognized, the effect of these changes was "to broaden the scope of their service." Whether this broadening represented an opportunity or an exigency depended entirely on the outlook of the individual architect.[116]

The FHA, with characteristic optimism, was disposed to the former point of view, which it repeatedly trumpeted in the sales manual given to those attending the Better Selling meetings and in numerous articles appearing in the architectural press. Selling modernization was simply "business building" that would enable the architect "to regain a profitable practice as a designer."[117] The problem, the FHA asserted, was that even in the midst of the Depression architects clung to a belief that in advertising and self-promotion they sacrificed their dignity and professional standing. But James Dusenberry, director of the FHA's Underwriting and Realty Division, was having none of this. In an article published in the AIA's monthly journal, he argued that the "so-called ethical inhibition against straightforward selling [was] often a cloak for ordinary laziness." Though the AIA had lobbied intently for the passage of the National Housing Act and had succeeded in making the architect's fee an allowable modernization expense under the MCP, architects had not adequately responded to the modernization drive that the FHA described as the "greatest single promotion ever given to this group."[118] From the FHA's point of view, the field of building modernization was "a market made to order for the architect," but to exploit it the architect had to become an "aggressive salesman." This was hardly a daunting prospect since, as a result of the FHA's national drive, opportunities for "selling architectural service and modernization" abounded—as long as architects knew where to look. The FHA was only too happy to point the profession in the right direction. As Dusenberry noted, "Main Street is lined with potential projects. Any architect, sitting at his office window, is looking down on many buildings crying for modernization."[119] All that remained was for architects to look at those buildings anew with the appraising eye of a modernization salesman sizing up his territory and his prospects.

Selling Main Street

Having convinced architects and other building industry sales representatives that their local Main Streets offered profitable work, the FHA directed them to "go after this Main Street business" and "sell the store owner." The counsel the agency offered was a typically slick mixture of hype and fact: "Rub-a-dub-dub, three men in a tub. The butcher, the baker, the candlestick maker . . . are now prospects for property modernization. . . . [S]ix out of every twelve stores on Main Street is in need of repair and improvement."[120] In emphasizing Main Street's needs, the FHA counseled architects and contractors to use their professional expertise to think creatively about the scope of modernization, since merchants could use the MCP for any improvements related to current retail operations: the baker could finance new ovens, the grocer new refrigerated cases, the clothier new fitting rooms; and all of them could finance new facades. If those merchants were also building owners, they could get loans for general real property improvements including structural and mechanical upgrades such as air-conditioning, heating, plumbing, and alarm systems. The FHA instructed architects and contractors to promote a broad range of such improvements, proposing that retailers and building owners undertake them jointly, as mutually profitable ventures. To clinch the Main Street sale, the FHA provided sellers with statistical evidence of that profitability, citing a Commerce Department survey that determined that twenty-five out of twenty-six modernized stores "increased their business to such an extent that added profits soon paid the cost of the job."[121]

What the FHA implicitly understood about "selling Modernization to Main Street" was that it was distinct from "selling property improvements on the Farm," for example. That *modernization* and *improvement* had very different connotations was not at all accidental, for the FHA was dealing with two very different markets. Farmers were interested in "common-sense repairs" and conveniences that tended toward running water and electricity. By contrast, Main Street merchants, whether they were independent or part of chains, were more concerned with intangibles like "desirability" and "customer appeal." This was what architects and contractors were really selling on Main Street: "You are now able to sell to merchants a way and means of protecting himself from the most relentless of all competition—obsolescence." Hence, the FHA encouraged modernization salesmen to tour their local business districts, taking stock of Main Street's buildings, noting which properties were obsolete and which were up-to-date. They could then use this information to create individualized modernization sales campaigns on their local Main Streets. Ideally, such campaigns would begin with their own offices and showrooms as they became, in effect, their own first modernization customers. If they truly wanted to be "merchants for modernization," as the FHA put it, their places of business should reflect this.[122]

The emphasis on Main Street in the spring of 1935 reflected a deliberate shift in FHA modernization policy and promotion. The BHP was well under way with 3 million door-to-door canvass calls made, 257 community property canvasses completed, $30 million worth of loans insured, total modernization work nearing $211 million, and 750,000 workers reemployed. However, for the FHA, these impressive figures represented only the MCP's "testing period.[123] There remained "a reservoir of work to be tapped," potentially worth many billions of dollars, but FHA statistics showed that this work would only begin to flow if the BHPs emphasized the modernization of commercial buildings.[124] In the MCP's first year, loans for commercial modernization represented only 11 percent of total modernization funds advanced, an insignificant percentage that the FHA blamed on program nomenclature that hindered borrowing for commercial property improvements. Despite the FHA's efforts to promote all types of building modernization, the MCP was frequently viewed as a housing plan, an understandable misperception given that it was sponsored by the Federal *Housing* Administration and promoted by the Better *Housing* Program. The trade publication *Stores* noted in February 1935, for example, that many merchants had not taken advantage of the MCP because they were unaware of its "commercial usage."[125]

To rectify this, the FHA now began promoting the MCP with a new marketing slogan, "Modernize Main Street: Better Housing for American Business." This local effort was paralleled by a new national campaign, as the FHA enlisted retail trade associations and corporate manufacturers to promote commercial modernization. The joint local/national effort worked: in 1936 modernization loans for commercial property increased to 47 percent of funds advanced as store building activity climbed.[126]

It was the imminent liberalization of the MCP in the spring of 1935 that led the FHA to formulate "Modernize Main Street" as a specialized sales campaign to stimulate more extensive commercial modernization projects than had been financially feasible before the $50,000 loan limit went into effect.[127] Even though the FHA predicted that the higher loan limit would encourage the modernization of such large revenue-producing properties as office buildings, apartment houses, and institutional structures, the agency was especially interested in capturing the store construction market historically lodged on Main Street. Because of what the FHA called the "numerical importance" of smaller stores, as a class they had the potential to generate a high volume of modernization activity.[128] Having determined that approximately 750,000 stores were in need of urgent modernization, the FHA estimated that 10 to 15 percent of those would modernize during 1935 and that it was reasonable to expect an annual modernization rate of 5 percent among all retail units.[129] Based on a minimum expenditure of $1,000 per store—just enough to purchase a new storefront of modest size and design—the FHA estimated that Main Street would generate a volume of modernization work between $75 and $100 million annually.[130]

Statistical data also indicated that the majority of Main Street retailers had deferred capital investments since at least 1932 due to a lack of available funds or a lack of available financing: "Many merchants have delayed plans for modernization because of a desire to conserve resources and keep their working capital free for operations."[131] Data collected by the National Retail Dry Goods Association (NRDGA) supported the FHA's claim: the trade group found that retailers in the under-$75,000-volume class, which included most independent stores, had been unable to finance even a normal program of modernization, estimated to be $2,384, simply because they lacked the funds to do so. Had sufficient financing been available, however, 75 percent would have modernized. This was in marked contrast to the chain stores, which had invested in capital improvements so regularly since 1929 that, according to the FHA, store modernization was now recognized as "the strongest trend" in retail. It was because independent Main Street stores had been unable to follow this trend that the FHA was now "offering government aid to smaller merchants," giving them "a clear-cut opportunity to modernize without any burden on present cash resources"—that is, through the instrument of the MCP.[132] Utilizing earlier industry analyses, the FHA understood that small retailers needed to modernize because of intense market competition. As the agency described the situation: "It is the modernized shops which attract neighborhood trade, and when one merchant makes improvements his competitors are literally forced to do so."[133] Without government assistance, independent retailers would be unable to modernize and unable to compete in the fierce Depression marketplace; and if they were unable to compete, they would be forced out of business at an even higher rate, worsening the social and economic effects of the Depression.

In directing its nearly eight thousand local BHPs to cultivate Main Street retailers, the FHA deliberately exploited the nature of Depression-era retail competition, especially between chains and independents, in order to convince the latter to modernize. In *Better Housing* the FHA stressed that "the small merchant particularly is affected when buying shifts into other channels and when sales volume that he has enjoyed is directed to other stores." It counseled the BHPs "to help merchants keep in step with Main Street"—a Main Street presumably lined with modernized chains, those *other channels* absorbing the small merchant's sales volume. While fierce competition made the small merchant a likely prospect for modernization, it was the job of each local BHP to make him realize that since "modernized stores had taken his trade away from him," only by modernizing his own store could he recapture that lost trade.[134] Despite numerous oblique references to chain stores, the FHA never explicitly blamed the chains for the predicament of the independents since it clearly did not want to offend the very retailers whose early and comprehensive modernization programs gave credence to the FHA's beneficial claims for capital improvements—programs that would continue under the liberalization of the MCP. In addition, the FHA recognized that the presence of modernized chain stores on Main Street served as a primary competitive example for the modernization of independent retail establishments that the agency was now promoting. Thus, the FHA realized that it would be counterproductive to criticize modernized chain stores since they were the formal model the agency hoped the independents would emulate. If there was a certain irony in encouraging the independents to make themselves over in the image of the chains, on whom blame for the present endangered state of the small retailer was popularly placed, no one seemed to notice.

Modernizing for Profit

This was probably because Main Street found itself in the midst of another FHA-sponsored promotional blitz as the BHPs distributed new commercially focused literature. The principal promotional piece, *Modernize for Profit* (FHA-180), was introduced in the summer of 1935 as "A Manual for Merchants" that explained the liberalized ($50,000) terms of government-insured credit and the supposed efficacy of store modernization (fig. 2.8).[135] The manual's initial distribution of 300,000 pieces was accompanied by a new series of direct-mail letters (500,000 pieces) addressed to the "Merchants of America" and to "Mr. Retailer."[136] In content, these letters ranged from simple explanations of the MCP to detailed store improvement checklists and always included, as did *Modernize for Profit*, before-and-after case studies to illustrate modernization's potential for architectural change and building improvement.[137]

Charged with following up on the government's mass mailings, participating BHP communities organized new store-to-store surveys intended to familiarize merchants with the Main Street program. In New Jersey the state BHP appointed a "special state-wide Modernize Main Street committee," which hosted more than three dozen "Modernize Main Street" dinners, including a banquet for five hundred in Newark attended by local businessmen and Chamber of Commerce members, with special invitations extended to small merchants and large retailers alike. Concurrently, paid "interviewers" swept through the business districts of Newark, Jersey City, Paterson, Trenton, Camden, and sixty-four other locales to cultivate Main Street modernization prospects. According to its organizers, this campaign "was in no sense a canvass but was presented as a business service."[138] In Missouri the state Chamber of Commerce promoted modernization among merchants and owners of commercial property through special "Main Street" meetings held in cities and towns with a history of organizing for town improvement. The Chamber of Commerce retained a local architect as a modernization adviser to provide free design advice to those in attendance at each meeting.[139]

In San Francisco the effort was even more intensive as the local BHP and the city's three merchants' associations sponsored a three-phase "Modernize Main Street for Profit" campaign. In the first phase, begun in the fall of 1935, unemployed members of the San Francisco Architects'

Figure 2.8 *Modernize for Profit: A Manual for Merchants, Manufacturers and All Owners of Business Property*. Published in conjunction with the liberalization of modernization credit in 1935, this manual detailed the operation and benefits of the MCP and had an initial distribution of over 300,000 pieces. The cover features shoppers on Fifth Avenue in New York. (FHA, *Modernize for Profit*, 1935, title page. National Archives and Records Administration, Record Group 31.)

Association photographed the city's principal and secondary commercial blocks and prepared sketches and cost estimates for modernizing every building. In the second phase, local merchants were invited to meetings with slide shows featuring before-and-after views of modernized San Francisco buildings and before-and-after sales figures intended to prove modernization's profitability. Finally, a merchant canvass commenced in the spring of 1936 beginning in the Presidio and the Marina and continuing in two dozen of San Francisco retail districts. The greatest successes were recorded on Market Street, the city's historic commercial core, and in Union Square, the city's destination shopping center in the 1930s. During the canvass, merchants were given renderings of design possibilities, along with copies of *Modernize for Profit*, and were informed that if they modernized their establishments, the California Institute of Cabinet Manufacturers would paint, free of charge, any empty buildings that might detract from the appearance of newly improved stores. The stores modernized in downtown San Francisco as a result of the local Main Street campaign demonstrate the range of styles, materials, and techniques that became standard to modernization practice in the 1930s, appearing simultaneously in the commercial districts of the country's largest cities and its smallest towns (fig. 2.9).[140]

While the FHA and its BHPs worked to promote the modernization of individual stores, they simultaneously encouraged a collective approach to Main Street improvements that might serve as the foundation for overall civic betterment and beautification.[141] Group modernization projects usually called for the improvement of all buildings on at least one side of a commercial block, though improvements on both sides of a block were obviously preferred, and multiblock sites were more desirable still. The goal was to stabilize property values, restore rentals to profitability, and counteract creeping blight, not only in individual buildings but in assemblages of buildings in which the physical and fiscal disposition of each affected the whole. According to FHA logic, modernization had a kind of reverse domino effect in a commercial district: if one unrenovated building would eventually bring a block down, then one modernized building would eventually pull it back up. To maximize this impact, the FHA stressed the benefits of collective modernization: "When area standards are raised—your own property naturally becomes more valuable."[142] Here, as usual, the FHA recognized that appeals to individualist self-interest were crucial to the success of the group project.

After selecting blocks that might benefit most from a group project, the BHP planning committee enlisted volunteer architects to prepare

Figure 2.9 Dunnes "When the Day Is Done" cocktail lounge, San Francisco. With its glass blocks, aluminum framing, and neon sign, this modernization typified the work generated by local retail property canvasses in the second half of the 1930s. (*Pencil Points* 20 [August 1939]: 500. Courtesy of the Avery Architectural and Fine Arts Library, Columbia University.)

renderings and detailed drawings of proposed improvements to the corridor or district, and these were usually accompanied by before-and-after views of the selected block or blocks. This was the case in Minneapolis, Minnesota, where several "obsolete" commercial blocks of Nicollet Avenue were selected for group modernization in the winter of 1935. In the 1930s Nicollet Avenue, a street rising from the banks of the Mississippi River and traversing the downtown core, was considered the city's principal business artery, the location of its largest department stores and best office buildings. As the city's commercial development shifted inland, the oldest blocks of Nicollet Avenue, those closest to the river, faced declining sales and property values and increased vacancies. The

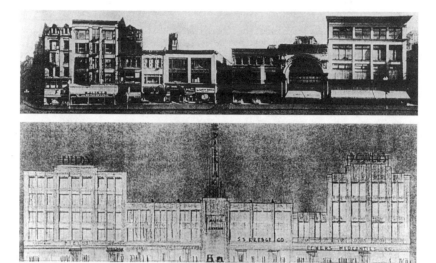

Figure 2.10 Nicollet Avenue in Minneapolis, Minnesota. The photograph shows an "obsolete" commercial block selected for a group modernization of its buildings. That scheme, depicted in the rendering, simplified and regularized the facades to give them the appearance of a newly built block-long structure. The proposal also included access to a rear parking lot through a midblock alley indicated by the tall pylon at the center. (*Better Housing*, June 10, 1936. National Archives and Records Administration, Record Group 31.)

designated downtown blocks were redesigned to create "a pleasing and harmonious appearance" that avoided monotony across the corridor by treating each side of the street as an autonomous unit. This produced four separate building ensembles, each in the guise of a newly built, block-long structure.[143] The most important element of the modernization scheme with respect to Nicollet Avenue's retail profitability was its accommodation of the automobile in off-street parking reached through a midblock alley and advertised with a large neon sign on a two-story stepped pylon. The intention was not simply to make the modernized blocks look "new and improved," but to make them appear as a modern shopping center, with as many shopping center amenities as could be fashioned out of the existing agglomeration of buildings (fig. 2.10).

After such group modernization schemes were prepared, the BHP planning committee would make public presentations to convince property owners to accept the proposed improvements. In outlining this general procedure, the FHA stressed the importance of soliciting and securing the participation of all building owners: "They must be made clearly to see the advantage to be gained from common action." At the same time, however, the FHA noted that no formal or legal "mutual bind" was necessary, only "a simple form of agreement among property owners to join in a group enterprise," as in Oakland, California, where downtown property owners participated in a "cooperative" modernization campaign to fight declining rents and increased vacancies in the oldest commercial section of the city.[144] Their goal was simultaneous improvement of the district rather than overall visual coordination, since this would have been too expensive to achieve given the diversity of the building stock.[145]

Overall coordination made more sense on a smaller scale, as in Weslaco, Texas, a small town on the Mexican border, where a modernization exhibition prompted merchants to "completely transform the appearance of Main Street" (fig. 2.11). The Weslaco Chamber of Commerce paid for an architect, R. Newell Waters, to prepare sketches of the town's business blocks showing how the buildings—mostly one-story, false-front brick structures—might be remodeled to "fit into a definite architectural pattern."[146] The sketches were turned into detailed watercolor renderings and displayed in a storefront remodeled according to Waters's scheme to serve itself as a graphic modernization display. While the majority of Main Street modernization schemes employed identifiably modern architectural styles, Waters wanted to "dramatize the romantic history of the region for tourist appeal." He made over Main Street in the Spanish Mission style, much like Santa Barbara, California, where zoning regulations of the 1920s prescribed the Mission style for all buildings.[147] In Weslaco this entailed the installation of a variety of "distinctive Spanish features": stuccoed facades studded with brightly colored tiles, clay tile roofs, archways and heavy piers, decorative projecting eaves, and uniform signage with a vaguely Baroque typeface. Romance aside, the modernization scheme still had to serve the requirements of contemporary merchandising, so Waters inserted modern glass storefronts into the spaces between the bays. All of this was made possible by the First National Bank of Weslaco, which provided $12,000 worth of FHA-insured modernization loans with building owners and merchant tenants sharing their repayment. By the summer of 1936, nearly all of the forty-five structures on Weslaco's two-block Main Street had been altered according to Waters's designs, including the local gas station "eyesore" and the Piggly Wiggly, a chain grocery store that replaced its standard black-and-metallic front to fit in with the community.[148] To celebrate the success of its modernization program—it reportedly generated a 50 percent increase in business—Weslaco held a Mexican-themed street festival that

Figure 2.11 Main Street in Weslaco, Texas. Not all modernization schemes relied on the imagery of modern architecture. Here, R. Newell Waters used the Spanish Mission style to transform a block of store buildings. His scheme was paid for by the local Chamber of Commerce and had the backing of the local bank, which extended $12,000 in modernization credit to realize the project. (*Architectural Forum* 66 [March 1937]: 60. Courtesy of the Avery Architectural and Fine Arts Library, Columbia University.)

complemented the "air of old Spain" that its *modernized* Main Street now possessed.[149]

For the FHA, the success of such enterprises depended upon a rhetorical balance between Main Street as a repository of hometown nostalgia and Main Street as a harbinger of progress:

> No longer need Main Street remain a row of antiquated and uninviting structures, offensive to the eye of every citizen who has pride in his home town, and unfitted to the requirements of those who tenant them. The old burg may put on a new front and a show of beauty and utility.[150]

While an investment in beauty satisfied Main Street's community orientation, an investment in utility satisfied its business orientation. This duality, permeating the entire BHP, was effective because it so accurately reflected the booster culture of Main Street in the 1930s. But another delicate balance also contributed to the New Deal's success in convincing Main Street to modernize—the balance between local and national support. Within the BHP, local campaigns relied on the extensive efforts of the federal government to promote modernization, and the same was true of the building industry as a whole. While local architects, contractors, and suppliers worked hard to sell modernization to Main Street merchants, the success of their efforts depended on support at the national level. To this end, the FHA would enlist corporate manufacturers of building materials to promote modernization the same way the BHP did, through a deft conflation of public and private, of patriotism and profit, and of civic and business interests.

CHAPTER 3

Marketing Modernization

Late in 1937 the Independent Grocery Association (IGA) ran a contest to encourage its grocer members to exceed their regular sales quotas of meat, can goods, and produce. Like many sales gimmicks of the era, the IGA contest relied on the lure of desirable prizes to motivate local merchants to outsell their rivals. In this case, winners were to receive not a trip to Hollywood or a late-model convertible, but something that a Depression-stricken independent merchant would have found far more appealing—a sparkling new modern storefront (fig. 3.1). This one featured blue-and-yellow structural glass and extruded aluminum framing and was intended as an IGA-branded facade, a standardized package of architectural features and signage that immediately identified the store as part of the IGA network.

This network was formed in the early years of the Depression by independent merchants who affiliated as a so-called voluntary chain to compete with corporate retailers, who had expanded aggressively in the grocery sector.[1] Participating grocers worked as national or regional groups to exploit the same economies of scale in distribution that gave the chains their competitive advantage. IGA members also cooperated in advertising and marketing, and here, too, they followed the example of the chains, paying close attention to the way they were actively modernizing

Figure 3.1 Storefront designed by Libbey-Owens-Ford for the Independent Grocery Association, 1937. This blue-and-yellow model, offered as a prize in a sales competition, was intended to give stores owned by members of the IGA voluntary chain a consistent, branded look. It was eventually installed on storefronts in Warsaw, New York; Wheeling, West Virginia; East Troy, Wisconsin; and Spokane, Washington. (Libbey-Owens-Ford, *1938 Advertising Scrapbook.* Courtesy of Libbey-Owens-Ford Glass Company Records, MSS-066, Ward M. Canaday Center for Special Collections, The University of Toledo.)

their retail units, updating standard storefront models with bold designs intended to grab consumer attention and, hopefully, scarce consumer dollars as well. By the mid-1930s, under intensifying competitive pressure and with the encouragement of the FHA, the IGA began to promote store modernization in its member newsletter, the *IGA Grocergram*, dutifully explaining the operations of the Modernization Credit Plan, the business benefits of building modernization, and the merchandising attributes of modern design.

For the latter, they turned to the expertise of building material manufacturers, many of whom had been promoting modernization throughout the decade. In fact, one of the nation's leading manufacturers of architectural glass and metal, Libbey-Owens-Ford (LOF), had designed the IGA's storefront and donated the contest prizes, all of which had been awarded and installed by the early spring of 1938. According to testimonials, the contest winners—member grocers in Warsaw, New York; Wheeling, West Virginia; East Troy, Wisconsin; and Spokane, Washington—were delighted with their prizes.[2] Their satisfaction is not surprising since these stylishly modernized storefronts were the products of a highly sophisticated marketing campaign, one that was orchestrated by U.S. corporations with the encouragement of the federal government in order to sell modernization on American Main Streets.

The National Housing Act will make it possible for many of your independent competitors, as well as yourself, to obtain money easily for remodeling their stores. That is why now is the time for you to remodel your stores with Pittsburgh Store Fronts to keep pace with the increased competition which the benefits of the NHA create in your markets.[3]

The Pittsburgh Plate Glass Company placed this advertisement, one of a series, in *Chain Store Age* in the fall of 1934. Intended to stimulate sales of PPG's storefront construction materials, these advertisements capitalized not only on the well-known rivalry between chain and independent retailers, but also on the recently commenced, federally sponsored modernization program. PPG was referring to the low-interest, government-insured loans newly available through the Modernization Credit Plan (MCP) enabled by the National Housing Act's Title I. The MCP, as the ad correctly stated, did provide independent retailers with access to capital they had previously lacked—capital that would help prime the pump of an economy in desperate need of stimulation once it was spent on architectural design, building materials, and construction labor. It was not coincidental that PPG mentioned the NHA explicitly in its *Chain Store Age* advertisements. The nation's largest glass manufacturer was simply following the Federal Housing Administration's recommendation that U.S. companies "further the successful operation" of the modernization program through a national publicity drive.[4]

Industrial Cooperation

From the commencement of the Better Housing Program in the summer of 1934, the FHA sought the cooperation of major industries, but initially the agency's energies were focused on the organization of local campaigns in those cities and towns where Main Street would become the front line of the modernization effort. With over three thousand local initiatives already in operation by September, the FHA's leadership turned its attention back to the national scene, laying plans for "a huge advertising campaign" intended to "give momentum to the program." In contrast to the local efforts, over which the FHA maintained careful control from Washington, the national efforts were more laissez-faire. "Industry understood that it would have to take the lead in modernizing," FHA head James Moffett declared.[5] To encourage such leadership, FHA officials traveled across the country, holding conferences, visiting trade group meetings, and attending businessmen's luncheons, addressing organizations such as the National Association of Manufacturers and the National Industrial Advertisers Association. In these addresses, the FHA made it clear that the government was not seeking the altruistic participation of American industry in some "educational campaign," but their participation *for profit* in what public relations director Ward Canaday called "a market greater in size and volume than any the world has seen before."[6]

By the end of 1934, this promise of market expansion had convinced over forty-six hundred manufacturers to "actively cooperate" with the BHP. This group included not only those firms who stood to benefit directly from modernization, but also those who understood that the program's potential for immediate economic revitalization would translate into improved business conditions in other spheres. Despite the FHA's focus on independents, chain retailers were among the earliest to join with the agency, eager to burnish their troubled reputations and recast their store expansion and improvement campaigns in a new light of government cooperation. The Kroger Grocery Company distributed modernization literature to customers and employees and displayed FHA posters in every store the chain operated, in addition to pressuring its bankers to extend modernization credit and allowing PPG to feature its stores in their *Chain Store Age* advertisements. However significant the promotions undertaken by firms like Kroger may have been, it was the cooperation of national companies in building and allied industries that the FHA deemed most essential to the effort to modernize Main Street.[7]

For manufacturers who had watched the demand for their building products shrink steadily since 1929, the FHA's promise of market expansion and positive public relations had no small appeal.[8] Indeed, many of the firms the FHA enlisted in the modernization drive had already demonstrated a public commitment to economic recovery by serving on Herbert Hoover's National Committee on Industrial Rehabilitation organized in 1932. Working to end the "prostration" of the capital goods industries, the short-lived committee promoted a nationwide effort to modernize factories, plants, and related retail establishments. Some of the same manufacturers had also demonstrated an active interest in finding greater markets for their products by organizing the Rehabilitation Corporation, a credit finance company specializing in the modernization of income-producing buildings. Even more recently, as the Modernization Credit Plan itself was in formation in the spring and summer 1934, these manufacturers met with New Dealer Raymond Moley to formulate their own approach to ending the Depression "by promoting cooperation between government and business." They eventually incorporated as the Committee for Economic Recovery to sponsor nonpartisan studies of national economic problems, including the depressed state of the building industry.[9]

Since the pro-business/for-profit orientation of the MCP and the Main Street initiative were sympathetic to these various enterprises, it is not surprising that the FHA found its earliest industrial supporters from within these ranks, including such blue-chip firms as American Radiator and Standard Sanitary, General Electric, Johns-Manville, Libbey-Owens-Ford, Pittsburgh Plate Glass, Ruberoid, U.S. Steel, Westinghouse, and Weyerhaeuser. The FHA expected these manufacturers to carry out the actual marketing and selling of modernization, for which the agency had laid the groundwork with its promotional blitz in the summer and fall of 1934. By its own account, the agency had worked hard to "drum up business for industry," using its considerable PR acumen to "rally publicity into more effective channels," including the press and radio. In the end, however, American manufacturers would have to "sell the products" themselves if they seriously wished to "bring about a re-birth of sales and production activity in the building and building materials industries" after five years of Depression-induced stagnation.[10]

While asserting that product sales were entirely the manufacturers' responsibility, the FHA was hardly suggesting that they undertake these promotional efforts alone. As detailed in the FHA's *Bulletin for Manufacturers, Advertising Agencies and Publishers*, architecture, building, and retail trade journals would assist them in this effort by simultaneously making modernization a "keynote of editorial campaigns" that promoted the New Deal initiative in the interest of national recovery, while presenting it as unbiased reporting of a topical issue.[11] These campaigns included an exhaustive array of modernization articles and regular columns, dealing with policy and finance, technique and practice, retail and material trends. Portfolios and "plate" sections, before-and-after case histories, and building-type studies offered graphic modernization illustrations to inspire architects and merchants alike. Like all FHA cooperation, this content was undertaken for profit. Modernization articles in magazines attracted modernization advertisements from manufacturers, and those advertisements produced revenues. It was a simple equation, but a crucial one: modernization's successful promotion hinged on it and, by extension, so did modernization's ability to stimulate depressed building activity.[12] This equation also reveals how what the government called *industrial cooperation* was, in fact, closer to a kind of industrial complicity, or at least questionable reciprocity as, in effect, big government was supporting big businesses to encourage them to support other big businesses.

Perhaps the most enthusiastic assistance was provided by *Building Modernization* magazine. With an editorial mission to "foster the building modernization movements [*sic*] as a step toward national recovery," it featured architects writing about their modernization and commercial design work. In articles such as "More Profit Store Fronts" and "Sales Psychology in Store Modernization," architects proffered practical advice based on their own experiences while also endorsing specific building products. In the fall of 1936, *Building Modernization* sponsored a Store Modernization Conference at Pennsylvania State College to promote "good design on Main Street." A rare event that included both sellers and buyers of modernization, the conference was attended by architects and contractors as well as retail executives and merchants, with architect Ely Jacques Kahn and store planner Charles Swanson as keynote speakers. The conference also included an exhibition of "successful store modernization work" that toured the state under the auspices of the American Federation of Art, indicating how far everyday commercial modernization had progressed in the minds of the general public, retailers, and the architecture profession in the short time since the national movement coalesced.[13]

Manufacturers also had the assistance of the government, with the FHA counseling that they link themselves as closely as possible to the federal program: "Tie your company or your products in with the Federal Housing Administration program," and declare that "its objectives are your objectives." This generally took the form of modernization-themed advertisements featuring the FHA, the National Housing Act, the Modernization Credit Plan, the BHP logo, and, increasingly by 1935, Main Street, which the federal government had effectively co-opted as New Deal territory.[14] Following the FHA directive to emphasize profitability as the main reason to cooperate, a U.S. Steel ad deftly cultivated interest in modernization practice among architects while it cultivated interest in sheet metal for modernization work: "There's Money in Remodeling Store Fronts. . . . [T]his modernization movement has proved a profitable one to the architect, the engineer and the builder." Revere Copper & Brass promoted the FHA admonition to "be your own first customer" with the headline "It Pays to Practice What You Preach" and an illustration of a Revere dealer's workshop modernized with a sheet-copper storefront to attract similar jobs.[15]

Such advertisements were the most common type of FHA tie-in since they required little additional expenditure if a manufacturer was already engaged in national publicity. Similar reasoning led many manufacturers to adapt other existing promotional materials for program tie-in, including a range of specialized literature—letters, flyers, booklets, and portfolios—demonstrating the general, artistic, and technical aspects of a given product. Manufacturers sent these directly to architects, contractors, and retailers, and placed them, in abbreviated form, in *Sweet's Catalogue File* and in retail equipment directories. Over the next few years, an incredible volume of tied-in promotional literature appeared, from Ruberoid's *Modernizing Money*, explaining the company's FHA-approved "Easy-Payment Plan," to Kawneer's *Book of Storefronts*, illustrating "what hundreds of progressive merchants have done to boost profits." Often these booklets were simply reissues of older publications updated for rhetorical currency by replacing "remodeling" and "improvement" with "modernizing" and "modernization."[16]

However successful print advertisements and promotional literature were, in the FHA's conception they were only the beginning of the manufacturer's campaign. For the FHA was not simply asking industry to "revive selling efforts"; the agency was asking it to *expand* those efforts until building material manufacturers were engaged in a range of promotional activities far more extensive than any they had previously undertaken.[17] By 1937 expanded PR activities had become common enough for *Architectural Forum* to remark that the "building industry was becoming aware of major advertising trends," as indicated by the adoption of "promotion methods customarily used to bolster sales of cigarettes, cosmetics, and breakfast foods"—in other words, gimmicks.[18] The advantage of using modernization as a sales gimmick was that it could be deployed with equal effect upon two particular market segments: architects and merchants whose joint interest in modernization as a building practice, a credit plan, and a putative business booster was crucial to the movement's success. The double appeal to architects and merchants was necessary for building material manufacturers because, unlike manufacturers of consumer goods, they had to approach their market by what one industry analyst called "a devious route." Since orders for building products did not come directly from the merchant/consumer, but rather from the architect, acting as a middleman, it was necessary for the manufacturer to sell both groups on the company's products.[19]

The manner in which manufacturers might effect this double selling via the modernization movement was explained in trade journals such as *Building Supply News* and *Building Material Merchandising Digest,* each of which devoted an entire issue to the sales opportunities presented by the Modernization Credit Plan late in 1934.[20] As detailed in the journals, this selling would ideally encompass a varied program of *nonprint* tie-ins as well, including nationally sponsored special events, industry-specific customer services, and product exhibitions and conferences. The latter were often sponsored by a group of manufacturers or a trade association. The Producers' Council (a coalition of manufacturers affiliated with the American Institute of Architects) and the U.S. Chamber of Commerce organized yearly Construction Industry conferences in which sessions on modernization and the Main Street initiative were regularly slated: architect Ralph Walker moderated a session on "Modernizing Commercial Buildings" and F. T. Brown, chairman of the Kansas City BHP, chaired one on "Modernizing Main Street."[21] As described by Dorsey Newson, special assistant to FHA PR director Canaday, these tie-ins were limited only by "the ingenuity of the Sales and Advertising Departments of national manufacturers."[22] Newson's comment suggests the degree to which advertising and marketing strategies would drive the modernization program throughout the 1930s. And as these strategies became more prevalent in the producer goods industry that had previously ignored them, the result was an unprecedented narrowing of the cultural distance between building and consumerism in the United States.

If promotions tied in with the federal modernization program offered, in the FHA's view, "great opportunities" to members of the building and building services industries, they also gave them "important responsibilities."[23] In practice, this duality became one of the tie-ins' principal attractions, allowing manufacturers to aggressively market their products to maximize sales while doing so under a banner of corporate responsibility, goodwill, and patriotism—a strategy as appealing during the Depression as it would be during World War II. This sort of nationalist emphasis is evident in a 1935 General Electric advertisement tying GE wiring materials to the expansion of the MCP, building modernization, and the Main Street initiative (fig. 3.2). The copy runs below a maplike image of the United States bisected by a banner carrying GE's civic-minded yet self-interested message to "Modernize Main Street Electrically." The banner itself resembles a coast-to-coast highway, an elongated Main Street lined with commercial, institutional, industrial, and residential buildings all apparently in need of GE products. Discreetly reinforcing GE's patriotic intentions, most of the buildings are flying flags. Explicitly reinforcing GE's selling intentions (and utilizing clichés of contemporary advertising), overscaled electrical outlets, switch plates, and fuses float disembodied above Main Street.[24] The remaining iconography, depicting a Spanish galleon and an ocean liner—emblematic of the antiquated past and the improved future—reinforced the modernization theme.

General Electric continued to tie its advertising to the Modernization Credit Plan throughout the 1930s, repeatedly deeming that the "electrical convenience" of its air-conditioning and lighting systems were most especially useful for "Main Street establishments" since they promised to attract customers and build profits. GE frequently borrowed one of the FHA's most familiar sales arguments, establishing the psychologically potent link between building improvement and business improvement that was crucial to modernization's appeal.[25] One of General Electric's earliest tie-in promotions was its credit finance subsidiary, the GE Contracts Corporation. Immediately after the MCP went into effect in 1934, GE reorganized the Contracts Corporation into an FHA-approved lender to take advantage of the obvious promotional value such an association held. The FHA clearly approved of GE's strategies, which it described as "impressive testimonials of cooperation."[26]

Figure 3.2 "Modernize Main Street Electrically," General Electric advertisement. This type of advertising tie-in by building material manufacturers became more frequent after the liberalization of modernization credit in 1935. It explicitly mentions the FHA and the new $50,000 loan limit while promoting GE products for modernization. (*Building Modernization*, March 1935.)

The country's leading manufacturer of asbestos and asphalt building materials also transformed its credit finance subsidiary into a modernization lender for promotional purposes and met with such success in extending government-insured credit that it was praised as an industry leader in the vanguard of recovery.[27] Johns-Manville had been working to change sales and promotional strategies in the building industry well before the Depression. Indeed, *Atlantic Monthly* gave J-M credit for "modernizing the building industry," an assessment that stemmed largely from its pioneering pre-Depression effort to bring such consumerist conveniences as installment buying and easy credit into the realm of durable goods.[28] In fact, J-M's Million Dollars to Lend program, administered through eleven hundred J-M agents nationwide, had been one of the credit finance models for the Modernization Credit Plan itself. Thus, J-M was in a unique position to take advantage of the marketing opportunity of the FHA's modernization program. After the start of the BHP, J-M sponsored FHA-related radio broadcasts, including high-profile speeches by officials James Moffett and Stewart McDonald, and organized a "motor caravan" that toured the country during 1935, stopping in over six hundred cities and towns to "capitalize on the NHA at the point of sale" by taking building products directly to Main Street.[29]

In the fall of 1935, J-M tied in use of its products explicitly to the Main Street initiative, demonstrating in a *Chain Store Age* advertisement how "Johns-Manville Modernizes a Main Street Shop." In the "before" photograph, the store had a pressed-tin ceiling, plaster walls, a jumbled arrangement of overstuffed furniture, and a checkerboard linoleum floor. In the "after" photograph, the modernized store has an integrated scheme with a drop ceiling, resurfaced walls with continuous decorative bands, streamlined combination display case/seats, and a lustrous striped floor—all fabricated with J-M products. In presenting its asbestos and asphalt products as a quartet of coordinated materials, J-M effectively *modernized* its product line for store installations, modifying the way it merchandised certain products to make them more appealing to retailers. J-M's Asbestos Wainscoting, a wall-cladding material, became Asbestos Flexboard. In transforming Wainscoting into Flexboard, the product shed any potentially negative associations with old-fashioned, heavily paneled interiors, replacing them with associations more appropriate to the fight-the-Depression ethic of the mid-1930s: flexibility, adaptability, and responsiveness to change. Equally appropriate to this ethic was the emphasis J-M placed on affordability. Not only did the company stress the low cost and "economy" of its products, but also the availability of its government-rate, deferred-payment plan for Main Street store owners who wanted to modernize but did not think they could afford it.[30]

In January 1936 a speaker at a J-M-sponsored building industry forum accurately explained what J-M and other building material manufacturers were doing "to spur a definite revival in the building industry." Because the Depression had effectively ended the "self-generating demand" for building materials, it was now necessary to actively stimulate demand by engaging in "creative merchandising." Though interest in modernization presented a great marketing opportunity, creative merchandising meant more than simply increasing advertising and the distribution of promotional literature.[31] It meant researching new uses and applications for materials already present in product lines and deploying these uses to reposition materials in the building industry through advertising and promotion. Ideally, in the mid-1930s, these new applications were compatible with the aesthetic and technical requirements of building modernization, permitting a tie-in with the FHA, the MCP, and the Main Street initiative.

Structural Glass: A Marketing Case Study

Of the numerous building materials subjected to this sort of creative merchandising during the Depression, including plastic laminates, porcelain enamels, extruded metals, even marble and terra-cotta, one material stands out
as a compelling example of a product marketed expressly for modernizing
buildings on Main Street America.[32] As a building material, structural glass
had been available since around 1900 when technological advances in the
manufacture of flat glass made possible the development of opaque, pigmented, highly polished, vitreous non-load-bearing slabs.[33] Since its non-
porous, hard finish made structural glass impervious to dirt and stains—
and supposedly to germs and odors as well—it was initially marketed as a
substitute for marble under trade names like Sani-Onyx and Novus Sanitary. These brands were used primarily in hospitals, lavatories, cafeterias,
and other environments in which cleanliness, sanitation, and hygiene
were of central concern.[34] In such interiors, structural glass was applied
to a variety of wall surfaces and fixtures, including wainscoting and base-
boards, table and countertops, and toilet and shower partitions. Though
color options were limited to white and black, the antiseptic gave way to
the glamorous during the 1920s, especially after the introduction of faux-
stone effects and sandblasted and inlaid decorative patterns. With the
dual influence of the 1925 Exposition Internationale des Arts Décoratifs
in Paris and Hollywood motion picture sets, especially Cedric Gibbons's
work at MGM, American designers were soon using structural glass to
panel the walls of chic foyers and voguish bathrooms. Though there were
nearly a dozen manufacturers of structural glass by the mid-1920s, two
brands dominated this market: Carrara, manufactured by the Pittsburgh
Plate Glass Company and introduced in 1906, and Vitrolite, manufactured
by the Vitrolite Company of Chicago and introduced in 1916.

By the time the stock market crashed, U.S. production of structural
glass was nearly 5 million square feet per year. This was less than 4 percent of the total plate-glass output, but it was significant enough for the
trade journal *Glass Industry* to boast that "structural glass has arrived,"
coming into its own as "a modern, efficient, economical material"—
characteristics that would make it especially compatible with storefront
use in the coming decade.[35] The glass industry's enthusiasm for the material was echoed by the design community. In 1930 furniture designer
Paul Frankl regarded structural glass as one of the new industrial materials most "expressive of our own age." Two years later industrial designer
Walter Dorwin Teague lauded it as a material that "fit in particularly well

with modern design trends" and predicted that it would "figure prominently in buildings of the future."[36] Despite these positive assessments,
as the Depression set in yearly structural glass production declined to 1
million square feet, and when construction activity hit bottom in 1933,
the material's market prospects appeared as gloomy as those of every
other building product.[37]

Pittsburgh Plate Glass

That year, as glass manufacturers regrouped after numerous bankruptcies, mergers, and acquisitions, PPG emerged as the industry's leader,
dominating the depressed flat-glass market with its Polished Plate and
Carrara products. As the New Deal got under way, PPG president H. S.
Wherrett was already implementing recovery measures initiated by the
National Committee on Industrial Rehabilitation, carrying out the company's $350,000 pledge to modernize PPG's factories and equipment and
its promise to promote building improvements with glass.[38] Though the
latter effort was fairly limited, it must have alerted PPG executives to
the possibilities of promoting modernization to reverse the downward
trend of glass sales. When the MCP went into effect in 1934 and the
FHA sought the cooperation of leading manufacturers, PPG immediately
threw its corporate weight behind the Title I initiative, agreeing to "gear
advertising and selling plans to the Housing Act to the fullest possible
extent." That fall the company initiated a promotional campaign that
expanded in scope and intensity over the next several years, eventually
reaching yearly expenditures in excess of $1 million.[39] Crucial to this
campaign was PPG's successful market repositioning of its Carrara brand
structural glass from an interior paneling to an exterior facing easily
applied to run-down Main Street storefronts. By the end of the decade,
structural glass storefronts had become so nearly ubiquitous that *Glass
Industry*, in an article about the Carrara brand, described the material as
"a staple architectural item . . . familiar to the ordinary citizen."[40]

Since structural glass had been successfully repositioned once before,
from a sanitary to a decorative material, it was not fantastic to think that
the public would accept it in yet another new context, as a wall surface on
the outside of buildings, where the product had not generally appeared.[41]
Already in 1932, when Walter Dorwin Teague praised Carrara by name,
he noted that the very same qualities that made it so advantageous in sanitary installations made it equally practical for "exterior purposes." In fact,
architects were employing it on building facades in sufficient quantities

that the exterior use of black structural glass trimmed in chrome had apparently become "a vogue" in urban centers by late 1933.[42] At that moment, however, while PPG and the Vitrolite Company both acknowledged the potential of structural glass in "refined exterior settings" and "modern storefront work," they were not yet marketing it for this purpose beyond scant advertising references.[43] Though the 1933 Committee for Reconditioning had the idea to "remodel store fronts in glass" as the "basis for a merchandising campaign," for PPG this did not yet include structural glass.[44] Indeed, when the company listed its products for storefront use in *Chain Store Age*'s 1933 "Equipment and Construction Directory," PPG's Polished Plate and EasySet Metal were the only "essential materials" included.[45] Carrara structural glass was nowhere to be found.

One year later, however, PPG made Carrara the feature material of its storefronts, announcing in the 1934 directory that its metal settings were "new and improved . . . designed especially for use with Carrara Structural Glass." Now available in black, white, jade, ivory, and gray, Carrara was described "ideal for modern storefronts." In the 1934 edition of *Sweet's*, the first to place materials for storefronts together in a single catalog section, PPG further promoted "Carrara for Storefronts," claiming that the material had "been developed to meet the requirements of outdoor uses" and offering its first catalog of storefront designs with full-size storefront details.[46] When the FHA's Main Street effort commenced in 1935, PPG began featuring what it called "outstanding installations of Pittco Store Fronts," chosen as much for their geographic distribution—a shoe store in Wisconsin, a grill room in Texas, a beauty salon in Connecticut—as for their quality of design.[47] While PPG continued to market Carrara for interior use, its storefront applications became increasingly important to the company's promotional strategies since it allowed PPG to increase sales of a material already in the product line without retooling for the new application. While there were certainly compelling aesthetic reasons for promoting structural glass as exterior facing—namely, its perceived modernity—PPG was counting on simple economics to create market dominance: in terms of the combined cost of purchase, labor, and installation, structural glass was one of the cheapest facing materials then available.[48]

The Pittco Store Front

There was a larger sales strategy at work as well. Prior to 1934, as PPG later explained, "you bought your facing material from one source, your glass from another, your metal sash and paint and incidental materials from still others."[49] Though the plate glass used in display windows was arguably the most important of these materials, it was also the least expensive.[50] Of the remaining materials, there were metal frames manufactured by the Kawneer Company, which PPG distributed, and, if the bulkhead was not metal, facings of stone, marble, tile, or brick, none of which PPG supplied or manufactured.[51] From the company's point of view, it was losing out on two-thirds of the products required for a typical storefront at precisely the moment when the efforts of the FHA were creating a market for complete storefronts. By early 1935, however, PPG laid claim to the entire storefront of frames, facings, and windows when it introduced an extruded metal of its own design and manufacture to be used as a window setting, with Carrara as a bulkhead facing. PPG could now boast that it had developed "a new type of store front construction" with a product line that included all three components of the standard storefront—Polished Plate Glass, Carrara Structural Glass, and Store Front Metal—now marketed under the single "Pittco" brand name (fig. 3.3).[52] It was not by accident that the introduction of the Pittco Store Front coincided with the FHA's March 1935 announcement of the "Modernize Main Street" initiative. In conjunction with that initiative, PPG president Wherrett predicted "at least a 50% increase" in the number of stores that would install new fronts in 1935. He further estimated that the potential existed for $1 billion of modernization work—knowing full well that his company was poised to capture this Main Street business with its trio of Pittco products.[53]

Beginning in 1935, PPG promoted its Pittco line with a campaign built around storefront modernization, tied in with the FHA, and directed simultaneously to merchants and architects. The largest component of this campaign was print advertising created by Batten, Barton, Durstine & Osborn, one of Madison Avenue's leading advertising firms. These ads employed a variety of techniques current in the mid-1930s. Testimonial-style ads appeared in both design and retail magazines, and featured personal statements from satisfied PPG customers, those merchants who had modernized their stores with Pittco fronts and claimed that business had improved as a result.[54] Editorial-style ads featured page layouts that resembled actual editorial content and attempted to engage the reader's full attention. With so many trade journals running articles and special features about modernization and the MCP, PPG's three-column advertising format, densely worded copy, and FHA-inspired headlines had a definite editorial resemblance. Typical editorial copy not only explained the MCP,

Figure 3.3 "It Pays to '*Modernize Main Street*' with a New PITTCO Store Front." The editorial-style copy of this Pittsburgh Plate Glass advertisement was intended to blend seamlessly with the modernization articles that appeared in retail and architecture journals in the 1930s. (*Chain Store Age*, June 1935, 73.) The storefront pictured was fabricated of plate glass, black and jade Carrara, and extruded metal, all manufactured by PPG.

but also deployed nearly every sales pitch in the FHA's considerable arsenal to convince merchants that a Pittco front "makes an outmoded store new and attractive... impresses potential customers... [and] results in jumping sales."[55] Regardless of its content, advertising copy was often accompanied by photographs depicting run-down or abandoned stores transformed with Pittco products. The FHA encouraged the use of such photographic pairs, since they enabled merchants "to quickly see the point" of modernization and enabled architects to see how products were being used in modernization work. In their subject, layout, and captions, PPG's before-and-after pairs often resembled the modernization case studies alongside which they appeared in *Architectural Record*, *Building Modernization*, *Box Office*, *Progressive Grocer*, or any of the other specialized trade journals featuring them after 1934.[56]

If PPG's modernization advertisements were keyed to the needs and interests of merchants and architects, so, too, were its customer service programs, notably the Pittsburgh Time Payment Plan, introduced early in 1936. Though PPG distributors and sales representatives had already been assisting customers in securing modernization loans from private financial institutions, with the Pittsburgh Plan they were now in a position to make the loans themselves, speeding up the modernization transaction and adding to corporate profits, since PPG now collected the 5 percent interest on the notes. When describing the Pittsburgh Plan in retail advertisements, PPG claimed that its purpose was to "make it easy for [a] merchant or property owner to finance the *purchase of a new Pittco Store Front*"—a predesigned, ready-to-install unit, now as easy to finance and purchase as a new refrigerator or car. Here was a manufacturer of producer goods thinking like a manufacturer of consumer goods and engaging in a consumer-oriented merchandising of building materials that the FHA encouraged, since, for all intents and purposes, the MCP was a consumer credit mechanism. Lest architects be concerned that they were excluded from this storefront transaction, PPG revealed that the Pittsburgh Plan contained a provision for the architect's fee and assured them that the company claimed that storefront design should come from the architect and not the manufacturer.[57]

For the merchant determined *not* to use an architect, PPG maintained "a special staff of store front experts" available for field consultations. PPG claimed these experts were "perfectly equipped," with the assistance of PPG's nationwide distribution system, to provide "instant and efficient service"—whether the customer was an independent merchant seeking the design and installation of a single "individualized" store or a corporate retailer seeking "identical store fronts for a chain all over the country at the same time!" In a different context, PPG's merchant-oriented storefront experts became "a staff of special architectural representatives" whose main responsibilities were "rendering the architect every assistance."[58] These representatives were PPG's so-called missionary men, publicity agents who generated goodwill for the company by contacting architects and contractors to discuss and promote—but not sell—products in a relaxed professional dialogue. FHA cooperation provided the PPG's missionary men with an ideal opportunity to initiate contact, while the growing interest in Main Street modernization may have influenced the company's decision to identify their field representatives as "Store Front Specialists."[59]

When PPG's missionary men took to the field, they were equipped with a range of promotional materials issued in connection with the Pittco/FHA modernization campaign, most of it typical of the publications all building material manufacturers offered in the mid-1930s. In the fall of 1934, PPG introduced *How Modern Store Fronts Work Profit Magic*, "a helpful handbook of storefront facts," containing product information, price lists, before-and-after photographs, and "statistics on business improvement due to Pittco-remodeling."[60] Geared equally to merchants and architects, the booklet emphasized the profitability and economy as much as the aesthetic merits of PPG products. Publications intended specifically for an architectural audience, such as PPG's *AIA File Folders*, included full- and quarter-scale detail drawings of product lines along with examples of recommended applications.[61]

In 1936 such examples grew into a *Design of the Month* series, direct mailings intended to bring Pittco Store Fronts to the attention of architects on a regular basis, on the theory that repetition would lead to specification of Pittco products. Each mailing offered style suggestions and construction advice, as well as sketches and plans for a new storefront design.[62] Though PPG credited these monthly designs to its team of Pittco Store Front experts, in fact they were prepared by Walter Dorwin Teague, whom PPG retained as a research and design consultant in 1935. Having earlier sung the praises of structural glass for facades, Teague now had the opportunity to explore its potential for himself. By March 1936 Teague's firm had completed some three dozen designs for a variety of commercial establishments, representing nearly every type of store along a typical Main Street, including a bakery, grocery, drugstore, five-and-dime, shoe store, and cocktail lounge. Twelve of these were selected for the *Design of the Month* mailings; others appeared in PPG product literature as representative examples of the "modern store front."[63]

Store Front Caravan

In early September Teague's Pittco Store Front designs were exhibited in New York City and were about to embark on a 50,000-mile two-year tour, visiting major cities and towns east of the Rocky Mountains "to encourage retailers to modernize their establishments."[64] Plans, but not specifications, of the designs were available to the public upon request. As usual, PPG was careful to point out that the aim of the exhibition was not "to supplant the services of the local architect but rather to cooperate with him." The company would cultivate interest in Pittco Store Fronts, and architects would duplicate them for their clients from the *Design of the Month* portfolio.[65] For the New York City and touring exhibitions, the latter dubbed the "Store Front Caravan" because it was mounted on the back of a truck, Teague and his staff turned their storefront designs into scale models fabricated of actual Carrara, Polished Plate, and Pittco Metal and finished with a high-degree of detail (fig. 3.4). At one-seventh scale (approximately 3.5 inches wide), with fully detailed interiors and displays stocked with miniature merchandise, these models resembled the product samples that traveling salesmen used to demonstrate the quality of their wares. If merchants were satisfied, they would order the full-scale version from the salesmen, which was exactly what PPG hoped would happen with the Store Front Caravan.[66]

According to PPG, Teague's models embodied "the latest developments" in storefront design, construction, lighting, and color, which was accurate enough, though their formal vocabulary was fairly well-established by the time the caravan left Manhattan in September 1936. Each of Teague's designs was a legible composition of four basic storefront elements—entrance, bulkhead, window, signboard. These were arranged to meet the specific retail needs of the designated store type but were also intended for easy adaptation to a variety of uses by altering the color scheme, window size, or typeface. Most had flat facades with flush, off-center entrances. A few models had slightly recessed doorways accommodating curving bulkheads, two-sided display cases, or a shadowbox signboard. The goal of the storefront models was to show Pittco products to their best advantage and to demonstrate their potential range for architectural effects. To this end, Teague and his staff utilized as much Carrara

Figure 3.4 Pittco Store Front Models designed by Walter Dorwin Teague. These one-seventh-scale models of luggage, china, and gift shops were made of Pittsburgh Plate Glass materials. Regarded as the "latest" in storefront design, they toured the country in 1936 and 1937 as part of a "Store Front Caravan." Plans were available to merchants and architects upon request. (*Real Estate Record*, September 19, 1936, 14. Courtesy of the Avery Architectural and Fine Arts Library, Columbia University.)

and Pittco Metal as possible, often reducing the size of the display windows to provide a greater facing surface and sometimes producing fussy detailing (the jewelry store's excess of extruded bronze trim; the cocktail lounge's stepped-in bulkhead). Teague appears to have employed triple-color schemes for most of the models, with black, white, or ivory as the dominant facing color. Other Carrara shades (jade, orange, red) were used as decorative trim, which was the only way these colors were marketed at the time. Though the caravan models were more restrained than many of the modernized storefronts then appearing on the nation's Main Streets, they were representative in terms of color, massing, and signage, and *Architectural Forum* was probably right when it concluded that the models would be of "considerable influence in stimulating further remodeling plans."[67]

Judging from the amount of press it generated, the Store Front Caravan was an unqualified success, with favorable write-ups and photographs of the models appearing in numerous publications inside and outside of the building industry. The FHA featured the caravan in its January 1937 *Clip Sheet*, noting that it had been "planned in conjunction with the Modernize Main Street campaign" and offering free reproductions of the designs.[68] It was characteristic of the reciprocal nature of the modernization movement that the federal government would assist in the publicity efforts of one of the nation's largest manufacturers, with one of the nation's leading advertising firms in its employ. That reciprocity would be demonstrated repeatedly throughout the decade, especially after the nation's other leading glass manufacturer joined the FHA's effort to promote building modernization and national recovery on Main Street America. This new industrial cooperation stimulated a series of promotional reactions from PPG, beginning with the corporation's decision to hire Walter Dorwin Teague in the summer of 1935.

As PPG explained it, the company's decision to seek Teague's advice was motivated by "the belief that the next few years will see glass more strongly emphasized in building and decoration."[69] While PPG's anticipation of architectural trends may have appeared as a forward-looking public relations offensive, it was actually part of a defensive strategy, with PPG acting to protect its market share. But this was probably not obvious in the summer of 1935, when PPG dominated the field of storefront modernization and sales of commercial architectural glass. Its advertisements were everywhere; its press coverage was positive; and it had just released a series of films, coproduced with Westinghouse in conjunction with the FHA, championing store modernization as the path to national economic recovery.[70] The promotional effort that PPG began tentatively in 1933 had yielded impressive results, bringing a noticeable upturn in sales and a concomitant increase in the company's net profits. By July 1935 PPG reported a sales record of ten thousand modernized storefronts fully specified with Pittco products. Largely as a result of PPG's achievement, production of structural glass had rebounded; by the end of 1935, it had reached nearly 2 million square feet, double what it had been the previous year.[71] But PPG's leadership in storefront modernization, in structural glass sales, and even in FHA cooperation was about to be challenged. For in creating a promotional campaign that had so successfully attracted public attention, PPG had also attracted the attention of others in the glass industry, notably the firm of Libbey-Owens-Ford. At that moment PPG's chief competitor in plate-glass sales and overall corporate rival for the title of America's preeminent glass manufacturer was poised to take the lead in the nationwide effort to modernize Main Street with glass.

Libbey-Owens-Ford

In March 1935, as the FHA commenced the Main Street initiative and PPG officially launched its newly named Pittco line of storefront products, rival glass manufacturer Libbey-Owens-Ford (LOF) established a New Uses Department at its Toledo, Ohio, headquarters, charged with the task of "creating glass business." Neither a research nor a sales department, New Uses was a merchandising department, the company's first. Made necessary by the economic stagnation of the Depression, the department's business-creating agenda was clear: "to develop new uses of glass, to offer new designs of glass products, to stimulate glass in architecture." With LOF's product line then limited to plate, window, and safety glass, the department faced a formidable challenge, but over the next several years it developed a number of "specialty products" that became integral to LOF manufacturing and sales. All of these were storefront products; structural glass was the first.[72]

The company that set out to add structural glass to its product line in the spring of 1935 was still a relatively young enterprise, having incorporated only in 1930. Nonetheless, LOF was already the second largest glass manufacturer in the country, formed through the merger of two venerable American glass works, Libbey-Owens Sheet Glass and Edward Ford Plate Glass. LOF's size and heritage all but guaranteed that it would become a major player in the glass industry, but the new company did not fare well in the early years of the Depression: its profits declined every year after the Crash, hitting bottom in 1934—the same year that PPG, cooperating with the FHA, posted a 44 percent increase in profits.[73] According to its 1934 *Annual Report*, LOF had also been promoting the FHA program in the belief that it would help improve business in the short term. Though the company claimed to be "cooperating in every practicable way with the FHA," its efforts consisted mainly of internal promotion, with LOF encouraging employees to volunteer with the Better Housing Program and to modernize their homes.[74]

With PPG showing increased sales and profits, apparently as a result of its FHA tie-ins, and giving every indication that its promotion of modernization with Pittco-Carrara storefronts would intensify throughout 1935, LOF knew that to effectively utilize the FHA program, in-house cooperation was not enough. It, too, would have to undertake an aggressive, external effort to promote modernization on Main Street. LOF also knew that in its long-term potential for generating corporate goodwill, cooperating with the FHA had a business value greater than its immediate potential for increased sales. And since LOF president John Biggers was—like the heads of PPG, Westinghouse, and other early FHA partners—a founding member of the Committee for Economic Recovery, LOF's policies were bound to reflect that body's avowed interest in government/business interaction. LOF's decision to launch an intensive promotional program for modernization in 1935 may have also been influenced by the personal efforts of FHA public relations director Ward Canaday, whose hometown lobbying in Toledo on behalf of his agency would have been too persuasive for Biggers or his company to ignore.[75]

Thus, in March 1935, when LOF established the New Uses Department, it did so fully aware that the FHA was working to expand markets for building materials and create demand for "increased building and store front modernization." What LOF must have soon realized, however, was that the material that appeared most likely to "be in increased demand during the next few years" was precisely the material the company did not have in its current product line—structural glass.[76] LOF acted quickly in the spring of 1935 to develop a structural glass worthy of the LOF name, accomplishing this through a big-business tactic typical of the Depression: it bought a cash-strapped factory, the only one manufacturing a structural glass with enough brand recognition to seriously challenge PPG's Carrara. That brand was Vitrolite, manufactured in a Parkersburg, West Virginia, by the Vitrolite Company of Chicago, which became a division of LOF in May 1935.

Prior to its acquisition, the Vitrolite Company had done its best to remain competitive during the Depression, despite declining sales and PPG's increasing market presence. The company continued to advertise Vitrolite into the early 1930s and had recognized, earlier than PPG, the potential of marketing structural glass for modern design and exterior uses. In 1934 it published *Vitrolite Storefronts and Building Exteriors*, hoping to capture the burgeoning market for "modern storefronts."[77] Even before the Depression, Vitrolite had seen the advantages of promoting the modern characteristics of structural glass, rather than its associations with traditional cladding, and color, in particular, became an important marketing tool. Having introduced a range of hues as early as 1922, Vitrolite was publicized as "the colorful structural glass" at a time when PPG was emphasizing Carrara's resemblance to marble and jet.[78] Color was still Vitrolite's distinguishing feature when it was acquired by LOF: it was available in ten colors and additional variations, a veritable "rainbow of colors from which to choose."[79]

The Modernize Main Street Competition

In purchasing the Vitrolite Company in May 1935, LOF's timing was impeccable: a mere six days after the sale was finalized, President Roosevelt signed the amended National Housing Act into law.[80] By then LOF had already placed two-page advertisements in the June issues of the four major architecture journals announcing its sponsorship of an architectural competition timed to coincide with the $50,000 expansion of government-insured modernization credit. Calculated to make the LOF name synonymous with the FHA's effort to stimulate commercial building modernization, of stores in particular, the competition was called "Modernize Main Street." Though PPG had used this FHA slogan in its advertisements, LOF co-opted it, upstaging its chief competitor and garnering the equivalent of an official endorsement from the FHA in a letter from agency head Stewart McDonald, who congratulated LOF for its contribution to the implementation of the amended NHA:

> Your new "Modernize Main Street" Architectural Competition is a most constructive and timely development in the growing interest in modernization and reviving construction. Your plan will stimulate the interest of many architects and builders and will encourage the specific action of business property owners throughout the country.[81]

McDonald's letter appeared alongside the competition brief when it was published in *Architectural Record,* which conducted the competition for LOF under the guidance of professional adviser Kenneth K. Stowell, AIA.

Stowell's participation was auspicious. As editor of *Architectural Forum* (until May 1935), Stowell was a vigorous supporter of the National Housing Act who repeatedly used the pages of the *Forum* to call attention to its "great potentialities of good for the architect," knowing that the profession as a whole needed to be encouraged to take small-scale building modernization seriously as a legitimate form of practice.[82] This support included a series of modernization competitions in 1934 designed to stimulate architectural interest in "minor as well as major building rehabilitation."[83] By 1935 Stowell was also something of an authority on building modernization, having authored the book *Modernizing Buildings for Profit,* which appeared shortly before the competition was announced.[84] Intended as a practical manual for architects, building managers, commercial property owners, and their long-term tenants, Stowell's book was a comprehensive treatise on the subject, covering such topics as determining feasibility for modernization, financing modernization (he endorsed the MCP), and modernizing structure, equipment, and style in a variety of building types including offices and hotels, restaurants and bars, and shops and stores.

The latter were the focus of the LOF competition, which offered $11,000 in cash awards, including four $1,000 first prizes for the best design to modernize the interior and exterior of a drugstore, apparel shop, food store, and automotive service station. As Stowell crafted them, each individual store design problem allowed competitors great latitude in approach and execution: no fixed budget and "complete freedom" in terms of style, materials, and construction.[85] Nonetheless, entrants were well aware of the MCP's $50,000 loan limit and the competition's sponsorship by Libbey-Owens-Ford to promote its glass products in store modernization.[86] The use of Vitrolite was never explicitly stated in the program since this would have revealed the competition merely as corporate PR rather than as a corporate contribution to national recovery. To promote this latter interpretation, LOF sought to make clear that it was not only attempting to sell its glass products, but to foster an activity of national import: "The Main Street of every city, town, village and community has at least these four business establishments. Better merchandising demands the modernization of thousands of them and better financing makes it possible."[87] The competition announcements and program included photographs depicting those nationwide Main Streets whose stores *demanded* modernization (fig. 3.5). Though a few vacant buildings appeared as a visible reminder of the Depression, the majority of the buildings were occupied and ordinary. They were not especially in disrepair; they were merely undistinguished and old-fashioned, with painted valances, appended signs, and symmetrically disposed facades— emblematic of the architectural hodgepodge that characterized so many U.S. business streets.[88] This unrarefied tableaux of the everyday—the Uptown Pharmacist, the Downtown Market—mirrored the text of Stowell's program. At once civic-minded, democratic, and appearing to make a significant contribution to the architectural and planning problems represented by Main Street, Stowell directed competitors to assume that the stores were utterly typical, occupying standard twenty-five-foot frontages and serving "an average American community rather than the luxury class."[89] In other words, they were sufficiently quotidian that architects might have ignored them were it not for the extenuating circumstances of the Depression.

According to the program, successful modernization schemes would place the requirements of merchandising above all other concerns, focusing especially on the design of the facade to "establish the character of the store" in a manner "consistent with the quality of the merchandise." Here Stowell acknowledges a defining aspect of building modernization in the 1930s—its preoccupation with the store exterior as the principal carrier of all architectural and retail intentions. This facade orientation was necessary, as Stowell explained it, because the goal of modernization was to attract the attention of the public, "to make the passer *buy*, inviting him or her to stop and shop." Inside, the layout and appointments were required to "fulfill the promise of the front" in terms of its display of goods and services for sale, serving as a discreet architectural background for merchandise.[90] Stowell was clearly seeking what might be called universal solutions to the store modernization problem, but he was also interested in stimulating designs to serve as a corrective to what were regarded as Main Street's most egregious visual afflictions. Thus, he qualified the program's stated freedom of design: deeply projecting signs and show windows were not permitted, and designers were encouraged to carefully consider the relationship between sign, window, and facade, treating them as integrated, rather than independent, compositional units.[91] However preliminary Stowell's attempt at architectural intervention on Main Street, his larger purpose was not lost on the competition's jury. Indeed, in their report the jury went so far as to commend

Figure 3.5 Announcement for Libbey-Owens-Ford Modernize Main Street Competition. This announcement appeared in all of the major U.S. architecture journals in the summer of 1935. The photographs represent typical Main Street stores (food, drug, clothing, and gas station) that the competition sponsors determined were in need of modernization. (*Architectural Forum* 62 [July 1935]. Courtesy of the Avery Architectural and Fine Arts Library, Columbia University.)

Stowell for the service he rendered "in the interest of raising the standard of public taste and commercial design."[92]

The jury met in late August to consider the merits of designs submitted by more than three thousand architects—nearly one-third of all those registered in the United States in 1935—many of whom submitted multiple designs for more than one of the program's store categories.[93] Consisting of five architects and two merchandising experts, the jury clearly reflected the aspirations of the program and the prominence of the competition (fig. 3.6). Chaired by J. André Fouilhoux, the jury also included Albert Kahn, William Lescaze, John Wellborn Root Jr., and Frank R. Walker. Presumably each was selected for the expertise he would contribute to an evaluation of Main Street designs. Kahn's utilitarian approach to architectural problems, evident in his factories and commercial lofts, was well-suited to judging whether the entries satisfied the functional requirements of selling, especially in terms of plan and equipment. Lescaze, well-known for his PSFS Building, was able to appraise the street-level showmanship of the designs in terms of the modernist brio they displayed. The other members of the jury brought specific knowledge of retail environments the architects may have lacked. Kenneth C. Welch was a designer with the Grand Rapids Store Equipment Company, one of the country's largest manufacturers of store fixtures and furnishings. He was also a frequent contributor to the architecture journals of articles in which he demystified the science of merchandising for designers.[94]

It was most likely the input of the merchandising experts that allowed the jury to quickly eliminate those designs that, however "creditable" aesthetically, did not represent a "solution for successful merchandising." This issue appears to have been the single most important factor in determining the winning entries. Indeed, the consideration the jury gave to a design's materials, colors, and style was based on its contribution to this major objective of the program: to attract attention and display goods to their best advantage. The jury evaluated how well the architect had "analyzed both the actions and reactions of the purchasers, and the psychology, methods, and routine of selling."[95] In other words, prizes were awarded to those fifty-two designs that would appeal most directly to Main Street merchants contemplating modernization.[96]

As a group, these winning storefront designs were remarkably coherent in terms of site, style, and materials. Responding to the program's demand for typical solutions appropriate to any and all U.S. Main Streets, the designers completely disregarded urban context. Neither adjacent buildings nor upper stories appear in the majority of winning drawings,

Figure 3.6 Modernize Main Street Competition jury at work. Albert Kahn points to a competition board while other jurors—including Kenneth Stowell, William Lescaze, Frank R. Walker, and J. André Fouilhoux—look on. The jury concluded that the competition would raise standards of retail design across the country. (*Architectural Record* 78 [October 1935]: 209. Courtesy of the Avery Architectural and Fine Arts Library, Columbia University, and Libbey-Owens-Ford Glass Company Records, MSS-066, the Ward M. Canaday Center for Special Collections, The University of Toledo.)

so that the stores resemble newly built taxpayers or exurban commercial strips more than modernizations on densely built Main Streets. Nearly all the designs made extensive use of plate glass and, since the competitors were mindful of their sponsors, of Vitrolite as well. Most were trimmed with extruded metal fittings of chrome, stainless steel, aluminum, or bronze. Signage typically complemented the metal trim, frequently with the addition of neon, though cut-out Vitrolite letters were not uncommon. According to the jury, these materials were utilized with a high degree of "workmanship" in compositions distinguished by an overall "simplicity," rather than "extravagance" in design.[97] This was a crucial distinction in the Depression era, when formal concerns, especially in

Figure 3.7 LOF Modernize Main Street Competition winner (Honorable Mention): Joseph M. Hirschman, Apparel Shop. The exuberant asymmetry of Hirschman's design—achieved through his manipulation of entrance vestibule, display windows, and signboards—stamped the storefront as legibly modern. His scheme also called for blue, white, and yellow facing with stainless-steel lettering. (*Architectural Record* 78 [October 1935]: 233. Courtesy of the Avery Architectural and Fine Arts Library, Columbia University, and Libbey-Owens-Ford Glass Company Records, MSS-066, the Ward M. Canaday Center for Special Collections, The University of Toledo.)

the context of building modernization, were imbued with national social significance and the line between simplicity and extravagance was the line between a serious response to the economic crisis and a frivolous flouting of it. Circa 1935 formal extravagance was synonymous with American commercial design of the late 1920s—those skyscrapers, department stores, and movie palaces with lavishly decorated repeated fields of floral, chevron, frozen fountain motifs, patterned tiling and brickwork, and customized and hand-finished metalwork, much of it elaborately detailed and finely tooled. The winning LOF Modernize Main Street entries must be set in opposition to these immediate commercial precedents in order to properly understand their so-called simplicity. As will be discussed in chapter 5, this simplicity does not necessarily imply a visual austerity, but rather an effort, influenced in part by European modernism, to create visual interest more through the manipulation of the basic compositional elements of the storefront, rendered in a few basic building materials, than through additive decorative effects.

All fifty-two of the winning entries were articulated in a broadly defined modern syntax influenced by the International Style of European

ELEVATION ON MAIN STREET

Figure 3.8 LOF Modernize Main Street Competition winner (Honorable Mention): Now-land van Powell, Food Store. Van Powell's use of enlarged porthole windows was unusual for a grocery, but the overall effect of the storefront—with its speed lines, pylon-like sign, and neon channel letters—was typical of many competition winners. (*Architectural Record* 78 [October 1935]: 252. Courtesy of the Avery Architectural and Fine Arts Library, Columbia University, and Libbey-Owens-Ford Glass Company Records, MSS-066, the Ward M. Canaday Center for Special Collections, The University of Toledo.)

modernism. Modified by the requirements of competitive retailing, this modernism was transformed in the winning designs into a series of iden-tifiable features: flattened planes and poster-like facades, often highly colored, asymmetrical compositions with strongly defined horizontals and verticals, curved bulkheads, and signage expressed in bold graphics with contemporary typefaces (figs. 3.7 and 3.8). While many of these for-mal features were already gaining architectural currency in the United States, the Main Street entries surely fostered their further dissemina-tion. Indeed, the jury report was unequivocal about the impact these winning designs would have on the commercial landscape of the United States, concluding that the winners would have "a far-reaching effect on raising the standards of store design," on directing architects' interest in the modernization field, and on providing merchants with "a guide as to what an intelligent public taste will demand." Even more emphatically, it declared that the winning designs would "stimulate the interest and imag-ination of store owners throughout the country and induce them to bring their stores up-to-date," especially since the competition coincided with "the government's extensive program to 'Modernize Main Street.'"[98]

The jury also predicted that the winning designs would be widely circulated and much discussed in the fall and winter of 1935–36. To the undoubted satisfaction of LOF and the FHA, the results of the Modernize Main Street Competition were well-publicized in building industry and retail trade journals. In addition to the *Architectural Record*'s comprehensive coverage, *Pencil Points, Architectural Forum,* and the *National Real Estate Journal,* as well as *Drug Topics, Progressive Grocer, Apparel Arts,* and *Gasoline Retailer,* all published a selection of prizewinning entries, usually with pro-modernization captions enjoining architects to design and merchants to commission similar schemes for commercial property improvements.[99] *Building Modernization* used its coverage of the winning designs to inaugurate a new monthly feature, a "Modernizing Main Street" column.[100] The competition was considered newsworthy even by the advertising monthly *Tide,* which discussed the winning designs on its marketing page and hailed LOF's success in capitalizing on and fostering the public's interest in modernization.[101]

Not surprisingly, LOF promoted the results of the competition extensively in product literature and advertisements. Having sponsored the Main Street competition to "crystallize the most competent thought" on modernization, LOF could confidently announce that the prizewinning designs represented the "best" and "most authoritative" architectural consideration of the problem of modernizing for profit. According to the company, this consideration led to a significant conclusion: "Various kinds of glass, a comparatively inexpensive building material, dominate almost all current architectural treatments of the modernized store."[102] Since LOF now owned all submitted entries, it published them as graphic testimony to support such a claim. Even more importantly, the entries, especially the winning designs, filled a void in the company's promotional portfolio, since LOF did not yet possess those mainstays of modernization advertising—before-and-after photographs of buildings remodeled using the manufacturer's products. In fact, even after such images of Vitrolite installations became available, LOF continued to promote the Main Street designs. As late as 1939, winning entries appeared in a pamphlet prepared for distribution at the "Glass Carnival," LOF's corporate pavilion at the Golden Gate International Exposition.[103]

However convincing the competition designs were as advertising illustrations, this was not the limit of their promotional use. In November 1935 LOF released a full-color book reproducing every winning scheme with elevations, plans, sections, details, and specifications—but not working drawings, which would have rendered the services of an architect unnecessary. The book also included detailed descriptions of individual LOF products and concluded with a discussion of "FHA Financing," featuring a monthly payment calculation chart using LOF's MCP-insured Modernization Budget Plan. *52 Designs for Modernizing Main Street with Glass* was available through LOF dealers and was distributed to merchants, landlords, and all "logical prospects for modernizing."[104] For LOF, *52 Designs* was simply a lavish promotional piece intended to increase sales of its building products, especially newly acquired Vitrolite. For merchants and architects, it was a ready reference for effective modernizing ideas that, having been approved by leading retail and design authorities, could be consulted with confidence for solutions to merchandising or architectural problems.

The success of LOF's Modernize Main Street Competition led several other manufacturers to generate interest in their products by sponsoring architectural competitions with programs similarly focused on stores and modernization.[105] Most important with respect to the subsequent development of LOF's storefront products is the competition Owens-Illinois sponsored in 1939 to promote the use of Insulux Glass Block. The program called for the partial "remodeling of an obsolete block on Main Street" in the heart of "the women's shopping district" in a midsize midwestern city. The specific problem was to modernize three stores—an apparel shop, beauty salon, and restaurant—located in a single business property whose owner had been informed that his tenants planned to vacate their quarters unless they were "brought up to date." This property owner, according to the program, wished to use Insulux on the building's modernized store facades because it was equally effective day and night and because it connoted "a modern, up-to-date establishment."[106] That the program acknowledged a client and a commercial scenario indicates how much the climate for modernization had progressed since the 1935 LOF competition: from an abstraction to a fact, from a type of work generally eschewed by the profession at large to one regarded as "realistic" and "a problem of everyday practice."[107] In selecting the winning designs, it was the disposition of the "modern storefronts" with which the jury was most concerned. While some of the winning designs made extensive use of Insulux, rear-lit to create evenly glowing facades, most used it as a luminous accent, in multiblock panels of various sizes, and in combination with plate glass and structural glass, as was standard for store design by 1939.[108] The fourth prize went to M. Righton Swicegood, a 1931 MIT graduate, who had taken first prize for his drugstore in the LOF competition. His Owens-Illinois designs, particularly his restaurant—with its off-center entrance, glass-block panels, and structural glass signboard and bulkhead—were, as his drugstore had been before, utterly representative of the currents of American commercial architecture in the late 1930s. Between Swicegood's Vitrolite drugstore and his Insulux restaurant, there had passed four years of relentless promotion of storefront modernization by the building industry—by material manufacturers and the architecture profession alike. LOF, flush with the success of the Modernize Main Street Competition, carried its own promotional momentum well into 1936, the end of which would see the company record its most profitable year ever, due to increased demand for flat glass of all types and stimulated, according to President John Biggers, by interest in and sales of Vitrolite.[109]

The Colorful Storefront

That John Biggers could observe with satisfaction at the conclusion of LOF's 1936 fiscal year that Vitrolite was "subject to growing demand" was due largely to the tremendous marketing effort the company had undertaken since the conclusion of the Main Street competition. This effort represented a significant investment of corporate resources, not only in advertising and sales, but in product development, continually measured against the activities of PPG and other glass-manufacturing rivals.[110] The staff of LOF's New Uses Department, rechristened the Architectural Services Department, was traveling the country as missionary men, addressing architects and merchants and meeting with the company's independent distributors and local jobbers to encourage the use of Vitrolite in modernization. They provided technical data and sales information and supplied design ideas through "visual demonstrations," including displays of the Main Street competition designs and photographs of Vitrolite installations in modernized buildings, examples of which LOF began compiling early in 1936.[111]

At the same time, Vitrolite product manager Frank Sohn was preparing another series of designs in conjunction with the LOF Art Department to illustrate the use of Vitrolite in ways the Main Street competition entries had not. Sohn, the man credited with turning Vitrolite into "the colorful structural glass" in 1922, now demonstrated the product's additional "color possibilities," emphasizing veined agates—golden, orchid, jade, emerald, royal blue, and walnut—which were available in light, medium, and dark.[112] One reason LOF publicized Vitrolite's agates was that these colors distinguished the product from PPG's Carrara, which, early in

1936, was only available in five standard colors and four trim colors (i.e., sold only in small sizes). Vitrolite, by comparison, was available in sixteen colors, all sized for facing and trim. Vitrolite's finishes, also emphasized in Sohn's design series, similarly set LOF's product apart from Carrara. In addition to high polish, the standard structural glass finish, Vitrolite was available in chipped, mirrored, or matte finishes. By contrast, PPG's comparable "suede" Carrara would not appear until 1939.[113] LOF circulated Sohn's twelve storefront designs—including drug, food, and apparel types as well as a restaurant, bar, men's store, and bakery—through normal promotional channels: in *Sweet's*, in advertisements, in portfolios for jobbers and LOF distributors, and in pamphlets and circulars made available to LOF representatives for distribution to anyone interested in using Vitrolite to "transform the obsolete, characterless store front into the New, Modern, Outstanding Front."[114]

Sohn's storefront designs had a decidedly different look than the majority of the Modernize Main Street Competition winners.[115] One of the most striking differences was the conspicuous absence of the curved bulkheads and windows, which were one of the principal design features of the competition's winning entries. Present, instead, were faceted bulkheads and windows that stepped back toward recessed entrances in angles right, acute, and obtuse. While this lack of curved Vitrolite-faced bulkheads and curved Polished Plate windows may have resulted from the designer's personal preference, it was more likely informed by manufacturing realities. When Sohn was preparing his storefront designs in the winter of 1935, LOF had no facilities for bending structural glass.[116] The company's situation for bending plate glass was only marginally better. Though LOF had a licensing agreement with the Invisible Glass Company of America to bend glass for store installations, this remained impractical because of cost and limited distribution. But with *52 Designs* in release across the country, and including in its pages a great number of storefronts specifying curved architectural elements, it was only a matter of time before LOF jobbers would be called upon to deliver bent glass. Responding to apparent increased demand, LOF established a glass-bending department in the spring of 1936. By the summer that department was in commercial operation, and LOF was supplying its customers with curving panels of Polished Plate and Vitrolite, as well as ribbed Blue Ridge Glass. A year later the department had proven such a success that LOF was forced to install two additional bending furnaces in order to meet further increased demand, as this ubiquitous formal element of the streamlined storefront found its way to Main Streets across the country (fig. 3.9).[117]

Figure 3.9 Ostergaard's bakery, Racine, Wisconsin, 1937. Installed by the Patek Brothers of Milwaukee, this storefront featured the bent glass bulkheads that LOF began manufacturing in response to demand generated by the Modernize Main Street Competition. (Libbey-Owens-Ford, *Vitrolite Album*. Libbey-Owens-Ford Glass Company Records, MSS-066, Ward M. Canaday Center for Special Collections, The University of Toledo.)

Within LOF's corporate hierarchy, the responsibility for spotting a design trend like the use of curved glass on storefronts fell to the Architectural Service Department. This made sense given its mandate to find new uses and new markets for the company's products in anticipation of, but also in response to, growing demand. Having accurately gauged public interest in structural glass and bent glass, the department appears to have made two subsequent determinations in 1936, both related to the further development of what LOF called the Vitrolite Store Front and the further marketing of LOF products in store modernization. The first concerned the growing interest in storefront illumination, which had evolved alongside the interest in storefront modernization. This was partially related to the development and popularization of lighted signage, of neon in particular. However, following the 1935 introduction of Insulux glass blocks by Owens-Illinois, which achieved a glowing luminosity when back-lit, storefront illumination soon involved the development of modern architectural effects equally visible day and night. This gave a storefront what advertising ad copywriters called "24-hour selling power," providing a maximum return on an investment in storefront modernization, of particular concern during the Depression.[118] In 1936 LOF's Architectural Service Department determined that the company needed a material to complement Vitrolite, to be used to create interesting lighting effects, to enhance nighttime visibility, and, most importantly, to compete with Owens-Illinois's Insulux. In less than a year, the Vitrolite Store Front became the Luminous Store Front.

In developing a product to compete with Insulux, LOF was not interested in simply bringing out its own version of the glass block. PPG was already doing this in partnership with Corning Glass.[119] Seeking to replicate the effect of glass block rather than its look, LOF developed the luminosity of one of its existing flat-glass products. This, it was hoped, would minimize the company's investment of capital and time and enable LOF to get its Luminous Store Front product on the market as quickly as possible. Basically, LOF wanted to combine the facing capabilities and chromatic range of structural glass with the luminosity and brilliance of glass blocks, while exploiting the potential of a material preexisting in its product line. A short time from development to manufacture was crucial because Insulux, or some other product, might become fixed in the minds of architects and merchants as the luminous material of choice.[120] What emerged was a material that combined the properties of Vitrolite and Insulux into an ingenious hybrid—Vitrolux—that offered "luminous color as an integral part of the structure itself." This color-fused tempered plate glass was put on the market in the spring of 1937 as Vitrolite's "logical companion."[121] Since 1935 LOF had been tinting its clear Polished Plate Glass in shades of blue, green, and peach to "keep pace with modern architectural and decorative trends," and Vitrolux developed logically out of this colored product, broadening its storefront applications by providing a middle ground of light transmission.[122] Neither transparent, like tinted plate, nor opaque, like structural glass, Vitrolux was translucent. Produced by fusing colored ceramic coatings to the plate substrate, Vitrolux was also tempered, making it stronger than ordinary plate glass and able to withstand the heat of prolonged rear illumination.

If Vitrolite added color to the modernized storefront, Vitrolux made the color glow. Available in eighteen translucent colors, ten of which matched Vitrolite's non-agate tones, Vitrolux was used for flush or panel-type illuminated areas (i.e., affixed to the front of a lighting unit), especially storefront signboards and upper facades, and the ceilings of display cases and vestibules.[123] When lit, Vitrolux transmitted an even, diffused light, the intensity of which varied with the color; otherwise it had a soft

Figure 3.10 The Baron Stiegel Room in Lancaster, Pennsylvania, 1938. LOF promoted this restaurant design as an example of Luminous Store Front that combined Vitrolite bulkheads with a rear-lit Vitrolux signboard. (*Sweet's Catalogue File* [1940]: sec. 18, cat. 2; and LOF *1940 Advertising Scrapbook*. Libbey-Owens-Ford Glass Company Records, MSS-066, Ward M. Canaday Center for Special Collections, The University of Toledo.)

luster akin to Vitrolite. Opaque Vitrolux was also available, used mainly for sign letters set in a translucent Vitrolux field (the reverse was also possible). When used in these various combinations, Vitrolux's colorful luminosity provided a striking counterpoint to Vitrolite facing and plate-glass windows, giving the storefront "after-dark brilliance" that made "night brighter than day," as LOF's copywriters aptly put it (fig. 3.10).[124] Since Vitrolux had to be installed in conjunction with lighting units in order to take advantage of its luminosity, LOF marketed the product extensively to electrical contractors and utility companies, encouraging them to promote the Luminous Store Fronts in order "to increase the night time power load." Here LOF was coordinating its products with yet another New Deal initiative, notably the programs of the Rural Electrification Administration, which were expanding electrification nationwide. Claiming that American cities and towns were "being kept years behind the times" by un-illuminated storefronts, LOF offered a variety of electrically oriented sales aids, including a store modernization manual with illumination data supplied by General Electric and a Vitrolux Demonstration Kit that came with color samples and a miniature light box for convincing demonstrations of Vitrolux's luminosity and translucency.[125]

The Complete Storefront

According to the company's records, in 1937, with Vitrolux firmly established in its product line, along with Vitrolite and Polished Plate, LOF finally surpassed rival PPG in the marketing of glass for store modernization. But PPG still had the lead in storefront metal since Pittco sashes had already been on the market for two years. Hence, LOF determined that it needed a metal trim to "tie its store-front package together." Following PPG's example, LOF designers Dean Lowry and Robert Pinney developed their own extruded metal trim with a cushioned glass-mounting system, and in the spring of 1937 the company patented a pressure-controlled, shock-absorbing extruded aluminum sash.[126] LOF heralded Extrudalite as "revolutionary," referring not only to its mounting mechanism, but to its sash profiles, which, LOF claimed, represented the "streamlining" of traditional classical moldings, a stylistic change significant enough to prompt PPG to redesign its own sash profiles along more modern lines in 1938. Equally revolutionary, in LOF's own exalted view of itself, was its merchandising of Extrudalite in three sizes and three price ranges to satisfy budgets both modest and luxurious—a promotional pitch that clearly responded to economic realities (fig. 3.11).[127]

The introduction of metal sashes enabled LOF, like PPG before it, to market itself as a full-service supplier of modern storefronts, but before the company could market itself as such, the Depression intervened once more. The economy declined steeply in August, bringing on the so-called "recession" of 1937 and causing LOF, like so many other American businesses that autumn and winter, to experience "a substantial falling-off of sales."[128] Making matters worse for marketers of store modernization, the MCP and Title I of the National Housing Act had expired in the spring, in a stunning display of bad timing. Though LOF was in a position to continue modernization financing through its Budget Plan, the government would no longer insure the loans it made, a disquieting thought as this most recent manifestation of the economic crisis worsened. When it became clear in the late fall that Title I would be reinstated, American manufacturers undoubtedly breathed a collective sigh of relief.[129]

It was in anticipation of the MCP's renewal that LOF unveiled the Complete Storefront in November 1937 at the annual New York and

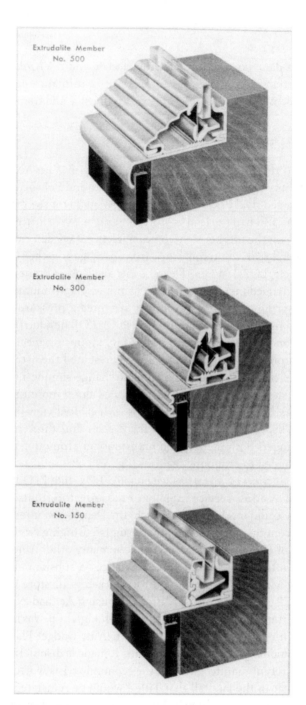

Figure 3.11 LOF Extrudalite Storefront Metal, introduced 1937. Standard extruded aluminum sash members were available in three sizes and styles that the company claimed were revolutionary for their streamlining of traditional molding profiles. The section cuts show the sash grips for window glass and facing glass. (*Sweet's Catalogue File* [1940]: sec. 19, cat. 6. LOF *1940 Advertising Scrapbook*. Libbey-Owens-Ford Glass Company Records, MSS-066, Ward M. Canaday Center for Special Collections, The University of Toledo.)

Figure 3.12 LOF, "Modern Shopping Center," 1937, rendering of retail units. This seven-eighths-scale model was displayed at the New York and Chicago auto shows in the fall of 1937. The five contiguous storefronts—for a florist, grocery, dry cleaner, bakery, and department store—were all fabricated with materials in LOF's Complete Storefront line. The colorful, high-gloss storefronts must have provided an ideal backdrop for the new model cars on display. (Libbey-Owens-Ford, "Colorful Storefronts" [1937]. Libbey-Owens-Ford Glass Company Records, MSS-066, Ward M. Canaday Center for Special Collections, The University of Toledo.)

Chicago automobile shows, the largest in the country, with combined attendance that topped half a million people.[130] LOF announced that it now offered "EVERY material required in the construction of the modern storefront," and as a demonstration LOF partnered with General Motors to produce an exhibition of model storefronts to serve as a setting for GM's display of its 1938 Chevrolets. This was no miniature caravan; it was a "Modern Shopping Center": a nearly full-scale (seventh-eighths) installation of five contiguous store units, fabricated entirely of Complete Storefront products (fig. 3.12). A decontextualized one-story strip containing a flower shop, food store, dry cleaner, bakery, and department store, the Modern Shopping Center was equally adaptable for Main Street modernizations or new construction on the urban periphery. Most likely designed by H. Creston Donner of the LOF Architectural Service Department, each store elevation was simplified for legibility of parts and materials, yet still recognizable as the modern(ized) retail types that had become common since 1935: broad, interior-revealing display windows and low bulkheads on the ivory (Vitrolite) and red (Vitrolux) Centre Food Store, round porthole displays fitted with plate-glass shelves on the white (Vitrolite) Modern Baker.[131] LOF placed great stock in the marketing value of such exhibits, observing of a similar Complete Storefront installation that Donner designed for its Toledo showroom that "a prospect who can leave without signing an order for a complete glass front most certainly has Herculean sales resistance."[132]

Though it may have fulfilled this sales function, it is questionable how successful the Modern Shopping Center was as a backdrop for the new model Chevys, given that the stated goal of the LOF storefront was "to compel attention." Surely, bulkheads, side panels, and signs of bright Vitrolite and glowing Vitrolux, trimmed in gleaming Extrudalite, were just as visually engaging as the Duco-lacquered teardrop fenders and chrome-plated, speed-lined radiator grilles of the Master De Luxe Chevrolet. It made sense that the storefronts on display had the potential to outshine the cars on display since both car and storefront were repackaged to sell during the Depression with new streamlined models introduced each year and available for purchase on virtually identical time-payment plans. That such formal and fiscal similarities existed was not, of course, coincidental. Not only was there a direct relationship between the auto financing offered by GM and the government-insured modernization credit offered by LOF, as discussed in chapter 2; there was an equally close connection between the appearance and aspirations of the streamlined car and those of the streamlined storefront, as will be discussed in chapter 4.

Following its introduction at the auto shows, the Complete Storefront was announced to the architecture community in February 1938 in simultaneous advertisements in the four principal professional journals, as well as in local architecture publications serving major markets like New York and Chicago. To architects, LOF offered the Complete Storefront as "a service" in which Vitrolite, Vitrolux, Extrudalite, and Polished Plate were brought together for ease of design and specification—and ease of promotion as well, since after 1938 LOF stopped advertising its storefront products separately.[133] The Complete Storefront was announced to merchants beginning in March, the delay allowing architects to familiarize themselves with the full product line in advance of their potential retail clients. LOF's promotional coverage in the retail field throughout the spring and summer was exceptionally thorough, with Complete Storefront advertisements appearing in *Baker's Weekly*, *FTD News*, *Meat Merchandising*, and *Motor Monthly*, among many others. LOF promoted the four-product line with what were, by then, routine modernization pitches: increased patronage, reduced maintenance, and an identification of the store owner as "a progressive retail merchant."[134] All of these sales angles came together in a promotional piece explaining why the Complete Storefront was "a business asset." The folder was lavishly illustrated with twenty "smart designs," photographs of LOF storefronts installed coast-to-coast, from Daniels Hat Shop in New York City (Phillip Associates, designers) to Foster's Restaurant in San Francisco (Farr & Ward, architects) with chain and independent dry cleaners, bakeries, markets, gas stations, movie theaters, and shoe stores at eighteen destinations in between.[135] These modernized stores are characterized by a series of familiar glass and metal elements: curved bulkheads, off-center entrances, deep vestibules, portholes and shadowboxes, enlarged signboards, and contrasting color schemes. As a group they serve as a graphic testament to the legacy of LOF's architectural competition, illustrating the degree to which Main Street had been modernized since 1935. But from the company's point of view, there was still much work to be done.

Three years after the FHA introduced the Modernize Main Street initiative, and three years after LOF began its campaign of promotional tie-ins, the company was still encouraging jobbers and architects to "look up and down Main Street."[136] Though by 1943 LOF had abandoned the Complete Storefront in favor of the Visual Front, as it began marketing Tuf-Flex tempered plate glass to meet the growing demand for "the open-faced architecture introduced pre-war," modernizing Main Street would remain a promotional touchstone well into the postwar era. In 1956, when LOF declared "Main Street open for business," it might easily have been 1936, so little had the promotional pitch changed. Merchants were still "discovering that attractive buildings are good business" and still seeking to replace "drab, uninspiring storefronts" with "the clean, uncluttered look of 20th century architecture."[137]

In the late 1930s, for Libbey-Owens-Ford and many other American manufacturers of building materials, store modernization had not yet lost its viability as a sales angle, nor had Main Street lost its potential as a territory for sales prospects. And neither was likely to in the near future—at least not until another national crisis would prompt another coordinated response, as the Depression had before (World War II and advertising supporting the U.S. mobilization). As a sales theme, the original FHA tie-ins had incredible longevity. Even if references to the FHA or the MCP were largely omitted by the end of the decade, modernization and Main Street had become apparently self-perpetuating, dominating building material merchandising until 1941 with nearly the same arguments and persuasions that were current circa 1935, though with varying degrees of intensity related to the life cycle of Title I. In 1939 Westinghouse introduced two new lighting units "designed for 'Main Street' Commercial Applications" and deemed appropriate there because they were "modernly-styled" and had a "low initial and operating cost." With equal confidence, Johnson Service Company proclaimed that "when Johnson controls the temperature on Main Street customers shop there *more* and *more*." Below the headline two stylishly dressed

Figure 3.13 "An appreciation of architecture long overdue." By the time this Owens-Illinois advertisement appeared in 1939, the modernized storefront had become ubiquitous on Main Street, but manufacturers of storefront materials continued to utilize the same themes that brought them success throughout the decade. Here Insulux Glass Block is described as a "merchandising asset" with the ability to stop traffic. (*Architectural Record* 85 [April 1939]: 125. Courtesy of the Avery Architectural and Fine Arts Library, Columbia University.)

shoppers head toward a modernized Main Street, its buildings and its cars clearly streamlined.[138]

As for the glass manufacturers, though LOF, PPG, and Owens-Illinois had used these themes longer and more consistently than any other marketers of storefront products, they were not about to tamper with such a successful formula—one that had spoken so effectively to architects and merchants that the glass-faced, modernized, streamlined storefront had already become very nearly a design cliché. Despite, or perhaps because of, this cliché, there was a real sense in 1939 that Main Street, to a great extent, had been modernized. That year, though Owens-Illinois proclaimed that "Main Street now recognizes sound architecture as smart business"—as if the goals of the movement were a fait accompli—the copy optimistically predicted that modernization would continue its work of "replacing those antiquated nightmares that are all too much in evidence on merchandising thoroughfares." These were represented by before-and-after photographs of the Walker Brothers Dry Good Company in Wichita, Kansas (fig. 3.13). What Owens-Illinois purposefully ignored was the fact that little more than the vicissitudes of architectural fashion separated the Luxfer Prism transoms of the old facade from the Insulux Glass Block windows of the new. But such was the nature of storefront improvement for, as *Architectural Forum* observed in 1934, "modernization is only relative."[139] That statement was more significant than anyone could have realized in the mid-1930s. As the movement to modernize Main Street gained ground through the efforts of the federal government and the building industry, the relativity of commercial design—its insistence on the mutability of architectural canons and on the ephemerality of consumer culture—would come increasingly to the fore.

CHAPTER 4

The Architecture of Consumption

In 1936 the Star Electrical Supply Company hired a young New Jersey architect named Barney Gruzen to modernize its premises on Market Street in downtown Newark. The existing turn-of-the-century structure was a small-scale loft building with double-height showroom space on the ground level and offices and storage space on the upper levels. Its architectural aspirations were modest and eclectic: a little gothic tracery, a bit of classical molding, some picturesque ironwork. These were largely overwhelmed by the various commercial proclamations Star Electrical had made over the years: a large billboard mounted above the cornice on the main facade and an even larger advertisement painted across all three stories of the blank side facade. By the mid-1930s, the building and its advertising superstructure were considered woefully out-of-date and insufficient for the merchandising demands of the consumer culture, not least because the products Star Electrical sold were so indisputably modern. To counter any potential perception of obsolescence by members of the buying public, the company modernized, determined to make its building appear as up-to-date as its inventory.[1]

Gruzen's redesign was exceptionally thorough and reflected the decade's dominant strategies of commercial modernization. He eradicated

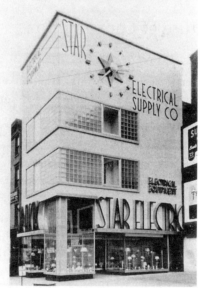

Figure 4.1 Star Electrical Supply Company, Newark, New Jersey, designed by Barney Sumner Gruzen in 1936. These before-and-after views demonstrate the dramatic impact that building modernization sometimes achieved, especially through the use of modern materials like glass block and enameled steel. Gruzen treated signage and advertising as integral to his scheme, transforming the entire building into a showcase of the electrical equipment sold within. This was especially evident at night. (*Architectural Forum* 64 [May 1936]: 426; and *Architectural Forum* 67 [August 1937]: 103. Courtesy of the Avery Architectural and Fine Arts Library, Columbia University.)

Figure 4.1 (*Continued*)

all traces of the original exterior, along with any architectural age markers, behind a wraparound facade of light blue glazed terra-cotta and bands of windows filled with alternating panels of glass block and plate glass (fig. 4.1). At the ground level, Gruzen opened up a dark, narrow vestibule into a boldly asymmetrical arrangement of glass display cases of varying heights and widths all showcasing Star Electrical's light fixtures. Treating the necessary signage as part of an integrated architectural scheme, Gruzen deployed oversize sans serif letters in orange porcelain enamel steel and ultramarine glazed terra-cotta to create a graphic sequence above the displays and below the cornice. However striking this composition was during the day, at night it was literally electrifying, as the entire building advertised the company and its wares: neon signs, an electric clock emblazoned with a star, rear-lit glass panels, and, of course, electric lamps, torchères, sconces, and chandeliers in the display windows.

In producing this legible and programmatic alignment between the building and the goods for sale inside, this modernization was emblematic of the relationship between architecture and consumer culture in the Depression era. Like so many streamlined consumer products, the Star Electrical building was repackaged to appear new and improved, even though in essence it remained the same store it had always been. But Star Electrical's proprietors, as well as its customers, willingly accepted this repackaged image because what they were looking at was more than simply a modernized building; it was an antidote to the Depression.

No doubt the ten years beginning with 1930 will be referred to by future generations as the Streamlined Decade.

So predicted the critic Emrich Nicholson in his 1945 book *Contemporary Shops in the United States,* a portfolio of mostly prewar commercial work culled from the pages of *Architectural Forum.* Nicholson used the term *streamlined,* in the broad sense of "improved in appearance or modernized," to characterize that recent period when "progressive design" found widespread public acceptance in commercial buildings as merchants and architects turned increasingly to "modern developments" in materials, technology, and style.[2] Time has borne out Nicholson's prediction about the decade: streamlining—with its speed lines, rounded corners, banded windows, and sleek facades—is regarded as a hallmark of the visual culture of the 1930s (fig. 4.2). Beyond mere prognostication, Nicholson's comments also make vivid an aspect of commercial architecture that has rarely been understood, especially as it relates to building modernization: its connection to consumer culture. This may seem like stating the obvious since commercial architecture, by its nature, is always in the service of commerce and consumption. But it was only in the 1930s, and largely through the widespread occurrence of building modernization, that architecture began to respond to consumer culture in explicit and deliberate ways by assimilating its aims, its practices, and its products.

In *Contemporary Shops,* Nicholson explained how streamlined buildings arrived on the nation's Main Streets as "an outgrowth of design in other fields," a shift in scale that was due "ironically enough to the economic depression beginning in 1929." Merchants, he implied, modernized their stores under increased competitive pressure, following the lead of

Figure 4.2 The Griddle restaurant, San Francisco, 1937. This storefront exemplifies the streamlining effects that were commonplace by the end of the 1930s, especially the rounded corners, speed lines, and sleek skinlike facades. Many of these forms originated in industrial design, especially the restyling of consumer products as a way to increase sales during the Depression. (Libbey-Owens-Ford, *Vitrolite Album*. Libbey-Owens-Ford Glass Company Records, MSS-066, Ward M. Canaday Center for Special Collections, The University of Toledo.)

manufacturers who had embraced product restyling to create "eye appeal and more sales." In his description, these were "styling jobs that aimed for the simplification of surface contour and the use of new color schemes" to produce "modern autos, railway cars . . . practical kitchens and shiny bathrooms."[3] Nicholson discerned a trend now acknowledged as historical fact: that the streamlining of vehicles and products emerged in the early years of the Depression under the aegis of corporate manufacturers to create demand for consumer goods glutting the marketplace in the wake of a 40 percent decline in consumer spending since 1929. Companies such as General Motors, General Electric, Hoover, and RCA brought in industrial designers like Raymond Loewy, Norman Bel Geddes, and Henry Dreyfuss to streamline a wide range of durable goods and household appliances, mainly by changing form or style and not function or technology. Simultaneously, they retained advertising agencies like Calkins & Holden and Batten, Barton, Durstine & Osborn to promote the new cars, refrigerators, vacuum cleaners, and radios by convincing the public that the appliances they currently owned were obsolete, out-of-date, and not modern.[4]

For Nicholson, there was an obvious connection between these streamlined vehicles and products and streamlined commercial buildings: "It is only natural that the buying public should expect our stores and shops to be as inviting, interesting, and up-to-date as the products on the shelves."[5] In other words, the improved appearance of stores was a necessary correlate to the improved appearance of consumer goods. Thus, in Nicholson's conception, the linkage between streamlined products and streamlined buildings was direct and causal. In this linkage, which Nicholson stated so matter-of-factly, was the foundation of a theory of building modernization during the Great Depression. Espoused by federal officials, corporate manufacturers, and architects and embraced by independent merchants and chain retailers, this theory was predicated upon the existence of a critical relationship between building modernization and consumer culture. Born of the Depression and fostered by it, this relationship would bring advertising, obsolescence, gender, and fashion to bear directly on the everyday architecture found on the nation's Main Streets.

Streamlining: A Metaphor for Progress

No group articulated this theory more clearly than industrial designers and advertisers. These so-called "masters of publicity" grasped the implicit lessons of streamlining in advance of their contemporaries in government, business, and architecture, and recognized the possibility of extending the restyling of individual products to the restyling of the broader environment.[6] Designer Norman Bel Geddes refused any fixed boundaries between architecture and design, embracing both in his totalizing vision of a present and future in which streamlining functioned as a metaphor for progress, prosperity, and modernity. Geddes tirelessly promoted this vision throughout the decade, in his 1932 book *Horizons*, in his unrealized projects for the 1933 Century of Progress International Exposition in Chicago, and ultimately in the Futurama, the pavilion and exhibition he designed for General Motors at the 1939 New York World's Fair.

Equally exuberant in promoting streamlining beyond product design was Egmont Arens, head of Industrial Styling at the advertising firm of Calkins & Holden. In 1934 Arens mounted a one-man campaign to promote streamlining as a boosterish slogan and a business method for national recovery through increased consumption. In Arens's view, streamlining was relevant to anyone engaged in the exchange of goods and services, meaning virtually all Americans, be they workers or managers for large corporations, small-town merchants, or members of the buying public. Determined to reach as many of these Americans as possible, Arens delivered slide lectures to civic groups across the country and in November sent a telegram to President Roosevelt explaining how his "streamlining for recovery" effort had "captured American imagination."[7]

Among scores of recovery schemes sent to Washington during the New Deal, Arens's proposal was taken seriously enough to be forwarded to an appropriate agency, in this case the Federal Housing Administration. At that moment, with the Modernization Credit Plan in operation and the Better Housing Program in place, the FHA was in the midst of its own national campaign to promote *modernizing* as a slogan and method for recovery. That New Dealers would have immediately recognized an affinity between Arens's streamlining scheme and the FHA's modernizing effort is not surprising, if only because by mid-decade the two terms were closely allied in the public's mind.[8] For its part, the agency also saw a correspondence between its goals and Arens's and arranged for him to meet with the advisory committee of its Industrial Division, whose membership included representatives from General Electric, Johns-Manville, Pittsburgh Plate Glass, and Libbey-Owens-Ford, all of whom were actively promoting modernization. With the committee's blessing, Arens designed a motor caravan fitted with building product displays and outlined a plan for the FHA to use streamlining as "a selling tool," thus transforming it "from a mere commercial enterprise into a movement of some national significance."[9]

Arens's concept of selling streamlining, though lacking policy specifics, was virtually identical to the FHA's conception of modernization as a "sales effort" designed to improve the appearance of the nation's buildings while improving the nation's economy. Despite these similarities, Arens, ever the ad man, regarded streamlining as superior to modernization from a marketing standpoint. In his report to the FHA advisory committee and in a telegram sent to President Roosevelt, Arens explained that because of its apparent psychological associations with products that were viewed by the public as "modern, efficient, well-organized, sweep [sic] clean and beautiful," *streamlining* was the most evocative, and thus appropriate, term to express the goals of the FHA's modernization program, especially since these went beyond improving buildings, credit availability, and even the economy to improving the American standard of living.[10] Despite Arens's entreaties, the FHA never substituted *streamlining* for *modernizing* in its promotional literature or in its program nomenclature, which was fixed by the congressionally approved mechanism of the *Modernization* Credit Plan. Nonetheless, streamlining was vitally important to the FHA's work even in advance of Arens's involvement in 1934. For the streamlining of consumer goods—a practice engendered by the Depression and conceived as a curative at once selfishly motivated by business concerns and socially meaningful as a psychological panacea—provided something far more significant than a slogan; it provided a model for the modernization program as a whole.[11] In 1924 Lewis Mumford suggested that it was "this side of exaggeration to say that today a building is one kind of manufactured product on a counter of manufactured products."[12] A decade later it hardly seemed an exaggeration at all, as the combined effects of the Depression and building modernization blurred traditional boundaries between producer and consumer goods and made a widespread, mass-produced architecture increasingly seem like a realistic possibility.

Modernized Buildings as Consumer Goods

In a general economic sense, consumer goods are a category of products including durables, like cars and refrigerators, and consumables, like food and clothing. They are distinguished from producer goods, those raw or processed materials and/or tools used to make durables and consumables. In a general cultural sense, while fulfilling certain basic needs or uses, consumer goods also satisfy less tangible desires and represent a network of social meanings or values shaped by producers and consumers and mediated by advertising and marketing.[13] As a theoretical and practical model

for the modernization movement, consumer goods—and more specifically the streamlining of consumer goods—must be understood in two
ways: economically, as a model for guiding the building industry in the
creation of new markets and the cultivation of new consumers for its products and services (as discussed in chapter 3); and culturally, as a model
for educating the consuming public to comprehend in buildings and architecture a range of associations and images the government deemed
necessary to help alleviate the crisis of the Depression.

This consumer goods model is firmly embedded in the discourse of
building modernization: in its rhetoric and propaganda (written by advertising and marketing specialists), in its procedural policies and fiscal
structure (modeled on consumer credit practices), in its formal expressions (borrowed from the restyling methods of industrial designers),
and in its distribution methods (influenced by door-to-door selling techniques). Embedded in this discourse are what can be called the *consumption constructs* of modernization, a series of analogies or paradigms that
effectively subsumed architecture into the consumer culture as they were
deployed by the corporate/government publicity machine. These constructs operated in two distinct ways, often concurrently: first in building
modernization as a consumption strategy, and second in the modernized
building as a consumer product.[14] Modernization's deliberate use of this
consumer goods model led to the increasing commodification of architecture in the 1930s. While architecture is always related to and influenced
by market fluctuations and the economy as a whole, as modernization
eroded distinctions between durables and consumables, this relationship
intensified. Now buildings—or parts of buildings—were produced, packaged, advertised, and sold on Main Street. There they were purchased by
a willing and able American public, members of an expanding consumer
culture who, in the words of Robert and Helen Lynd, were increasingly
"hypnotized by the gorged stream of new things to buy."[15] And during
the Depression, as that stream overflowed with storefronts, the purchase
of those *new things* was charged with social urgency as never before.

Historians of consumer culture have observed how the material abundance resulting from the gradual improvement of factory production at
the turn of the century, and especially after World War I, gave rise to new
imperatives for creating consumer demand. If consumption was to keep
pace with accelerated production, the stimulation of demand for goods had
to transcend utility and rely on other criteria. Manufacturers and their
publicist/apologists, the advertising agencies, began to promote a therapeutic social vision in which particular goods were explicitly associated

with particular states of well-being, a not insignificant claim in the rapidly changing and uncertain modern world. Consumption became a palliative, assisting in the supposed realization of aspirations or assuagement of anxieties, be they personal, public, local, or national. Though the crisis of the Depression revealed consumption's social curatives as illusory and precipitated a popular distrust of promissory advertising, as aspirations went unfulfilled and anxieties became more acute in the years after 1929, the therapeutics of consumption became even more potent.[16] In fact, in 1934 Robert Lynd commented in President Hoover's report on recent social trends that since 1929 "selling commercial products as substitutive reactions for more subtle forms of adjustment to job insecurity, social insecurity [etc.] had advanced to an effective fine art."[17] Indeed, manufacturers, their advertising agencies, and their industrial designers now facilely associated restyled consumer goods with a specific state of well-being adjusted to the realties of the Depression. Enter streamlining, with its evocations of a speeding machine, a smoothly functioning society, and a prosperous future all made available to consumers with an easily purchased promise of modernity.

The scope of that therapeutic promise widened in 1934–35 as the government and its corporate partners promoted building modernization through an association with consumer goods: "Now, for the first time in history, owners may repair, alter, and improve their properties on an even better basis than that upon which they have purchased automobiles, refrigerators, washing machines, and other accessories."[18] This may have seemed like preying on a consumer society already enthralled and over-extended with installment buying, but the government reassured the public that modernization was a national need and a patriotic duty. Seeking to allay consumer suspicion and relieve consumer anxiety, the government explained that modernization would "telescope the future into the present" by bring prosperity into the Depression.[19] Thus, without guilt, companies extending modernization credit during the Depression deliberately repeated the advertising mantras of the consumer credit craze of the 1920s: "easy payment" and "no money down."[20] Modernization— requiring no mortgage, collateral, or down payment—satisfied the supposed instant gratification desires of the American consumer's restless "installment soul" and, at least in the government's view, proved un-equivocally that "building owners like to buy improvements this way just as they do automobiles."[21] This therapeutic satisfaction was true whether they were buying an entire storefront or facade or merely some of its individual elements, such as a sign or a display case.

It is not surprising that the federal government so easily assimilated a therapeutic vision of consumption. Not only had consumer goods manufacturers like General Motors and General Electric played a key role in the formulation of the modernization program, but many New Dealers, including FHA officials, subscribed to the belief that under-consumption was to blame for many of the country's current economic and social problems. If under-consumption of the products and services of the building industry, implicit in deferred maintenance and repair, was responsible for the run-down state of the nation's buildings, then it followed that renewed consumption through modernization would serve as an economic and social palliative. If modernized storefronts fulfilled this therapeutic function more convincingly than restyled consumer goods, this was more a matter of scale and site (a building on a public street) than of a significant qualitative difference between the two, since both were products of the same corporate capitalist machine. As with consumer goods, the storefront's success or failure as a therapeutic image of prosperity hinged on its legibility to the American public. Of course, by the time the Depression hit, the public was fully equipped to read such imagery, having been long exposed to the visual, linguistic, and psychological practices of advertising, to such an extent, in fact, that some critics, such as Soviet writers Ilya Ilf and Evgeny Petrov, bitingly observed that without advertising the average American would no longer be able to cope with modern life.[22]

At a basic level, the modernized storefront *was* an advertisement, selling both a product, the store's actual merchandise, and a promise of prosperity, progress, and modernity. As the FHA noted, "The front of a business house is its best advertisement." Modernizing this front would not only "convert a building into an efficient salesman," but also "display national spirit . . . and a commitment to broad recovery."[23] While the Depression produced the explicit social content of the storefront's advertising message, the concept itself was already present in commercial architecture before the Crash. In 1929 the critic Shepard Vogelgesang wrote in *Architectural Forum* of "America's return to architecture as advertisement" after decades of suppressed commercialism when "commerce took refuge in palazzi or retired behind columned arcades." According to Vogelgesang, increased competition in the late 1920s led merchants and store designers to reconsider the storefront as a means of attracting public notice. Influenced by the 1925 Exposition des Arts Décoratifs in Paris, they began to realize that attention could be directed to the store as much through distinctive architecture as through appended signage. This led to the emergence of so-called "advertising fronts" or "billboard" type stores, as they were known in the 1930s.[24] Both terms referred not only to a storefront's promotional intent, but also to its architectural expression, in which signage and facade were treated as an integrated whole.

According to store designer Morris Lapidus, the billboard-type facade had "the same principles as a poster," with displayed merchandise and sign letters instead of an image and text.[25] The poster-like qualities of the billboard front were enhanced when the modernization encompassed the building's full facade. With the upper stories, including existing windows, clad in structural glass or porcelain-enameled steel, the facade became, essentially, a two-dimensional field. The treatment of the "billboard" could be straightforward, a flat background for signage, or more elaborate, as in Lapidus's abstract, almost cubist, composition for the Peggie Hale clothing store in Birmingham, Alabama (fig. 4.3). Lapidus arranged colored bands and rectangles to create a visual play of projection and recession that would distinguish the store from those adjoining it. The goal, obviously, was to turn the modernized facade into "savvy advertising" that would, according to *Building Modernization* magazine, "act as the merchant's brass band," drawing in customers.[26] Lapidus used similar terms, noting the "pulling power of storefronts" and likening them to "circus barkers" and "ballyhoo artists" soliciting passersby.[27] In making this architectural equivalent of a sales pitch, the modernized storefront attempted to convey an essential message: "Here is a progressive, up-to-date store."[28] While comprehension of this message required that the public recognize certain architectural forms as progressive and up-to-date, legibility was equally predicated on the opposite. It was necessary that the public recognize other architectural forms as unprogressive and out-of-date. Modernization cultivated this awareness through the most important concept it borrowed from advertising—obsolescence.

Obsolescence

The FHA was unequivocal in acknowledging that obsolescence lay at the foundation of its modernization program. In *Modernize for Profit*, the widely distributed merchant's manual used to introduce the $50,000 loan limit in the summer of 1935, the agency declared, "Here, then, is opportunity for the business men of America to protect themselves against the costly results of obsolescence." This was represented in visual terms by a spectral collage of apparently antiquated buildings calculated to scare merchants and business property owners into modernizing, lest they, too, fall victim to obsolescence.[29] While *Modernize for Profit* identified

Figure 4.3 Peggie Hale clothing store in Birmingham, Alabama, designed by Morris Lapidus in 1934. This chain store typifies the billboard-type approach to building modernization. Here Lapidus treats the whole facade as a two-dimensional graphic field for advertising the retail occupant. Such billboard facades became commonplace as the Depression worsened and many buildings were abandoned above the ground floor. (Photo permission from *Chain Store Age,* November 1934, 116. Copyright Lebhar-Friedman, Inc., 425 Park Avenue, NY, NY 10022.)

the dangers of obsolescence as a loss of customers, increased operating costs, and decreased profits and property values, the term's actual meaning remained obscure. Though the FHA specified the necessity of improving antiquated mechanical systems (heating, lighting, plumbing, etc.), this referred exclusively to technological obsolescence of the sort the real estate industry had promoted since the 1920s when it began to call for the modernization, and even the demolition and replacement, of tall office buildings from the nineteenth century. For the FHA in the

1930s, obsolescence was a much broader concept, one the agency defined as "the loss of value due to all causes except physical deterioration."[30] This was also confusing because the physical deterioration of buildings through outright neglect or slackened maintenance had been one of the principal justifications for the government's modernization program. Indeed, physical deterioration was linked directly to the loss of property values. In *Bulletin No. 1*, for example, the FHA stated that the nation's buildings were suffering from "the ravages of five years of depreciation and obsolescence," with an implied distinction between the two terms.[31]

Arthur C. Holden, an architect and consultant to the National Recovery Administration, clarified this distinction in the *Survey Graphic* in an article titled "Modernization—Ballyhoo or Progress?" Arguing, like the FHA, that "depreciation and obsolescence [were] serious problems," Holden defined the former as "the physical wearing out of property" and the latter as "the psychological wearing out of property." Depreciation, Holden contended, was controllable and even avoidable through adequate maintenance and repair to offset deterioration. Obsolescence was more problematic because it introduced potentially elusive criteria for evaluating whether a building was worn out: "Obsolescence takes place because styles change."[32] Here the determinants for worn-out property seemed to move far away from a building's utility, or even its state of repair, toward factors that, in the words of Robert Lynd, were "less tangible [but] scarcely less potent" in the pressure they exerted on the building owner–cum-consumer.[33]

Within this concept of obsolescence, the power of style was largely psychological and lay in its very intangibility. Understood to be artificially created and socially controlled—produced by some complex of factors known as "public taste"—style was restless and changeable. It accelerated in tempo with modern life and was just as destabilizing to the individual consumer, who barely had time to acknowledge the "style of today" before it became the "style of yesterday."[34] A Libbey-Owens-Ford promotional pamphlet prepared for the 1939 Golden Gate Exposition in San Francisco vividly demonstrates this in relation to commercial buildings (fig. 4.4). Using an 1839–1939 timeline of shopkeeping similar to Raymond Loewy's product evolution charts, LOF depicted a "modern age characterized by fast tempo [with] every phase of life...stepped up to a new high."[35] Predicating a building's need for modernization on a style-based concept of obsolescence allowed government and corporate publicists to manipulate merchants and property owners more easily than if modernization was based simply on the necessity of physical repairs, since, like most

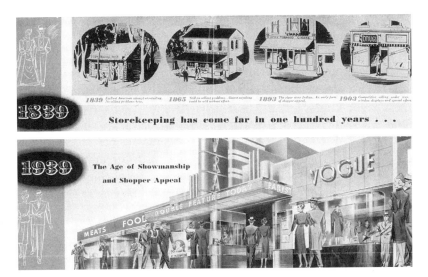

Figure 4.4 *Keeping Store Today*, 1939. This LOF pamphlet depicts a century in the evolution of the American store, from the frontier trading post to the contemporary shopping strip. According to LOF, intense retail competition had created the "age of showmanship" in which stores must continually keep pace with design trends lest they become obsolete. (Libbey-Owens-Ford Glass Company Records, MSS-066, Ward M. Canaday Center for Special Collections, The University of Toledo.)

consumers, they were thought to be psychologically vulnerable on matters of taste. Adding further complexity, merchants were not modernizing simply for themselves, but for their customers, who, the FHA argued, would "ordinarily avoid stores of obsolete appearance."[36] Borrowing this concept intact from the marketing of consumer goods, modernization publicists inculcated a fear of obsolescence—that "most relentless of all competition . . . applying to our greatest national asset, our real property"—in order to create a desire for its antidote: the modernized building.[37]

Style obsolescence emerged as a codified marketing strategy sometime around 1930, as manufacturers and advertisers attempted to increase demand for surplus goods born of overproduction. As promoted by advertising executive Earnest Elmo Calkins, so-called "artificial obsolescence" was intended to encourage "new buying" through the redesign of products to make them look "markedly new"—exclusive of any technological improvements. These redesigns were intensely promoted through marketing that cultivated contempt for a product's former appearance in order to convince consumers that they could not be stylish without purchasing the different-looking, but functionally unchanged object.[38] The psychological manipulation inherent in artificial obsolescence gave rise to complaints from consumer advocates like Stuart Chase, who campaigned against mass psychology and urged consumers to resist artificial demand. Even Calkins himself was uncomfortable with the implications of artificial obsolescence and ultimately came to believe, like Chase, that the strategy was foisting unnecessary products on an unsuspecting, gullible public.[39] The FHA seems to have suffered no crisis of conscience about obsolescence, possibly because of the advertising and business backgrounds of FHA officials and their close relationships with corporate manufacturers.[40] Even so, it was somewhat problematic for the government to borrow as potentially exploitative a marketing strategy as artificial obsolescence for a program intended as a sincerely civic-minded, grassroots fight against the Depression.

Progressive Obsolescence

By the time the government co-opted style obsolescence, the general concept had already been redirected away from the *artificial* toward an ideology known as *progressive* obsolescence that appeared as pro-active and consumer-oriented. Though the term was coined by business publisher J. George Frederick, progressive obsolescence's chief apologist was his wife, Christine Frederick, home economist, consumer advocate, and author of the influential *Selling Mrs. Consumer*. Frederick defended progressive obsolescence as the consumers' "willingness to take hold of anything new either in the shape of a new invention or new designs or styles or ways of living." For Frederick, the consumer, as much as the manufacturer, was controlling obsolescence. In her conception, the consumer was not a passive object, but an active subject making deliberate choices and decisions in his/her free acceptance of the new. Frederick's use of the term *progressive* was particularly important since it suggested "progress" and "the modern world" while dispelling any negative associations of falseness and wastefulness connoted by *artificial* obsolescence. The latter she defined as "a readiness to scrap or lay aside an article before its natural life of usefulness is completed," with the implication that this discarding or rejection was purely arbitrary.[41] The difference between the two forms of style obsolescence was principally a matter of intent: artificial obsolescence lacks clear motivation, while progressive obsolescence is motivated by the dynamic impulses of modernity. Three aspects of Frederick's progressive obsolescence are especially relevant to building modernization. First, the wholehearted acceptance of the new requisite in progressive obsolescence was understood as endemic to the United States as "a common-clay American trait." Second, style obsolescence was just as important as technological obsolescence and represented the "principal operative" in contemporary American consumer society. Third, progressive obsolescence was both a consumer practice *and* a producer gimmick since, according to Frederick, consumers were as eager to buy the new as producers were to sell it.[42]

Corporate and government modernization literature is filled with similar conclusions. Modernization supporters consistently posited the urge to fight obsolescence as a natural and national compulsion, part of a characteristically American anxiety complex. A writer for *Building Modernization* commented that "no one is more willing or anxious than the American to keep up with the times, to keep up with the Joneses"— referring to Arthur Momand's popular comic strip of the 1920s in which the mere presence of the wealthy Jones family compels their middle-class neighbors to excessive spending in order to rival their standard of living.[43] FHA radio publicity used a similar argument but emphasized the common-man angle typical of Depression-era advertising: "ordinary, average, run-of-the-mill, matter-of-fact American citizens" had no desire to be "the bob-tail and the fag-end of the procession." Rather, they desired "to be modern," which meant "keeping up-to-date."[44] Contemporary critics and consumers would have recognized the marketing code words in each of these statements. By the end of the 1920s, many Americans were familiar with, if not wholly literate in, such parlance, and certainly by the mid-1930s phrases like *up-to-date* and *keeping up with the Joneses* were not only in common usage, but were understood as advertising slang for the aspirations of material modernity.[45]

This desire to "keep up" manifested itself on a personal and communal level, in the individual merchant and the town as a whole, bound up with ideas of progress and betterment fundamental to the Main Street booster culture, as discussed in chapter 1. Since there was always someone or someplace that was bigger or more prosperous, the keeping-up mentality fueled the competitiveness on which the modernization movement was founded. "Rivalry," according to the FHA, was an "incentive to modernization."[46] In the overheated Main Street marketplace that pitted the independent merchant against the corporate chain over scarce consumer spending, keeping up with the store next-door was the only way to survive: "The one sure way of keeping a step ahead of the competition."[47] Following the advertising stratagem of therapeutic consumption, modernization propagandists contended that this innate American up-to-dateness extended almost empathetically, from the individual to the

building, with modernization itself posited as an obvious "cure for obsolescence." Architects John A. Holabird and John W. Root (who would
later serve as a juror for LOF's Main Street competition) agreed with this
assessment, commenting that building modernization meant "to fall in
line and keep step with the times." LOF noted that "it is essential that your
store be as modern in its appearance as you are yourself."[48] Evidently,
up-to-date Americans required up-to-date buildings. The president of a
Chicago-based grocery chain admitted as much when he accepted progressive obsolescence as the rationale for a corporation-wide store modernization program. Because "people crave newness," R. V. Rasmussen
explained, it was necessary to alter the store design every few years.[49] By
the end of the 1930s, even the F.W. Dodge Corporation took an "obsolescence factor" into account when compiling statistical data on commercial
alterations and repairs, noting that the need to attract "public attention" was responsible for much minor building activity.[50] In the FHA's
words, a "modernization-minded public [was] not likely to be attracted to
an unprogressive-looking building." Hence, the FHA advised merchants
that "customers coolly pass by the stores that do not keep in step with
the times and patronize those that do."[51] The title page of *Modernize
for Profit* offered apparent photographic proof in an overhead shot of
a shopping street crowded with women in cloche hats and fur-trimmed
coats and men in fedoras and business suits: such smart and stylish consumers would patronize only those stores that were "as modern as tomorrow"[52] (see fig. 2.8).

The FHA's most outright, yet eloquent, defense of consumer-driven
progressive obsolescence in architecture occurs in a five-minute speech
prepared by the PR division in the spring of 1935 and released in a
portfolio of radio publicity as a "Talk for Merchants." More than any
other statement found in the broad literature of modernization, this
speech reveals the movement's underlying ideology, demonstrating once
again how fully modernization borrowed from the consumer culture:

> It is a matter of historic record that when buying is resumed after any
> period of depression, the buying public demand [*sic*] the new and the
> different in merchandise. They are not interested in old merchandise,
> dusted off and marked down. They are no longer interested in the old
> stores, unless the old stores feel the urge to newness and the call of a new
> day. When prosperity dawns after depression, we suddenly realize how
> utterly tired we are of the fashions of yesterday. We tire not only of last
> year's fashion in clothing. We tire of old packages. We tire of old

architectural forms. We tire of old methods of doing business. And this is a form of restlessness that is absolutely right. It explains why tenants move from old buildings into modernized structures. It explains why obsolete stores lose patronage.[53]

Interspersed with advertising phraseology emphasizing up-to-dateness and contemporaneity, the speech also displays a calculated empathy with American consumers as it shifts pronouns from the distancing "they" to the inclusive "we." In addition, FHA speechwriters are offering historical precedent, as well as extenuating circumstances circa 1935, as rationale for shifting consumer preferences and a reorientation of consumer demand from the old to the new. "Newness," that all-encompassing grail of consumption, was apparently denied the buying public during the austerities of the economic crisis, making the desire for it all the more acute.[54] In the FHA's reasoning, after a period of deprivation, the desire for the new was so strong that building modernization was required perforce as a logical extension of Depression-induced consumer ennui. Following the logic of progressive obsolescence, the FHA validated a nation growing tired of merchandise and even of architecture solely on the basis of style. This was hardly a startling development: style has been a basis for architectural restlessness at least since the Renaissance, and even in the 1930s in the emerging conflict between modernism and historicism. Within the modernization movement, however, style consciousness and the cultivation of mass taste in architecture were privileged as never before to the near exclusion of other considerations whether functional or technological.

As is evident in the "Talk for Merchants," the government was using the economic hardships of the Depression to legitimize consumer demand for new merchandise and new architecture based on aesthetics and not necessities—thus simultaneously legitimizing the efforts of manufacturers to stimulate that demand. Arguably, the determination of necessities was entirely subjective. While some business leaders worried that style obsolescence engendered self-indulgent, luxury consumption, modernization experts argued the opposite because the nation's buildings needed some kind of repair and improvement after five years of deferred work. However, as already indicated, under the influence of obsolescence ideology, modernization implied something more than paint and plaster, stimulating style-based renovations in which the visual trappings of modernity were far more important than efficiency of plan or equipment. In fact, it was in the presumed obsolescence of architectural style itself that one could argue for the necessity, since within the prescriptions of modernization, a building's obvious display of the "fashions of yester-day" and "old architectural forms" would lead to an inevitable decline in business, rent, or property values. With advertising legerdemain, building modernization's publicists neatly resolved the vexing moral dilemma of style obsolescence. Far from encouraging extravagant and wasteful consumption in Americans, modernization encouraged the kind of therapeutic consumption on which the dawning prosperity supposedly depended. For the Main Street merchant, the government's stamp of approval in the form of loan insurance transformed the purchase of a new storefront from a luxury into an economic exigency. But the style-based rationale articulated in the "Talk for Merchants" does more than simply disclose the operation of obsolescence in the creation of consumer demand for modernization. It also makes explicit analogies between architecture and consumer goods and, by extension, implies that the modernization consumer was no different from the so-called "typical consumer," as understood by manufacturers, advertisers, and designers in the 1930s.

Gendered Consumption

According to the marketing experts responsible for constructing *her* identity, the "typical consumer" of the 1930s was categorically assumed to be a woman. This was because American women were understood to have enormous buying power, with as much as 85 percent of all consumer spending attributed to them.[55] In particular, women were assumed to be the principal buyers of so-called style goods, products redesigned to make them beautiful and/or fashionable, thus appealing to the supposed changeability of the female sensibility. Indeed, American women were thought to possess a psychological love of change and a natural predisposition toward stylishness and up-to-dateness, an extreme manifestation of what was regarded as a characteristic American trait. This essentialist view—held by the majority of advertisers and marketing experts, and even women's consumers advocates—assumed that women valued style and appearance above all else.[56]

As participating manufacturers and prospective modernizing merchants were well aware, the modernization program could hardly overlook the female consumer, since it was so driven by sales and preoccupied with appearance. LOF and PPG consistently emphasized gender in storefront advertisements, insisting that "the modern market owner ... realizes the vital importance of attracting women into his store."[57] The government was also aware of the importance of the female consumer, as evident in FHA PR director Ward Canaday's frank assessment: "The women of America control our spending, and because they do control our spending they have largely in their hands the ability to determine when this depression shall end."[58] Because consumption was marked as female, this statement seems to give women critical power to end the Depression; but following the causal theory of under-consumption, it also places responsibility, if not blame, for the Depression upon female shoulders. Nonetheless, the government viewed women as important modernization consumers, even though their actual consumption of modernizing products was largely limited to the home, since few women were in a position to make purchases for commercial buildings. This was the purview of men, as the nation's principal merchants and landlords.

Despite their apparent exclusion, women were not uninvolved in commercial modernization; to the contrary, their influence was pervasive.[59] Controlling consumer spending enabled women to exert power in the commercial sphere, influencing not just style goods, but the space of the marketplace, sites of consumption that were now, themselves, designed and marketed for female appeal. This power may have been illusory in reality, since the female appeal potentially embedded in those sites was, itself, largely a construct of male-dominated corporate marketing. Nonetheless, it was still a crucial determinant of the architectural form and meaning of modernization within the commercial sphere, and another example of the way that the consumer goods model shaped both the modernized building and building modernization.[60] Recognizing their purchasing power, building modernization appropriated female consumption habits, producing in the modernized building the imprint of the female consumer and reflecting what Ward Canaday called her "needs and desires."[61] These are especially evident in those formal and psychological elements that occur simultaneously in marketing and design, supplying the modernized building, and the storefront in particular, with a desired female charge.

In his 1935 book *Modernizing Buildings for Profit*, Kenneth Stowell, sometime architectural editor and organizer of LOF's Main Street competition, posited an evocative analogy between modernized buildings and style goods. He compared commercial buildings in need of modernization to automobiles, noting that "even Ford found that it was not enough to produce a car which would run at a low price. It must also have eye appeal for the customer."[62] Stowell's choice of Ford as style exemplar was hardly accidental. The last of the Big Three automakers to introduce the yearly model change (following General Motor's 1924 lead), Ford finally succumbed to marketing pressure in 1927, offering color options and a new body design in the Model A. Stowell's analogy had a further implication: style consciousness, that perceived female trait, was so forceful that even the great industrialist Henry Ford eventually capitulated. He did so only grudgingly, however, with the complaint, quoted triumphantly by Christine Frederick, that "we are no longer in the automobile, but in the millinery business."[63] Ford's ultimate recognition of the necessity of appealing to women is the basis of Stowell's argument for the importance of gendered "eye appeal," especially as related to obsolescence ideology.

While a new car model might possess a variety of technological improvements appealing to consumers, these were almost irrelevant if the car's styling had the appearance of last year's model. To sell these improvements (or to sell the car even if there were no improvements), it was necessary for the new model to possess some visual cue or hook—a change in color, an added compound curve—that canceled the perceived obsolescence and gave the car an aura of the new. Modernization was the functional equivalent of the model change, serving to transform an out-of-date building into one physically and psychologically in vogue. Modernization, like the model change, gave a building "new character and atmosphere through style and design" that was intended to lure customers and boost sales.[64]

The chains were among the earliest retailers to pursue the parallels between automotive and storefront model changes in the early years of the Depression. Thom McAn Shoes, for example, introduced seven new model storefronts during its first decade of existence, each one an "evolution" from its basic "Model A" or original "white front" store. While the new models were sufficiently recognizable as Thom McAn stores, they were varied enough to "meet new conditions" in retailing caused by the intensified competition of the Depression era.[65] The government also recognized the value of the restyled car analogy, with the FHA counseling building material manufacturers to update their product lines and "bring forward any 'new models' with the latest improvements" that might attract modernization consumers.[66] The building/car style construct was equally explicit in an LOF advertisement appearing in *Motor Magazine*: "A smart-looking modern LOF storefront is to an up-to-date place of business what the beautiful finish is to a modern motor car—a becoming dress that sells through the eye."[67] The added analogy to women's clothing underscores the gendering of style consumption in modernization.

Facadism

The transformation of an old model building into a new model building was achieved in modernization the same way it was achieved in car styling: by removing the visual appearance of obsolescence from the body of the object. Modernization experts agreed that what marked a building's exterior as obsolete was the manifestation of past architectural styles, what Stowell called "excrescences" and "superfluous ornaments and gimcracks." To a consuming public being educated to recognize heavy molding, pronounced cornices, jutting dormers, elaborate masonry, and cast-iron storefronts as signifiers of age, these features rendered a building "an antiquated nightmare"—but not irrevocably. As the FHA put it, "Buildings can be rescued from obsolescence by a few simple operations on their exteriors."[68] The building, like a streamlined consumer good, was stripped of ornament and details and sheathed in a veneer of materials perceived as modern: Carrara and Vitrolite structural glass, Formica and Micarta laminated plastic, or Enduro and Veribrite enameled steel.[69] Manufacturers also recognized this as a basic strategy of modernization: "Fussy details are discarded and clean lines and broad surfaces are the rule. Color, too, is playing an increasing part in outside decoration."[70] Such surface restyling had proved a workable strategy for cars and refrigerators: that the gadgetry underneath the streamlined shell was messy and the technology unchanged was inconsequential as long as the product's exterior was pristine and stylish. If the typical (female) consumer was interested only in style, and never went beneath that shiny new surface, she willingly drew the conclusion that if it looked new, it was new. The surface restyling of the storefront operated similarly: the effacement of obsolescence through stripping and sheathing branded the building with an emblematic visual newness that supposedly stimulated a positive psychological reaction (or asserted a psychological control) to influence the consumer's decision to enter the store.

This psychology was apparently at work even in commercial establishments in which the decision to enter was more likely predicated on the quality and price of the products for sale. In a movie theater, for example, it would seem that the films being shown, rather than the appearance of the facade, would have the most influence on box office receipts. But the psychological power of visual obsolescence was apparently so all-embracing in the 1930s that the architectural antidote of modernization could single-handedly alter consumer habits, a claim that trade publications like *Better Theaters* and *Box Office* emphasized throughout the decade.[71]

This was also the argument the General Porcelain Enamel Company used to explain the success of the modernized Rialto theater in Waukegan, Illinois (fig. 4.5). Age-marking elements like classical moldings, decorative parapets, and a guy-wired sign were effaced by a cladding of black Veribrite, stainless steel trim, and a cantilevered, streamlined marquee with neon lights. General Porcelain readily heralded the inevitable effectiveness of the Rialto's modernized facade: "Increased attendance? Of course!"[72]

Following a logic of surface, Kenneth Stowell argued that regardless of structure or mechanics, "exterior design and decorative changes that make the newness of the old building apparent" were most important for attracting style-conscious tenants and customers. Surface restyling was "the design that attracts the people that pay" and "the first line of attack in the competition for customer patronage." This fact alone, Stowell believed, made exterior restyling of the facade the most important type of modernization, and the one that should precede all others.[73] Storefront manufacturers and the government wholeheartedly agreed with this argument: the former because facade modernization offered the best opportunity for increasing sales of their products; the latter because through facade modernization a Main Street building might best function as a public symbol of recovery during the Depression.[74] For both, modernization effectively became facadism—"architecture as shelter with symbols on it," as Robert Venturi would later put it.[75] Three decades before Venturi's famous formulation, modernization's publicists and practitioners were well aware of the scenographic and symbolic potential of the restyled facade. This emphasis on the architectural surface produced the most compelling implications of consumer goods as a model for modernization theory and practice. Through it the modernized building was transformed into a colorful package, a streamlining skin job, and a stylish costume, not only in corporate marketing, but on Main Street America; and what was remarkable in the 1930s was that making these analogies clear was the stated goal of much of the modernization work.

The Packaged Facade

The storefront is *facade* by definition, representing exteriorly all advertising and architectural intentions. The storefront's facadist strategies during the Depression were simply the varied ways that exterior representation was conceptualized within the discourse of modernization filtered through the consumer culture. As already suggested, within that culture women were thought to be especially responsive to the type of

BEFORE The Rialto Theatre of Waukegan, Ill., was renewed through *Veribrite*. The two photographs show the decided improvement gained. Increased attendance? Of course!

Figure 4.5 Rialto movie theater in Waukegan, Illinois, before and after modernization in 1936. The decorative grilles, parapets, and moldings were replaced with black Veribrite facing and a cantilevered marquee. So strong was the supposed psychological power of visual obsolescence that modernization alone was credited with increasing attendance at this cinema, regardless of the film showing. (*Architectural Forum* 66 [March 1937]: 61. Courtesy of the Avery Architectural and Fine Arts Library, Columbia University.)

re/styling recommended for the modernized storefront, its experts assuming that women would find colorful and shiny surfaces as appealing in a streamlined building as they did in a streamlined car or refrigerator. A basic marketing equation emerges here: a product designed to visually appeal to women should be sold in a store possessing the same visual qualities. In other words, form follows not function, but merchandise.[76]

As early as 1928, Randolph Williams Sexton, a contributor to *American Architect*, wrote that "the architectural treatment of the shop [should be] as modern as the wares on sale." Creative advertising writer Ralph Richmond agreed, noting that the stylistic linking of the storefront and the goods on sale would announce to the prospective customer: "Here is modern merchandise, modernly offered for moderns."[77] This was also the rationale behind the FHA's repeated declarations to merchants that "buyers demand not only the new and different in merchandise, but they instinctively purchase that merchandise in places of business that present a new and different appearance." Thus, the buyers would equate an "ultra-modern front" with "the latest and most up-to-date of anything" for sale inside.[78] Industrial designers seeking to extend their sphere of influence had been making similar claims since the beginning of the decade. By 1940 Harold Van Doren argued for a progressive modernizing process that started with the redesign of a package or a product, then moved on to commercial fixtures and ultimately to the store or showroom itself.[79] This was clearly the progression when Texaco inaugurated a chainwide improvement campaign in 1934 to overhaul its forty thousand existing units and to establish design guidelines for the construction of new units. Under the guidance of Walter Dorwin Teague, the service station became the largest and most visible element of Texaco's corporate identity program, the stylish purveyor of Fire Chief Gasoline and Havoline Wax Free Motor Oil. Teague's modernization scheme replaced the picturesque "house with canopy" of the typical Texaco station with a flat-roofed box whose vague factory aesthetic and bright architectural trademarking were deemed appropriate to that most modern of machines in the 1930s—the automobile.[80]

While the degree of stylistic correspondence between store and product ranged from a generalized affinity to a literal equivalence (a programmatic packaging of the facade in the form of the goods sold within), this was invariably achieved through the use of those materials and forms comprehended as modern by the consuming public. The use of glass or metal veneers and plastic laminates, rounded edges, and bold graphics—characteristic of any number of products found in Main Street stores of the 1930s—amounted to a visual re/packaging of the storefront as a deliberate replacement of those old packages/architectural forms decried in the FHA's "Talk for Merchants." It bears repeating that as a way of conceptualizing exterior modernization, the packaged storefront directly paralleled contemporaneous efforts to make a product look new and improved by changing the outward appearance, but not the contents of a given container—be it a restyled cereal box or refrigerator case. Such an idiom was sufficiently popularized in the coming years that by 1941 the editors of *Architectural Record* cautioned store designers against "the notion that all architecture is packaging."[81]

By then, architects had been making this analogy for well over a decade. As early as 1928, Morris Lapidus designed a "modern drugstore" in New York City that, by his own admission, took its cue from the colorful packages of drugs and cosmetics sold within. These, as Christine Frederick noted, had themselves been restyled through "modernistic art" to specifically appeal to women (who made nearly 90 percent of all drugstore purchases).[82] Following a similar storefront correspondence, Horace Ginsbern designed a new front for a Chock Full o' Nuts coffee shop that borrowed the company's trademark black, yellow, and red color scheme and patterning (fig. 4.6). This decorative device, along with Ginsbern's composition—which broke up the facade into small display units—led *Architectural Forum* to favorably comment that the store's design reflected its function of vending "small packaged goods": the familiar Chock Full o' Nuts coffee cans and vacuum bags.[83] When Cushman's Sons Bakers began modernizing its three hundred nationwide units in 1935, it, too, sought to establish a clear formal relationship between the storefront and its trademark package—a white bakery box with a blue script logo and a blue "Grade A" ribbon. The earliest Cushman's modernizations clad the facade in white enameled steel, trimmed it in blue, and treated the signboard as an oversize bakery box top. Eventually, Cushman's brought in Raymond Loewy to restyle the chain's already updated image and to provide a prototype for subsequent modernizations. Loewy redesigned and significantly enlarged the signboard logo and transformed the standard display window into a semicircle, giving the whole storefront a more emphatic streamlining effect (fig. 4.7).[84]

Even without obvious trademarking, a literal visual coordination of storefront to product was a common modernizing strategy that often resulted

Figure 4.6 Chock Full o' Nuts in New York City, designed by Horace Ginsbern in 1936. An example of a packaged facade, the black, yellow, and red color scheme and forms of the display cases took their cues from the coffee cans and vacuum bags sold inside. (*Architectural Forum* 65 [October 1936]: 317. Courtesy of the Avery Architectural and Fine Arts Library, Columbia University.)

in humorously programmatic facades. In Boston an abandoned dry cleaner was renovated into a cocktail lounge with a display window shaped like a cocktail shaker and the glass panes of the entrance door shaped like a martini glass. On Wilshire Boulevard in Los Angeles, architect Marcus Miller inserted an eight-foot tall camera of black Carrara, plate glass, and metal trim into the facade of the Darkroom photography shop. In a general way this display unit resembled cameras restyled in the 1930s by designers such as Walter Dorwin Teague (fig. 4.8).[85] Such packaging of the storefront was concerned with transforming the modernized facade into an easily apprehended image and a legible symbol for consumption. Like other facadist strategies, the packaged storefront focused on surface effects, but this focus had more to do with the literal location of the modernization than it did on its significance as an idea or metaphor. By contrast, within the other facadist strategies, it is possible to identify three distinct metaphorical surfaces, each laying atop the other on the restyled storefront.

Figure 4.7 Cushman's Sons Bakers, modernized unit designed by Raymond Loewy in 1938. The white-enameled steel cladding and the blue lettering were meant to evoke the chain's trademark boxes. (Photo permission from *Chain Store Age*, November 1936, 114. Copyright Lebhar-Friedman, Inc., 425 Park Avenue, NY, NY 10022. *Architectural Forum* 70 [February 1939]: 105. Courtesy of the Avery Architectural and Fine Arts Library, Columbia University.)

Figure 4.8 The Darkroom on Wilshire Boulevard in Los Angeles, designed by Marcus Miller in 1935. Here, the packaged facade is taken to a programmatic extreme that was not unusual in Los Angeles. Miller gave the projecting display unit the appearance of a streamlined camera, complete with lens, aperture ring, shutter release, and flash. (Library of Congress, Prints & Photographs Division, HABS-HAER [HABS, CAL,19-LOSAN, 33-2024-1].)

The Youthful Facade

The first of these surfaces is epidermal, conceptualizing facade modernization as a skin job and evoking a typical approach to product restyling in the 1930s.[86] Skin in that industrial design context is a sleek membrane stretched over the body of an object. But a building has a face as well, and in modernization that patch of skin—the anthropomorphized facade—was the most prominent. As the government noted in 1934, "The modern American store should have a clean, inviting, smiling face."[87] A year later the FHA's promotional *Clip Sheet* announced the start of a trade-specific campaign to modernize the nation's seventy-five thousand beauty salons: "Beauty Shops Will Have 'Face Lifted.'"[88] Given that the accompanying article was intended for publication in newspaper women's pages, the likening of facade modernization to face-lifting was probably intended as cute wordplay, a double-edged cosmetologist's pun. It would prove a potent neologism. Today, referring to a building's exterior restyling or refurbishment as a face-lift is commonplace, but this was not the case in the 1930s when the cervicofacial rhytidectomy was still a relatively new procedure in the burgeoning field of cosmetic surgery. However, as historian Elizabeth Haiken has shown, though the face-lift had not yet become popular as elective surgery, the idea of the face-lift had already emerged in the 1920s and 1930s as "a rational response to the higher standards set by consumer culture and a way to achieve psychic balance," particularly for women. Further supported by a long-standing tradition of self-improvement and an ardent belief in the efficacy of scientific progress, the face-lift was viewed as an extreme but acceptable form of therapeutic consumption.[89] Its purpose was obvious: to counteract the aging process and improve the appearance of the skin by removing age markers such as wrinkles and bags. The resulting face supposedly looked younger and more beautiful; the face-lifted person, typically a woman of a certain age, apparently regained her powers of physical attraction and was thus able to socially compete with those younger than she. In a nation enthralled with the ideals of youth and beauty, the face-lift was fraught with cultural significance in the 1930s—for women and architecture.

Industry experts, government officials, and building material manufacturers all recognized the metaphorical power of the face-lift as a synonym for facade modernization. The suggestive potency of this metaphor clearly stemmed from its stability of meaning even when introduced into the seemingly disjunctive context of architecture, for the purpose of the building face-lift was basically the same as the human face-lift: to counteract the aging process and improve the appearance of the surface by removing age markers, specifically those architectural elements deemed stylistically obsolete. The resulting (modernized) facade supposedly looked youthful and beautiful, modern and up-to-date, enabling the face-lifted building to retain its power to attract customers and tenants and to gamely compete with newer buildings. Though Kenneth Stowell cautioned that "it would be foolish to think that all properties can be brought to the credit side of the ledger by a face-lifting treatment," he concluded that such a treatment would make "the old building as new and modern in design as any of its younger competitors," giving it "a new lease on life and a change of character."[90] The FHA concurred: noting that at least 90 percent of all American stores were "drab and uninteresting in appearance," the agency concluded that "Main Street face-lifting" was a necessity, and that it would do "more toward renewing the youthful appearance of a building than almost any other rejuvenating operations."[91] Such cosmetic surgical characterizations appeared with increasing frequency as the modernization movement became widespread. In *Middletown in Transition*, the Lynds cited a newspaper editorial that observed: "If Middletown is not so improved pretty soon that she will not be able to recognize her 'lifted' face, it will not be the fault of good old Uncle Sam."[92] Though the use of a feminine pronoun to personify place was not unusual, it surely gained rhetorical strength in the gendered context of cosmetic surgery.

Not surprisingly, manufacturers of storefront products were most enthusiastic about the face-lift as a cure for the blemishes of architectural old age. PPG described how "attractive" the City Drug Store was after "it had its 'face lifted.'" Republic Steel urged architects to "modernize Main Street with new faces for old buildings," noting that "there's a lot of plastic surgery going on all over the country today." Here the standard before-and-after photographic pair was supplemented by a drawing of an old man before and after his face-lift, showing the renewal of his youthful appearance—a surprising image given the infrequency with which men elected to have cosmetic surgery in the 1930s (fig. 4.9). At the opposite extreme, Chase Brass and Copper, a manufacturer of pipes and fittings, warned of "the penalty of 'skin-deep' modernization," which only covered flaws and did not correct them.[93] Writing in the municipal affairs journal *American City*, architect Henry Churchill also employed a negative metaphor to condemn all modernization as ineffective, but his indictment that "facial uplift can no longer hide the wrinkles [of American cities]" was driven by larger ideological arguments about the need for comprehensive planning to forestall the spread of urban blight.[94] The

Figure 4.9 "New Faces for Old Buildings." This Republic Steel advertisement makes explicit how building modernization used analogies to the face-lift and plastic surgery to promote the idea of the youthful facade. (*Architectural Forum* 62 [June 1935]: 45. Courtesy of the Avery Architectural and Fine Arts Library, Columbia University.)

existence of such dissenting advertising and architectural voices demonstrates how fully the face-lift was assimilated into the discourse of modernization. It existed as a rhetorical expression of modernization's potential to counteract the real and symbolic ravages of the Depression and as an architectural procedure—an operation that was, ironically, more prevalent in the 1930s than the surgical procedure that inspired it.

The Beautified Facade

Though face-lift served as a general analogue to exterior modernization, as an architectural procedure performed on the storefront's surface, it seemed to refer more to the first step in the modernization process, the stripping away of a building's age markers, than to the equally important second step, the surface sheathing or recladding in a veneer of new materials. As a concept this application of materials utilized a set of consumer culture referents closely related to those of the face-lift. Concerned with youth-enhancing, beautifying effects, these referents were likewise gendered, since women more than men were socially programmed to desire a youthful and beautiful surface appearance. They were, however, far more quotidian, engaging not "that strange new form of surgery," as Frederick Lewis Allen labeled the face-lift in 1931, but rather what he called "the vogue of rouge and lipstick" and "facials . . . to restore the bloom of youth." In other words, they engaged cosmetics and the beauty culture.[95] Thus, Vitrolite was marketed in terms not merely suggestive of lipstick, but worthy of Max Factor himself: "Beauty always Pays! For color—depth of color, choice of color, permanent color, sheer loveliness of color—there is nothing that holds a candle to Vitrolite." Applied to the surface of the building, Vitrolite was also analogous to a cold cream applied to the face of a woman: "It glows. It gleams." But it did not require continuous application, for unlike human skin, Vitrolite did not "grow dull with age." Instead, it offered "ageless beauty" without the use of elaborate beauty treatments: "a damp cloth is the only facial treatment Vitrolite ever needs."[96] Such allusions to the products and services of the female-oriented beauty industry in advertisements for a building material directed at predominantly male architects and merchants clearly reflect the consumer culture's ever-widening sphere of influence. In addition, however, there existed an obvious correlation between modernizing products and beauty products—a correlation recognized at the time and manifest not just in the marketing of these products, but in their meaning as well.

Consumption of personal care products in the United States, of which women purchased over 80 percent, had risen steadily since 1900 and even during the Depression fell off only slightly. With this increased consumption came a decided shift in the beauty culture. Women moved away from the use of soap and water with an occasional application of powder toward what historian Kathy Peiss has called "everyday cosmetic practices," the regular, if not daily, use of facial preparations and makeup.[97] These practices, actively cultivated by beauty product manufacturers beginning in the 1920s, were explicitly tied to the therapeutic consumption of cosmetics as aids to the attainment of those same heightened standards of appearance that created desire for the face-lift. Of course, cosmetics were far more accessible, available for purchase at the corner drugstore or the local beauty shop—sites that, themselves, were also increasingly subject to these standards.

The modernization of the Lantieri Beauty Salon in New York, for example, responded equally to heightened standards of appearance for women and stores. In 1935 what had formerly been a parlor for hair styling and manicures became a full-service salon, offering hair and nail treatments, electrolysis, reducing, chiropody, facials, and cosmetology. But in attempting to prove itself an "outstanding authority on beauty culture," Lantieri's had to look the part (fig. 4.10). As redesigned by Vahan Hagopian, its low storefront with old-fashioned signs, painted transoms, and heavy framing was replaced by a tall and slender storefront with a nearly double-height extent of plate glass, neon signs, and two-tone enameled steel facing. To enter the salon, customers passed beneath a projecting signboard depicting a woman's stylized head, her hair colored and waved, her eyebrows plucked, her cheeks rouged, her lips painted. Once inside the customer could choose to have any of those "improvements" done to herself, or she could proceed directly to a streamlined "powder bar" opposite the door to purchase customized beauty preparations.[98]

While increased consumption of cosmetics was related to women's oft-stated interest in appearance and enthusiastic pursuit of youth and beauty, it was also related to the emergence by 1930 of the *made-up woman* as a female ideal. Dramatically reconceived in the post–World War I era, this ideal was explicitly tied to larger social concerns as women, however much their thinking was influenced by the sales efforts of beauty marketers, began to look upon the use of makeup as an emancipating form of self-expression. In the 1920s the lipstick, rouge, and mascara once associated exclusively with prostitutes and actresses were suddenly emblematic of social and sexual freedom, and the painted face functioned

Figure 4.10 Lantieri Beauty Salon in New York City, designed by Vahan Hagopian, 1935. The before-and-after photographs show how Hagopian beautified the storefront by making it appear more slender, with double-height display windows, and more colorful, with a two-tone enameled steel cladding. (*Real Estate Record*, November 16, 1935, 19–20. Courtesy of the Avery Architectural and Fine Arts Library, Columbia University.)

as a highly visible rejection of the past and a repudiation of Victorian manners and morals. In the 1930s it was "a sign of the times," according to Kathy Peiss. No longer shocking and virtually the norm, color applied to a woman's skin had become an expression of the present, of a woman's up-to-dateness and glamour. The painted face was thus a mark of modernity—utterly intentional, freely displayed, and purposefully calling attention to itself.[99]

In relation to beauty culture, it is possible to understand building modernization as an architectural extension of everyday cosmetic practices. What was facade modernization if not color applied to the surface of the building to enhance appearance and make modernity visible? What were modern surfacing materials if not architectural cosmetics rendered accessible in the 1930s through the mass-marketing efforts of manufacturers? Indeed, in his 1930 book *Contemporary Art Applied to the Store and Its Display*, architect Frederick Kiesler had already referred to storefront materials as "decorative cosmetics."[100] Just as powders, rouge, and lipsticks were newly available in an astonishing variety of shades and colors ("28 shades to fit 28 types of skin"), aiding in the transformation of the

Figure 4.10 (*Continued*)

lily-white complexion (the Victorian ideal) into the modern painted face,
so storefront materials were increasingly varied in the 1930s.[101] Vitrolite came in sixteen colors, including "suntan," a cosmetic shade that
emerged circa 1929 reflecting the vogue for tanned skin. Kawneer porcelain enamel came in twenty-seven (including five shades of blue and
six shades of green), Formica and Micarta in nearly forty each. Just as
women supposedly needed expert advice in the application of makeup
lest she "overdo her cosmetics," as Christine Frederick warned, so the
merchant needed the advice of the architect who might, according to

Kenneth Stowell, "use his materials and colors in producing designs that people cannot resist."[102] Of course, even the architect ran the risk of *over-doing* the modernized facade through applied colors: George Ketchum's redesign of the Kallet movie theater in Pulaski, New York, utilized seven shades of Vitrolite: black, walnut agate, and red on the bulkheads; red, gray, princess blue, jade, ivory, and gray on the billboard-like upper area.

In the journal *Architecture*, W. F. Bartels warned against such potentially immoderate surface applications, offering the architect cosmetically inflected design guidance that analyzed the storefront in terms analogous to the made-up face: the storefront should not be "garish" or "repellent," but "in good taste" and "attractive." It should not give the effect of "a Coney Island side show" (a reference to the bearded lady or the reptile girl?), but should instead possess "a sleek, clean-cut appearance." It is not insignificant that these latter terms were increasingly gendered as masculine in the advertising parlance of the day. They were particularly utilized in the promotion of men's toiletries, especially shaving accessories such as Gillette safety razors and Williams's Aqua Velva aftershave. For Bartels, the designer had to be ever mindful of applying his storefront materials, lest they create the wrong "psychological effect," which in his conception seemed to range from the chastely demure to the whorish or freakish.[103] Here he seems to echo Frederick Kiesler's identical argument about the "psycho-function" of a storefront's materials and colors and his warning against their excessive use.[104] Ultimately, the psychological goal was to achieve something in between Bartel's extremes, as the architect, through the colorful application of surface materials, creates a storefront that, as PPG put it, "catches the eye, arouses interest, and issues a special invitation"—modernizing cosmetics enhancing the come-hither look of the store facade.[105]

The Fashionable Facade

As the most significant modernizing action, the application of colored materials to the surface of a building was metaphorically fluid: one architect's colored face paints became another's colored fabrics without any conceptual slippage. While modernization was largely unconcerned with polemical distinctions between cosmetics and clothing, the latter provided the most crucial paradigm of surface—the facade as fashion. In this paradigm, architecture clothes a building as fashion clothes a body, and there exists a literal analogy between the modernized building and stylish clothing—the old storefront clad in new materials. In advertising its Vitrenamel surface cladding, U.S. Steel claimed that it provided "good sheets to clothe modern buildings." The architect would design the clothes and the company would produce them "'tailormade'" to fit the front of a given building.[106] Similarly, LOF directed the merchant to "dress your store in modern selling clothes," positing modernization as the architectural equivalent of dressing for success.[107]

The relationship between the storefront and clothing went deeper than simple advertising analogies. Indeed, the very concept of the modern storefront was, to a certain extent, dependent on a fashion strategy known as the ensemble. Promoted by makers of women's apparel and accessories beginning in the mid-1920s, the ensemble was a series of goods offered to the consumer as a complete, matched set. The appeal of the ensemble lay in the degree to which it overrode consumer decisions regarding personal appearance and taste by predetermining stylistic coordination. By the 1930s the ensemble, especially the color-coordinated ensemble, was a popular merchandising technique used to sell all manner of matching goods from clothing, handbags, shoes, and lipsticks to cameras, cars, home furnishings, and eventually storefronts.[108] As noted in chapter 3, prior to the modernization movement, PPG, LOF, and other companies marketed storefront materials individually, offering product lines of facings, trims, or window glass. By the mid-1930s, many of these companies, especially glass manufacturers, were selling complete storefronts as fully accessorized ensembles for modernizing buildings, despite the fact that these were not marketed directly to women.

LOF's "Complete Storefront" line featured products with evocative, coordinated names like Vitrolux, Vitrolite, and Extrudalite. According to the company, these products were brought together "in ensemble" as a line that was "pacing the vogue of modern merchandising," but it is unclear whether this referred to LOF's own sales techniques or those of its merchant customers.[109] Brasco's Modern Store Front line was "comprehensive and complete" with all products "in harmonious design." It also included "such important complementary items" as doors and frames, awning hoods and boxes, grilles and sign letters, and bulkheads.[110] PPG's Pittco Store Front—consisting of Carrara structural glass, Pittsburgh Plate glass, and Pittco Store Front Metal—was promoted as the "first complete line ever to be designed deliberately, all at one time, with a pleasing harmony and relationship of appearance, a real *unity* of design."[111] In each case, the language is clearly informed by coordinated merchandising, for stylistic unity and harmony were the primary lessons of the ensemble. As Christine Frederick observed in *Selling Mrs. Consumer*,

"What building a complete costume ensemble has taught the American woman is to buy her clothing, not as unrelated units, but with a harmonious costume effect in mind."[112] Like a woman buying a harmonious costume, a merchant could purchase "a unified storefront of coordinated materials—products meant to be used together."[113] The facade was now as easily harmonized as a woman's outfit, from shoe to hat or, as Brasco advertised, "from sidewalk to coping, unified in character."[114]

When government modernization strategists turned to the idea of the ensemble, they were well aware of its impact on consumers and of its consequences in the marketplace, where it was credited with encouraging increased consumption. Operating in tandem with style obsolescence, the ensemble trained the consumer to recognize potentially discordant elements within a given visual field and to reconceptualize what had formerly been individual or periodic purchases as part of a unified whole. In this respect, the ensemble was understood to have profoundly altered American purchasing habits, of women in particular, by expanding the definition of necessities. The FHA's Ward Canaday noted this in 1935: "The psychological fact is that American women do not stop with single item buying. When they reach the point of buying a new dress, nine times out of ten it means, new hat, new shoes, new gloves, in fact, a new outfit."[115] According to Canaday, this female propensity for ensemble buying could be exploited to stimulate home modernization and, depending on the susceptibility or willingness of the woman, could lead to full-scale exterior and interior residential redesign. But it could also be exploited to stimulate commercial modernization by convincing the merchant that his ensemble-savvy customers would instantly identify, and disapprove of, any uncoordinated element in the storefront just as they recognized unmatched or out-of-date items of clothing or accessories. In the competitive world of Main Street, the poorly accessorized storefront would cause those customers to patronize other establishments. Thus, the merchant required a storefront in which signage, bulkheads, display windows, and entrances were consciously coordinated. As the consumer turned to the department store stylist, who could assist in the building of clothing ensembles, so the merchant turned to the architect, who utilized matching building products to create appealing storefront ensembles. As a storefront stylist, the architect would, in effect, put together facade "outfits" that possessed a stylistically correct harmony of facing materials, metal moldings, colors, and textures.

The objective of the ensemble, which so thoroughly informed the relationship between fashion and modernization, was candidly stated by

George D. Buckley of the FHA's public relations division: "Before we are through, we hope to have everybody thinking about his own property the way every woman thinks about her clothes"—mindful of appearance, desirous of current styles, and aware that the latest architectural fashions were as easily purchased as the latest dress.[116] While obviously acknowledging the significance of fashion in the architecture-as-clothing sense, Buckley's statement also evokes fashion's temporal quality: its inherent dynamism or "system of rapid change" that enables it to represent that which is the newest and most up-to-date, desired by at least some portion of the consuming public.[117] When FHA head James Moffett announced the necessity of "making modernization fashionable," he implied this changeable sense of fashion.[118] As an economic emergency measure, modernization could not wait for gradual acceptance by the public; to be successful it had to be in vogue, seized immediately as a fashion, or the latest trend, to motivate style-conscious, obsolescence-fearing Americans to modernize their buildings.

This had a clear implication for the fashionability of Main Street's architecture. Some critics have viewed the relationship of architecture and fashion as paradoxical because fashion's temporal and transitory nature is seemingly antithetical to architectural practice, in which factors such as size or scale, cost, and time lag from design to production appear to limit a building's capacity to respond to fashion's stylistic vicissitudes.[119] In the 1930s, however, largely as a result of government intervention and corporate cooperation, modernization practice obviated these factors, collapsing the time lag, reducing the scale of projects, and making cost less pertinent through the availability of insured credit. Modernization's raison d'être was to force architecture to respond to the pressures of fashion in order to stimulate the economy, creating, as FHA Deputy J. Howard Ardrey observed, "an interest in up-to-the-minute ideas on building materials, equipment [and] styles of architecture."[120]

From Wallflower to Belle

Modernization's double fashion sense was explicitly demonstrated in a 1939 LOF advertisement that placed two gendered pairs of before-and-after contrasts in evocative opposition as "the Wallflower of Main Street becomes the Belle of the Avenue," following a complete makeover of woman and store, or woman-as-store (fig. 4.11).[121] Verbally and visually, the wallflower and the belle represent the opposite extremes of the American woman as popularly understood within the consumer culture. At the

Figure 4.11 "The Wallflower of Main Street Becomes the Belle of the Avenue." This LOF advertisement makes explicit how the distinction between old-fashioned and up-to-date was frequently coded in terms of gender and sexuality. (*Architectural Record* 85 [April 1939]: 17. Courtesy of the Avery Architectural and Fine Arts Library, Columbia University.)

same time, they were made to represent the opposite extremes of the American store, popularly understood as an architecture subsumed into the consumer culture. In both pairs, the old-fashioned and out-of-date becomes fashionable and up-to-date through the palliative of consumption. The wallflower, presumably unattractive and dowdy in her high-necked frock with ruffled sleeves, stands alone, unable to attract the male gaze. Similarly, the unmodernized store is unable to attract the customer's gaze because it is negatively marked by the obsolete features of its front: scalloped-edged sign, cast-iron lintel with decorative rosettes, right-angle bulkheads, and display windows out of scale with the merchandise. The belle, by contrast, is good-looking and alluring in her revealing evening gown, able to solicit the attention of three men.[122] Simultaneously, the modernized store—sleekly *dressed* in green and blue Vitrolite and accessorized in Extrudalite trim with a yellow Vitrolux sign—attracts multiple shopping (female) customers.

Deploying "colorful, swanky" LOF products, the architect as a modernizing stylist at once dress designer and beautician, has made over this wallflower into a belle. Through color, the architect gives the modernized store *her* "looks," making her "radiant with shopper-appeal, tenant-appeal and sales-appeal." As with a woman's painted face or modish dress, the application of surface color has apparently introduced into the storefront a sexual charge, expressed euphemistically in text but more blatantly in image.[123] In becoming a belle, the modernized store has become "a profit maker," literally trading on her good looks to move merchandise—an architectural expression of the advertising adage that sex sells. Morris Lapidus eventually theorized the storefront's sexual charge in terms close to those presented in the LOF ad. According to Lapidus, the storefront should attract and seduce by displaying both merchandise and itself, as a woman in an evening gown displayed her décolletage or as a female model in a life-drawing class draped and undraped her body (fig. 4.12). In either case, Lapidus echoes Frederick Kiesler's assertion that the storefront must "stimulate desire."[124]

In the modernized storefront, it was the architect (usually male) who had the agency, orchestrating the display by manipulating window and wall surface to attract and seduce the consumer. This may explain why a male figure, standing in the foreground in front of the modernized store, is given prominence in the predominantly female shopping/consuming tableau of the advertisement. Whether he is the architect, the merchant, or simply a pedestrian, he looks toward the store, seeming to gaze less at the shoes on sale than at the shoe store itself. Actively looking, passively

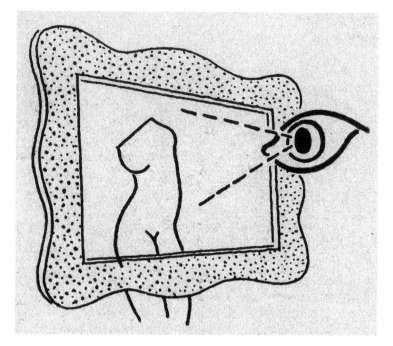

Figure 4.12 Diagram of storefront display by Morris Lapidus. Here Lapidus explains how the store should attract the shopper's gaze as a female nude attracts a viewer's gaze. The analogy applies equally to the merchandise and the storefront. (*Architectural Record* 88 [February 1941]: 118. Courtesy of the Avery Architectural and Fine Arts Library, Columbia University.)

shopping, he is still consuming the other *goods* on display—the made-up face, the draped body of the modernized storefront—as the three men in the vignette above look at the belle. Ultimately, however, the male gaze was secondary to the modernized storefront.

In the actual commercial sphere, the female gaze was far more critical. Fixing upon the storefront and its products, assessing the style and fashion being displayed in both, the female gaze was directly linked to the purchasing power of the female consumer. She, too, is present in the LOF advertisement. Standing close to the storefront, her torso is reflected in the polished Vitrolite that seems to garb her, as it does the facade, in the fabric of modernity. Her head is not reflected; through transparent plate glass, shoes appear instead. Woman, merchandise, and storefront merge on the modernized surface, each assuming and displaying characteristics of the other—youth, beauty, fashion, color. Down below, however, where the storefront meets the street, a strategically placed mirrored baseboard reflects the woman's own shoes as she stands before the facade. While she window-shops, her shoes are displayed with a critical clarity. Self-consciously, she examines them, judges them, and finds them wanting. In that moment the storefront gives architectural expression to a principal determinant of the consumer culture, the exploitation of consumer anxieties to produce an increased desire for goods. But if this is the implied strategy of the mirrored baseboard and the woman's inspection of her shoes, it is also the strategy in the advertisement as a whole—where it is simultaneously at work upon the merchant as he inspects his store. For however much he may have been a savvy marketing expert himself, within the realm of modernization, he was also a consumer, and as a consumer he was subject to the same concerns as his customers—was his store up-to-date and fashionable, or was it obsolete and old-fashioned? Was he, in other words, a wallflower or a belle?

The contrast between the two becomes even more potent in the context of the specified loci: "Main Street" and "the Avenue." The former is that ubiquitous commercial corridor identified as old-fashioned and obsolete by no less an authority than the federal government. The latter refers to Fifth Avenue, that exclusive commercial corridor regarded at the time as the epitome of style and up-to-dateness, the antithesis of Main Street. As it was understood in the 1930s, the oppositional pairing of Fifth Avenue and Main Street served to distinguish between the perceived extremes of American life, between the big city and the small town.[125] In a broader cultural sense, Fifth Avenue embodied change and modernity (the rapid tempo of modern life), while slow-moving Main Street was viewed as a repository of tradition and old-time values. In reality, as discussed in chapter 1, expanding consumerism was obviating these distinctions by cultivating Main Street's aspirations toward and fashion-consciousness of Fifth Avenue. What was true of clothing and cosmetics was also true of commercial architecture: building fashions appeared first in New York and then spread across the country. In both cases, the national chains played a significant part in the style progression and fashion acceleration.

In the late 1920s and early 1930s, as the chains engaged in expansion and modernization, they developed new designs for their flagship stores in New York, on Fifth Avenue in particular. If these designs were deemed a success, as judged by public approval and sales volume, they would be utilized for new or modernized retail units elsewhere.[126] The storefront that served as the Wise Shoe Company's chain standard for nearly eight years was originally designed for a store Wise opened on Fifth Avenue in 1925. In its location and (modernistic) style, this store, the company's first in New York, was regarded as "the ultimate in storefront architecture."[127] It was that Fifth Avenue *ultimate* to which Main Street aspired as fashion and modernization accelerated. Such was the implication of *Architectural Forum*'s favorable review of the modernized Abraham (drug/smoke) Store, whose black glass and aluminum facade would not have been out of place in the country's style centers: "Neither New York, nor Chicago, but Burlington, Vermont offers this shop of contemporary design."[128] Thus, the architecture/fashion analogy implicit in the wallflower/belle opposition was not simply a marketing strategy or advertising angle. It was the reflection of a contemporary, consumer-driven trend in commercial architecture that had, by the time the ad appeared in 1939, already produced countless modernized and modern belles on American Main Streets.

CHAPTER 5

Modernism on Main Street

In 1937 a saloon keeper named John Francisco decided to transform his corner bar on Park Street in Anaconda, Montana, into the Club Moderne (fig. 5.1). At the time of the modernization, Anaconda was a classic company town of twelve thousand people, dominated by the smelting works of the Anaconda Copper Mining Company (ACM). One of the largest employers in Montana, the ACM had ensured that Anaconda would become a thriving industrial and commercial center and the leading metropolis of the northern Rockies. Though far removed from any large metropolitan centers, Anaconda saw itself, at least in the recollection of many longtime inhabitants, as a cosmopolitan community every bit as sophisticated as New York, Chicago, and Los Angeles, and just as up-to-date in terms of fashions, tastes, and habits.[1]

If the contemporary consumer culture in the United States left its mark on Anaconda, so did American economic realities. When the price of copper plummeted after the stock market crash in 1929, the ACM reduced its workforce and its wages by 30 percent. The company tried to find new channels for copper and its alloys, even marketing Anaconda bronze for modernized storefronts, but demand remained flat. As the Depression worsened, the corporate paternalism on which the town had relied

Figure 5.1 Club Moderne bar and lounge in Anaconda, Montana, 1937. Designed by Boze-
man architect Fred Willson and built by Fred Wallus with materials supplied by W. P.
Fuller Paint of Butte. The Club Moderne demonstrates how deeply modern design pen-
etrated the American heartland in the 1930s and illustrates how the formal elements of
modernism served as a recognizable iconography of prosperity during the Depression.
(Library of Congress, Prints & Photographs Division, HABS-HAER [HABS, MONT,12-
ANAC,1-A-1].)

for half a century was met with increasing skepticism, and Anacondans turned to the relief programs of the New Deal and to their own informal networks centered on the town's bars and social clubs to make it through the crisis. Disillusionment with the ACM also reinvigorated the local labor movement, culminating in a strike during the summer of 1934 that changed Anaconda's balance of power and helped shape a community identity independent of the company. Though unemployment and poverty remained critical issues after the strike, according to local accounts, the town possessed a new sense of optimism about the future.[2]

It is against this social, economic, and political backdrop that John Francisco's Club Moderne must be seen. Surrounded on both sides by modest brick-faced commercial blocks, the club's four-color Vitrolite facade (ivory, black, yellow, and cadet blue) stood out as a modernization of conspicuous individuality. Even without its tall pylon and perpendicular sign, both sporting neon graphics, the building was noticeable for a design that was strikingly modern: smooth curves on its corner entrance and canopy, ribbon-like treatment of its windows, and the simplicity of its detailing. As much as this appearance of modernism in Anaconda reflected the success of corporate marketing and progressive design in penetrating the remoter regions of the American West, it also reflected the degree to which small-scale commercial architecture embodied the symbolic amelioration of the upheavals of the Depression—even in the remoter regions of the American West. For the Club Moderne was more than just an up-to-date storefront; it was a resonant symbol of Anaconda's Depression-era self-image, its name and its forms shaping an iconography of prosperity as meaningful in Anaconda as in the rest of Main Street America in the 1930s.

It is at the eye level or thereabouts that most of the changes have taken place—not new buildings so much as new show windows and shop fronts. This is mainly the work of the department stores, the specialty shops, and those particular friends of a rather blatant form of modernism, the shoe shops.

Here, in a 1937 *Sky Line* column, critic Lewis Mumford described the modernized storefronts and refurbished commercial exteriors that were appearing regularly on the streets of New York City for nearly a decade. As Mumford surely realized, by the end of the decade what was true of Fifth Avenue was also true of Main Street, and his observations would have accurately characterized virtually every commercial corridor in the

United States in the later 1930s. One of the things Mumford appreciated about the new storefronts—and that was valid whether they appeared in big cities or small towns—was that they were helping to disseminate European modernist architecture in the United States. However, though he strongly advocated modernism, Mumford did not uniformly approve of all the new designs. In fact, he found many storefronts to be "overemphatic and strident" and too often employing only the "slogans and catchwords" of modernism rather than its "intellectual discipline."[3] In this criticism, Mumford articulated a crucial aspect of the small-scale American modernism of the Depression decade.

When chain and independent retailers with stores lining U.S. Main Streets embraced Mumford's "blatant" modernism as their own, they did so in conscious emulation of urban prototypes that had been among the earliest buildings in the United States to reflect architectural trends emanating from Europe and stylistic trends emanating from the discipline of industrial design. One reason this occurred was that distinctions among local, regional, and national consumer markets had largely collapsed since the end of World War I, and retailers had begun to embrace the idea that, in the words of architect Morris Lapidus, "selling the same products to the same people is the same everywhere"[4] (fig. 5.2). As that sameness of products spread across the United States, it was inevitable that spaces for selling would respond in kind; but within American consumer culture in the 1930s, it was also inevitable that the architectural response would be far more complex than a simple homogeneity of stores all following, or at least borrowing from, the precepts of European modernism. The complexity of this response was, of course, rooted firmly in that consumer culture, in those same anxieties that made the facade so important in the modernized building.

Architectural Anxiety in the Modern World

The rhetorical strength required to convince merchants to train their fiscal resources and competitive energies upon the storefront and to deploy a popularized modernism as a retail strategy emanated from a very precise, and obvious, source—the social importance placed on exterior appearance. The government itself articulated this clearly when the FHA, cautioning merchants to "consider first your store front," further advised them to "remember that even as the character of an individual is first judged by outward appearance, so does the public judge a store by its front."[5] In emphasizing the importance of exterior appearance in an

Figure 5.2 "Selling the same products to the same people is the same everywhere." In this collage Morris Lapidus superimposed shoppers on Congress Street in Portland, Maine, onto the sidewalks of Dauphin Street in Mobile, Alabama, to illustrate the degree to which U.S. consumer markets were increasingly homogenized. (*Architectural Record* 89 [February 1941]: 132. Courtesy of the Avery Architectural and Fine Arts Library, Columbia University.)

individual's relations with others, the FHA referenced two crucial social impulses that would influence not only why but how buildings were modernized: the first was the reconceptualization of the self that emerged in American society after 1900; the second was the related trend of societal self-diagnosis that it produced. By the 1930s both of these had become accepted facts of life in modern consumer society.

In an oft-cited essay on American culture in the twentieth century, Warren Susman characterized the development of consciousness of self, an awareness of one's own being and actions, as a critical aspect of the modern world, noting how changing visions of self and changing methods of presenting self to society have marked particular cultural moments of modernity.[6] The decades after 1900—which saw the rise of consumer society in the United States as manufacturing, distribution, and sales of consumer goods intensified—represent one such moment, when the culture of *personality* superseded the culture of *character*. As a result, self-worth based on one's intrinsic moral qualities gave way to self-worth based on one's ability to impress others through surface projections of comportment, manners, speech, and dress that were now understood as accurate indicators of inner character. It was this latter idea, popularized as the "personality ethic" by Dale Carnegie, to which the FHA referred in the statement cited above, but the government was hardly alone in articulating this cultural shift in the context of modernization.

Advertising executive Earnest Elmo Calkins betrayed his awareness of the power of the surface when he admonished Main Street Rotarians to "give your town a personality" by improving its appearance through coordinated building modernization.[7] LOF, too, recognized the currency of the outer self, observing in *52 Designs to Modernize Main Street with Glass* that the storefront that "expresses the character of establishment to the buying public" was performing the same function as "the 'suit of clothes that makes the man' and stamps him as successful and progressive."[8] Even more explicitly, PPG asked merchants to scrutinize their storefronts as if they were scrutinizing job applicants: "When you hire employees, why do you choose the ones you do? Past records being equal, isn't it because of personality and appearance?" While PPG used "personality" often in its advertisements, the term was never precisely defined, though it was linked to abstract ideas of attractiveness, stylishness, and up-to-dateness and to architectural forms borrowed from modernism.[9] The emergence of this outer expression of self as a determinant of relative quality was evident even in the architecture journals. In a 1935 store design portfolio, *American Architect* declared that "the personality of a store is stamped upon the front" and was indicated by an arrangement of its forms and materials to reveal the character of the establishment within.[10]

The importance attached to personality and the outer self, first in people and then in buildings, was predicated on a belief that in the competitive, fast-paced modern world superficial appearances—perceived in an initial, momentary appraising glance—would determine one's success or failure in all social interactions, whether personal or professional. This belief, simultaneously cultivated and exploited in U.S. advertising in the late 1920s, gave rise to one of consumer culture's most potent narratives, the parable of the "first impression."[11] The first impression was employed initially to sell products related to personal appearance, especially clothing, personal care items, cosmetics, and even plastic surgery. When the modernization effort commenced in 1934, its governmental, corporate, and architectural publicists seized the first impression as a viable promotional theme. There was a certain logic to using the first impression to sell modernization, one that even made it seem less manipulative than when it was used to sell other consumer goods. Even the most cynical person might hope that an individual would be judged on something more substantial than a dingy smile, bad breath, or unfashionable clothes. But how else would an unknown commercial establishment be judged if not by the appearance of its front, by the way it impressed shoppers as they passed it on the street—especially if it was an independent store lacking the name recognition of a national chain? It made sense for the National Retail Dry Goods Association to offer its merchant members this frank assessment of their potential customers: "Let us make no mistake. People are impressed by appearances—by first appearances." According to the association, the only way a merchant could guarantee a favorable first impression was for the store to "put on a new front [by] modernizing the exterior."[12] LOF related the idea of personality and outer self to the storefront graphic terms when an exhortation to "put on a good front" was accompanied by a pair of photographs that would not have been out of place in advertisements for toothpaste or shaving cream: first, a frowning man with messy hair, slumped shoulders, and a wrinkled collar; second, a smiling man, with his head up, his hair smoothed, and wearing a bright tie—presenting his "good front" to the world. As the smile and fresh appearance paid off for the man, so Vitrolite would pay off for the store and "transform the obsolete characterless store front into the New, Modern Outstanding Front," thus winning public approval.[13]

The goal of the first impression was to make consumers desire an appearance that others would judge favorably, but first they had to understand how others saw them. Thus, it was necessary to cultivate self-consciousness and to encourage rigorous self-scrutiny, forcing consumers to look at themselves objectively as "today's critical public" did.[14] Earnest Elmo Calkins regarded "a local self-consciousness . . . which will soon seek community pride" as a prerequisite for any Main Street modernization effort.[15] At the same time, the individual merchant-cum-consumer was repeatedly admonished to be critically self-aware: "Examine your establishment with the eye of a customer."[16] If, in cultivating an awareness of the stranger's critical eye, advertising ran the risk of producing in the individual an excessive self-consciousness and a pronounced sense of inadequacy and unease, such emotional disturbances had already been normalized, though not entirely neutralized, by widespread acceptance of the existence of a psychological state known as the inferiority complex.

Recognized first by Freud's associate Alfred Adler, the idea of the inferiority complex was introduced in the United States in the mid-1920s through Adler's lectures and especially his best-selling book *Understanding Human Nature*. In the trend-driven 1920s, discussing the inferiority complex became a fad, popularized as a justification for all manner of personal difficulties. In the Depression-ravaged 1930s, when self-confidence was profoundly shaken, both collectively and individually, the inferiority complex seemed to offer a genuine social salve and a reasonable explanation for a demoralized populace. In both decades it turned up regularly in newspapers and magazine articles and also in product advertisements, since the tradition of therapeutic consumption was easily adapted as a confidence-building, anxiety-soothing palliative for feelings of inferiority and insecurity.[17] The success of the first impression as an advertising parable lay in its ability to exploit Americans' collective inferiority complex regarding social interaction and then offer a corrective through consumption of some appearance enhancement, be it toothpaste, Vitrolite, modernization, or modernism.

In explaining the cultural power of the inferiority complex in the 1920s and 1930s, Warren Susman found that, like personality, it was deeply rooted in certain anxiety-producing conditions of the modern world: fear of losing one's individual identity in the impersonal, anonymous crowd of mass society and fear of not fitting in with the crowd, of not being liked and thought well of by others. These fears, according to Susman, had correlate desires: a need to stand out from the crowd and express individuality, and a need to be a part of the crowd, to conform and be appealing lest one stand out too much or call unfavorable attention to oneself.[18] Already present before the Crash, these anxieties were exacerbated by the Depression. As the social and economic crisis worsened, and general insecurities increased, the need for the reassurance of the collective grew, and the desire to belong intensified. At the same time, the necessity of millions of Americans having to accept charitable and government relief weakened the nation's mythic self-reliance, thus increasing the need to express autonomy and individuality—however bootless or purely symbolic.[19]

As it assimilated the psychosocial impulses of personality and inferiority, via the strategies of advertising, modernization also assimilated these anxieties. These, in turn, produced two distinct approaches to the storefront, both of which informed modernization's embrace of modernism: one stressed the distinction of the individual store; the other stressed the coordination of the commercial corridor as a group of stores. While both of these approaches were evident on Main Street during the Depression, they occupied almost antithetical positions, expressive of an opposition between the Main Street corridor as a commercial reality and an architectural ideal. To some degree, all efforts to encourage modernization on Main Street played off the anxiety of conformity and fitting in regardless of the architectural style displayed. Certainly, at a basic level the social urge to belong informed the competitive urge to keep up, serving as the underlying motivation of the FHA's assertion that "when one merchant makes improvements his competitors are literally forced to do so."[20] The psychological operation was obvious: the fear of not fitting in and being judged inadequate was so great that competitors would follow the modernizing lead of a nearby store. No Main Street merchant wished to stand out unfavorably as the only unmodernized establishment—the one that was old-fashioned and un-civic-minded. As *Architectural Forum* noted in 1939, "As more and more stores on Main are improved, modernization tends to become not a question of choice but of survival."[21] The comprehensive modernization campaigns of the chain stores certainly enforced this tendency for the independent Main Street retailer.

Some modernization advocates, including Arthur C. Holden of the American Institute of Architects and S. R. DeBoer of the American Planning and Civic Association, optimistically believed that the pressure to fit in might be exploited to spur group improvements. In this way, agglomerations of unmodernized Main Street buildings could be converted into coordinated assemblages of complementary modernized units in emulation of the uniformity and clean lines of the modern shopping center. However, while Holden was hoping to realize the "architect's dream for a modernized Main Street" and DeBoer was calling for "a harmonious whole," both men overestimated the strength of the urge to fit in.[22] A willingness to participate in the modernizing trend was not the same as a willingness to forsake storefront identity to the "architectural control" of visual coordination. In other words, a desire to be a part of a modernized group was not the same as a desire to be part of a group modernization.

The more Main Street's merchants felt compelled or required to modernize as a necessity of belonging, the less the simple determination to modernize as an act of therapeutic consumption offered adequate compensation for social and competitive insecurities. Modernizing to fit in was not enough; it was necessary to modernize in order to stand out—a fact that was critical in understanding the role that modernism was to play on Main Street. Thus, the modernized storefront, as responsive to the anxieties of the day as other consumer products, became a vehicle for the expression of individuality—an apparently unique projection of the outer self that could conquer anonymity and, to paraphrase Warren Susman, make a nobody into a somebody.[23] As the urge to stand out from the Main Street crowd overwhelmed the urge to fit in, individuality asserted itself in the discourse of modernization as a promotional strategy and an architectural practice.

Individuality through Modernization

In 1936 PPG declared in a *Chain Store Age* advertisement that "individuality" in the storefront was the "most important of all qualities" since it enabled stores to "stand out from their competitors." Without it, PPG insisted, business would go elsewhere. Three years later individuality was still a prerequisite for storefront success whether a particular design strove for a "simple" or "pretentious" architectural effect.[24] When PPG and other storefront manufacturers utilized individuality as an advertising theme, they were simply appropriating what had already become accepted storefront practice and a point of critical debate. In 1936 *Architectural Forum* complained that the contemporary storefront was too often the embodiment of "a peculiarly obnoxious form of rugged individualism," but this was less a denigration of specific individualized designs than a commentary on the standing-out-from-the-crowd ethos that dominated Main Street during the 1930s.[25] As Depression-stricken merchants desperately sought to distinguish themselves from neighboring retail premises, considered direct competition for consumer attention even when they offered dissimilar services or merchandise, individuality of design, and the unique storefront expression it implied, became a veritable holy grail of modernization. This was true not only for independent Main Street merchants, but for chain retailers as well. Always alert to national changes in consumer attitudes and consumption habits, whether these changes involved shoppers buying consumer products or merchants buying modernization, the chains sought to adjust their storefronts accordingly.

Prior to the Depression, nearly all national chains adhered to a rigid architectural policy of "complete standardization" in which chain identity was established through the use of unvaried trademark fronts. By the early 1930s, in the face of deepening competition and mounting anti-chain sentiment, some chains began to modify their trademark types to respond to specific market demographics and local communities, but the practice of "keying stores to locations" was not yet universally adopted. By the mid-1930s, however, as the chains expanded and intensified their improvement programs in reaction to the government-assisted entry of the independents into the store modernization arena, many chains allowed storefronts to be redesigned with "a reasonable degree of individuality."[26] The modernization programs of Regal Shoes and Childs restaurants illustrate the breadth of this approach, from modest contextualizing to a virtual retreat from standardization.

For Regal Shoes, Morris Lapidus preserved certain visual elements that readily characterized the chain, but transformed these as necessary to suit particular locations and the chain's desire for a more modern identity. He retained the company's trademarks—its green-and-gold color palette, Old Modern typeface, and Cavalier boot logo—but simplified them into a straightforward arrangement of signboard and bulkhead with reduced but more emphatic display windows between. In a further nod to the Regal's wish for an updated image, whenever possible Lapidus created a storefront approximation of a Corbusian free facade, emphasizing the distinctions between the structure (mirror-clad piers) and the enclosure (plate glass extending across the front) that created a curtain-wall effect duly appreciated by the editors of *Architectural Forum*. The new front was intended to give the shops a "brightness" that would attract attention within the typical Main Street commercial strip and prevent them from being "blotted out" by other stores in a given block. However recognizable the modern green-and-gold Regal facade, it was apparently not appropriate for every locale, and when Regal opened its first store on Fifth Avenue in New York, chain executives requested that Lapidus consider the existing atmosphere of the nation's premier shopping corridor (fig. 5.3). Though the rarefied atmosphere of Fifth Avenue was gradually eroding in the 1930s due, in no small part, to the incursion of the chains, Lapidus responded to its supposed "dignity and richness" by toning down the Regal color scheme and trademarks: gold became bronze (Anaconda Architectural Extruded Bronze); green porcelain enamel became green cast granite; the logo became bronze casts of the Regal boot and a bronze shadowbox sign. The vestibule, by now the chain's standard, had three curving displays arranged almost like pinball bumpers, to shunt the shopper from side to side ever closer to the door, placed deliberately off-axis from the vestibule entrance. The result, according to contemporary observers, was a subtle "family" resemblance rather standardization.[27]

Though the movement away from standardization risked diminishing chain identity, store executives deemed this necessary to mediate against the corporate anonymity now closely associated with their trademark facades, as the modernization program of the Childs restaurant chain demonstrates. Until the mid-1930s, the white-tiled "dairy-room" fronts of Childs restaurants were immediately recognizable across the country, "from Portland, Oregon to Portland, Maine," according to the company. Designed and built in the early 1890s and standardized by 1900, the dairy rooms typically featured a double-width storefront of white glazed terra-cotta with glass entrance doors flanking a large display window

Figure 5.3 Fifth Avenue storefront of Regal Shoes chain, New York City, designed by Morris Lapidus in 1936. By the middle of the decade, many chain stores moved away from the strict standardization of their storefronts. The goal was to maintain chain identity while giving each unit an individualized treatment. (*Architectural Forum* 65 [October 1936]: 316. Courtesy of the Avery Architectural and Fine Arts Library, Columbia University.)

emblazoned with the chain's script logo (fig. 5.4). This transparent front provided unobstructed views inside the restaurant—a single open room with white tiled walls and floors and a long structural glass counter from which food was dispensed by white-uniformed servers. The whiteness and openness provided Childs' patrons with the "visible proof of sanitation" upon which the chain's reputation and success were based. According to Childs' executives, "It was good business to subordinate decorative effect and even comfort to obvious cleanliness." From the chain's point of view, the standard dairy front was utterly utilitarian, and it was precisely this quality that Lewis Mumford had viewed as an accidental, incipient modernism, praising it as "the beginning of a real machine form."[28] Childs was unimpressed with its unintentional avant-gardism, and by the mid-1920s the chain felt that the dairy rooms were too antiseptic and out of step with the American public's taste in dining. However, though it introduced scenographic decor into newly built restaurants, the chain continued to construct its standard white tile and glass dairy front, feeling that it had become too widely recognized a "landmark" for alteration.

Figure 5.4 Childs Restaurant, circa 1900–1910. The standardized dairy front, emphasizing cleanliness and openness, immediately identified the restaurant as part of the Childs' chain. (*Architectural Forum* 67 [July 1937]: 15. Courtesy of the Avery Architectural and Fine Arts Library, Columbia University.)

A decade later these fronts were still in use throughout the chain and, from a marketing standpoint, still "signalized Childs" in the public's mind. Now, however, in the altered climate of the Depression, company executives regarded the standardized front as nothing more than a "stumbling block in its effort to keep up with the times." In 1934–35 the chain determined that "the old white tile places must be brought up to date," but in establishing modernization policy for its restaurants, Childs did not merely "abolish the dairy room"; it unilaterally abandoned the standardized unit, adopting a policy of "individualization" that rejected "duplication of style" in order to give each restaurant "its own distinctive atmosphere." Though the determination of that atmosphere was left to the discretion of the individual architect hired for each modernization job, designers were instructed to examine the surroundings of each unit and select a "suitable" style. Among the first twenty-five units selected to "go modern," as Childs put it, nearly half were located in New York City. These restaurants were chosen not only because they were among the chain's oldest, but also because chain store executives regarded New York as the best place for trial runs of the latest storefront fashions.

Ultimately, these modernized Childs encompassed an eclectic stylistic range that, significantly, the company regarded as entirely modern. "Modernity" in this context appeared to be based less on the storefront's specific stylistic character than on the degree to which the modernization departed from the appearance of the standardized front.[29] Thus, the modernization of the two-story unit on lower Broadway was considered modern because it represented a "striking change from the old dairy-room front," even though that change was accomplished by sheathing the facade with half-timbering and installing casement windows and a steep tiled roof. A central display window and Childs' logo were the only standard elements retained from the dairy-room front, and even the logo was transformed into a rounded, enameled steel marquee. That this streamlined marquee coexisted with the neo-Tudor storefront may indicate the depth of Childs' yearning for architectural individuality and also the ease with which that yearning could slip into a kind of stylistic schizophrenia.

The first Childs to be modernized in Times Square represented an equally extreme departure from the classic dairy front and a radically different solution to the problem of individualization (fig. 5.5). As redesigned by George Sweet in 1936, the Childs on Seventh Avenue and Forty-second Street was visually too high-pitched for the conservative taste of critic Talbot Hamlin, but it possessed a "vulgar vitality" that Lewis Mumford applauded as in keeping with "the spirit of Broadway."[30] In fact, given a locale of unsurpassed visual noise, with Rosario Candela's flamboyantly modernized Rialto Theatre right next door, Sweet's facade was relatively low key. Nonetheless, it was a dynamic composition unified through the architect's trebling of its principal formal elements. Three colors—white, black, and blue—were aligned with three cladding materials—enameled steel, structural glass, and mirrored glass—into an asymmetrical composition enhanced by three levels of surface reflectivity with aluminum trim and speed lines tying the whole together.[31] By substituting modern flash for Childs' standard restraint, Sweet's modernization ably met the company's mandate for individualized, contextually appropriate schemes, here gleefully reflecting the "naughty, gaudy, bawdy, sporty" atmosphere of the Times Square entertainment district in the 1930s.[32] Upon completion of the first phase of its chainwide modernization program, the company ran newspaper advertisements asking readers, "Can this really be Childs?"[33] Through a tone of gentle self-mockery, the implications of the question were patently obvious. A nationwide chain that had successfully established in its trademark white-tile dairy front the architectural equivalent of its "cleanly" reputation boldly dispensed with thirty years' worth of accumulated brand identification by commissioning modernizations that were purposefully anti-trademark, unstandard, and highly individualized. But such was the nature of the American commercial corridor during the Depression, a high-pressure marketplace that drove chain retailers and independent merchants alike to the expressive visual extremes of the modernized storefront.

If those storefronts were too often characterized by "strident individuality," as George Nelson observed in his foreword to Emrich Nicholson's *Contemporary Shops in the United States*, this was the unavoidable consequence of the "strenuous—and frequently anti-social—competition" that had so marked the decade in trade, causing merchants and their designers to pay "more and more attention to the exterior." Perhaps, as Nelson conceded, the storefronts of the 1930s did "try much too hard to catch the eye and what they have to say is sometimes said too loudly," but at least Main Street now regarded modern design "as a major weapon in its arsenal."[34] Writing in 1945, Nelson was reiterating what storefront critics in the previous decade, Lewis Mumford chief among them, had already lamented. While Mumford found much to admire in the apple-green porcelain enamel and molded steel facades of Horace Ginsbern's ultra-modern Hanscom's Bake Shops (1934–38), he complained of the "decibels of visual noise" they created. "What," Mumford wondered, "would a street of such shops sound like?" In posing that question, Mumford was addressing architectural and retail concerns more than broadly social ones. In response to the former, he understood that in the midst of this visual cacophony of colored glass and curving bulkheads, of neon signs and metallic speed lines, the message of each individual store was all but drowned out by that of its neighbor. This was the reason he suggested a judicious return to "quiet, civilized, uniform design."[35]

What Mumford failed to acknowledge is that even while the modernized storefronts shouted to be heard above their competitors, their collective Depression-era social message was still resoundingly clear. Despite the architectural babble, the storefront was a legible advertisement for a modernity and prosperity promised by consumption. For as much as store design and modernization was responding to the pressures of consumerism, it was likewise responding to the pressures of the Depression. Indeed, within the federally sponsored and privately promoted modernization movement that was responsible for stimulating so much of this commercial design, the Depression's economic, social, and political exigencies were even more critical to Main Street's acceptance of modernism than the relentless consumer culture.

Figure 5.5 Childs restaurants, Times Square (Seventh Avenue at Forty-second Street and at Forty-ninth Street), designed by George Sweet, 1936–37. In 1934 the chain decided to "go modern" and began updating its units, giving each a style deemed suitable to the immediate locale. Here, Sweet's designs captured the "vulgar vitality" of the area in their forms, colors, and materials. (WPA Tax Photographs of New York City, 1014-33-M. Courtesy NYC Municipal Archives. *Architectural Forum 67* [July 1937]: 15. Courtesy of the Avery Architectural and Fine Arts Library, Columbia University.)

An Iconography of Prosperity

Within the sociopolitical and socioeconomic landscape of the Depression era, the movement to modernize Main Street was unique. Though predicated upon everyday practices of shopping and selling, and therefore attempting to meet a retailer's merchandising needs, it also sought to fulfill a community's social imperatives. And as the appearance of Main Street's stores changed, so, too, did their meaning, blurring the boundaries between private and public sectors, between consumerism and civicism, between consumption and good citizenship to embody the fiscally dubious, yet easy-to-swallow proposition that the nation could literally spend its way out of the economic crisis and buy its way into a prosperous future. With building modernization as a requisite first step toward the completion of this project, the iconography of the modernized storefront was doubly consumed as shopping *and* recovery, as marketplace *and* modernity—the real and metaphorical terms of which were well understood by men and women walking down any Main Street in the 1930s.

It should not be surprising that an architectural manifestation as banal and quotidian as the Main Street storefront should have been imbued with such obvious representational power during the Depression. In an era rife with the rhetoric of social and political populism, the storefront's everydayness contributed to its agency, as New Dealers clearly recognized. These buildings were understood as transmitters of core cultural values, a signification that was evident from the earliest moments of the federal modernization movement. The FHA's *Bulletin No. 1*, although little more than a dry procedural manual for financial institutions, opened with an exhortation attaching unmistakable social good to the extension of modernization credit. The MCP was posited as a relief measure, not for the building industry, but for the buildings themselves, here identified as the "other victims" of the Depression. In this analogy, run-down buildings were "casualties" as seriously stricken by "the ravages of five years of depreciation and obsolescence" as the Depression's "human victims" were by unemployment and hunger.[36] In a nationwide radio address broadcast live from Radio City in November 1934, FHA head James Moffett rendered the social significance of Main Street's dilapidated buildings equally unmistakable, declaring that they represented the "break-down of the American living standard" and a "comradeship of poverty" that emerged during the Depression, making it acceptable to "get along with the old and worn-out." At a public rally in Los Angeles two months later, Moffett further declared that worn-out buildings were "signs and reminders of hard times."[37]

In retrospect, Moffett's use of such a familiar Depression-era phrase allows these buildings to be understood as the architectural equivalent of the decade's "official" images of hard times—the photographs by Dorothea Lange, Walker Evans, and others produced by the Historical Section of the Farm Security Administration beginning in 1935.[38] Like the FSA photographs of destitute farm families and urban breadlines, run-down or untenanted buildings possessed a currency enabling them to represent with apparent truthfulness the conditions of the Depression in American cities and towns.[39] But this documentary truthfulness was somewhat distorted for, like the FSA photographs, run-down buildings were also subject to ideological construction that assigned to them a burden of meaning outweighing their actual economic status as symptoms of retail and real estate decline. Thus it was that administrator Moffett, speaking with the authority of the New Deal state and backed by the corporate-bureaucratic publicity apparatus of the modernization movement, described these buildings as "a barrier between American people and prosperity." Moffett identified this barrier to prosperity as both physical and psychological, though he was aware of its fiscal dimension as well, and he challenged the American public that it would remain impenetrable until there was "free spending in every community" to modernize Main Street's buildings.[40]

In its potential for modernization, the run-down storefront possessed the ability to transform its documentary significance. A testament to present hard times before modernization became an exposition on future good times after modernization—a conceptual dyad with its own photographic representation in the before-and-after pairs that typically accompanied government publications, trade journal portfolios, and corporate advertisements. If the run-down storefront may be aligned with the FSA's iconic images of human despair, the modernized storefront finds a correlate in other artifacts of New Deal visual culture, especially the murals produced under the auspices of the Federal Art Project of the Works Progress Administration and the Section of Fine Arts of the Treasury Department. Whether these murals trafficked in nostalgia or progressivism, they possessed an underlying optimism that sought to suppress the traumas of the Depression through an inspirational iconography of historical persons and events, vignettes of small-town life, heroic workers, or streamlined trains and airplanes.[41] Though architecture is, by its nature, abstract and is thus denied the easily comprehended narratives of this sort of figural painting, the iconography of the modernized storefront was just as legible as the typical WPA mural. And by virtue of its serial existence on Main Streets across the country and its realistic engagement with everyday life—at the most basic, and during the Depression, most anxiety-producing level of economic exchange—the modernized storefront possessed an even greater therapeutic potential as its architectural optimism became a psychological salve.

This potential was fully evident in a simple corollary that expressed the storefront's public meaning and was implied throughout the FHA literature. If a run-down building betokened social and economic depression to the general public, then the opposite was also true: a modernized building could signify the positive outlook and revived prosperity of a commercial corridor, an entire town, or even the country as a whole, regardless of the actual state of the local or national economy. When presenting its building statistics for 1935, the F.W. Dodge Corporation observed that "the modernization of the main street of trade constitutes definite evidence that the recovery cycle is underway."[42] The government pointed out that while modernizing a single property surely served the individual owner, it was also a "definition of civic pride" that "benefit[ed] the whole community" and generated "a new spirit of hopefulness . . . a feeling of confidence . . . [and the knowledge] that a brighter day is coming and coming fast."[43] Robert and Helen Lynd discovered similar optimism in Middletown following the "external improvement and sprucing up" of the business center. Modernizing Main Street's buildings was regarded as "a symbol of recovery," which seemed to revive Middletown's "civic spirit" and engender a jocular denial, at least in the middle class: "What depression? We haven't had a depression here." This, despite the fact that in 1935 Middletown's industrial activity was still in decline, that retail volume on Main Street was half of what it had been in 1929, and that genuine civic improvements (to infrastructure, services, etc.) were "largely standing still." Noting this paradox, the Lynds concluded that the Depression had made more urgent "the need to 'put on a good show' to reassure the groundlings [and] to 'doctor up' the morale of the rank and file."[44]

In putting on a good show, assisted by the architectural masquerade of the new facade, the modernized storefront functioned to convince the American public that "the innate dynamism of the modern economy," in Marshall Berman's phrase, was proceeding apace, despite the rupture of the Depression.[45] By disguising or effacing the Depression's physical effects behind that new facade, modernization operated socially to minimize or even deny the rupture's psychological impact. But as the

Lynds observed in *Middletown in Transition*, this impact had registered with the public as "an elemental shock" at once universal, prolonged, and nearly primal in its deeply felt trauma.[46] Some critics have argued that in terms of image-making this trauma precipitated a nostalgic return to an idealized small-town archetype that would forever remain, as Terry Smith called it, "an obvious domain of the not-modern." For Smith, the small town was "crucial to the visualization of modern America" in the 1930s, but only as it stood in opposition to the factory, the skyscraper city, and other generally recognized landscapes of modernity—a last line of defense against the onslaught of inevitable cultural modernization that the Depression had barely halted. Smith claimed that the small town, "the quiet look down Main Street," became a symbol of recovery within the decade's visual culture (principally photography) precisely because it appeared to resist external modernizing forces through a show of old-fashioned independence expressed in archaizing imagery.[47]

If, however, visual culture is defined broadly enough to include everyday architecture, a different Main Street emerges, one that became a symbol of recovery not through resistance to modernization, but through its acceptance as localized practice that transcended the sphere of retail and commerce and was in keeping with the progressive self-improvement that typified small-town culture. On this Main Street, the traumatic shock of the Depression was ameliorated not through a backward slippage toward a nostalgic haze, nor through a heroic leap forward toward a tabula rasa utopian future, but rather through a brisk walk toward the light of tomorrow as embodied in a gleaming modernized storefront. To signal this imminent return to prosperity, modernization required an architectural imagery that might serve as a countershock, unabashedly expressing progress and optimism, and boldly advertising an ever-brightening future. Modernization required the architectural imagery of modernism.

Enter the International Style

Of those varied modernisms available to American architects in the mid-1930s, not all could satisfy the iconographic requirements of "building modernization as national recovery." Stripped classicism was too closely associated with civic or institutional authority and timeless solemnity, and its stone revetment and sculpture were too costly and too staid for average Main Street modernizations. It represented the state, not the people; them, not us. Modernistic, or art deco, design was more appropriately commercial and quotidian, as well as exuberantly and fashionably contemporary, but therein lay the fault: it was too closely associated with the excesses of the 1920s. Its floral fields and zigzags seemed frivolously out of place amid Depression-era austerities when unemployment was high and the breadlines were long.[48] Of course, there was another modernism, one possessing sufficient quantities of simplicity, economy, and a crucial shock of the new to auger the popular perception of the contemporary American character and to embody the architectural resuscitation of America's failing Main Streets.

In the years prior to the commencement of the modernization program in 1934, American architects had become increasingly familiar with the International Style of European modernism. As historians such as Richard Guy Wilson and David Gebhard have shown, the term was current in their vocabularies and, if they were sympathetic but not especially dogmatic, they viewed it as one of several plausible modern modes.[49] This familiarity came from a number of different, mainly secondary, sources. The most obvious and accessible were journals and books that published images of European buildings and, in addition, sought to explain what the new architecture was all about. George Howe's 1930 *American Architect* article—"What Is This Modern Architecture Trying to Express?"—for example, described how modernism emerged in response to modern life, deriving its essential elements from the social and technological progress of the twentieth century. The accompanying illustrations—of Bijvoet and Duiker's Zonnestraal sanatorium in the Netherlands, Erich Mendelsohn's Universum Cinema in Berlin, and Laprade and Bazin's Marbeuf auto showroom in Paris—were meant to demonstrate the simple and direct methods that architects used to satisfy such modern programmatic issues as accommodating hygiene and health, focusing attention on the screen, and selling cars.[50] Catherine Bauer's 1934 book, *Modern Housing*, served a similar function as it used text and illustrations to introduce the urban and architectural principles of modernist planned communities and housing estates to an American audience.[51] By the mid-1930s, European modernist buildings, especially commercial ones, were also appearing regularly in articles dealing with store design and modernization. One of the most comprehensive of this sort was "Retail Store Planning," which *Architectural Record* published in July 1935 in conjunction with the Libbey-Owens-Ford Modernize Main Street Competition.[52] In addition, they could also be found in such specialized publications like Frederick Kiesler's *Contemporary Art Applied to the Store and Its Display* (1930) and Adolf Schuhmacher's *Ladenbau* (1934), as well as advertising journals like *Gebrauchsgraphik*, which Morris Lapidus claimed as an

Figure 5.6 "Asymmetrical Store Front Composition" designed by Frederick Kiesler from *Contemporary Art Applied to the Store and Its Display*, 1930. Kiesler reduced the storefront to an enlarged plane with an abstract arrangement of display windows. (© 2006 Austrian Frederick and Lillian Kiesler Private Foundation, Vienna; and the Avery Architectural and Fine Arts Library, Columbia University.)

important influence in the early 1930s (figs. 5.6 and 5.7). However important their exposure to actual commercial examples from Europe, as American architects began to grapple with modernist imagery, typological consistency was not foremost in their minds. Lapidus, for example, modernized a building on Fordham Road in the Bronx that borrowed heavily from Le Corbusier's houses at the Weissenhof Siedlung and William Lescaze's townhouse in Manhattan, despite the fact that the building was occupied by a men's clothing store.

Exposure to the new architecture also came through buildings in the United States that were understood as responses to immediate European precedents, including those at the 1933 Century of Progress International Exposition in Chicago, which critics at the time linked directly to the work of those architects most closely identified with the International Style. Writing in *American Architect*, Arthur Woltersdorf observed that the buildings displayed ample borrowing from the work of Walter Gropius, Ludwig Mies van der Rohe, Le Corbusier, "and others to whom the American designers, no doubt, grant first place among their preceptors for modern architecture." Writing in the *New York Times*, R. L. Duffus described the buildings in modernist terms: they were "dynamic and functional," rejecting all historical form in favor of horizontality, undecorated flatness, and bold color. But for Duffus, the contemporary parallel was less to European buildings than to American streamlined cars, planes, and trains.[53] For both critics, however, the buildings possessed a distinctive modern sensibility that portended a new direction in American architecture—one that drew formal and rhetorical strength from both modernism and streamlining, combining the two into a potent commercial hybrid.

Encouraging a hybrid modernism was the last thing that curator Philip Johnson hoped to achieve when the Museum of Modern Art's Modern Architecture exhibition opened in New York in February 1932. Rather, he hoped to stimulate "really comprehensive and intelligent criticism in both architect and the public" by presenting them with the best examples of "the New Architecture."[54] To this end, Johnson arranged for two different versions of the show to tour the country for almost two years after its successful run at the museum. A full version, with models and drawings, traveled to Hartford, Worcester, Rochester, Buffalo, Cleveland, Cincinnati, Toledo, Milwaukee, and Kansas City, as well as to Philadelphia, Los Angeles, and Chicago; the smaller version, without models and consisting mostly of photographs, was on view in Poughkeepsie, Denver, Troy, St. Paul, Indianapolis, and Kalamazoo, as well as Pittsburgh and San Francisco. In several locations the show was installed in major department stores, including Sears, Roebuck, Bullock's, and Gimbels, which undoubtedly extended its public reach.[55] Included in both exhibitions, in the catalog, and in the subsequent publication, *The International Style*, were such major European modern buildings as Walter Gropius's Dessau Bauhaus, Mies van der Rohe's Barcelona Pavilion, and Le Corbusier's Villa Savoye, as well as such Euro-American examples as Howe & Lescaze's PSFS Building. Also included were a number of

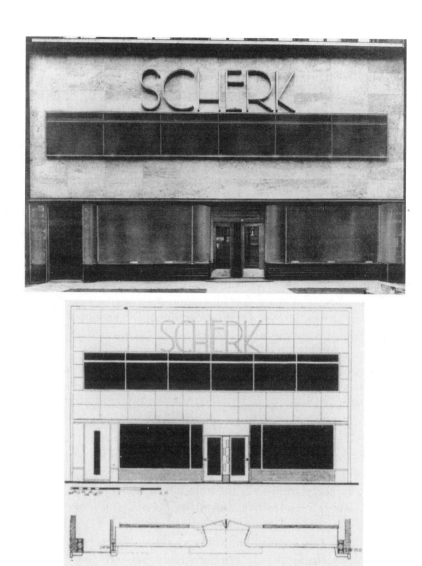

Figure 5.7 Scherk perfume shop, Berlin, designed by O. R. Salvisberg in 1929. General view, elevation, and plan. Throughout the 1930s, American architects became increasingly familiar with this type of modern European design through international publications available in the United States and in U.S. professional journals. (*Moderne Ladenbauten*, 1929, 134; *Architectural Record* 78 [July 1935]: 64. Courtesy of the Avery Architectural and Fine Arts Library, Columbia University.)

minor modern buildings, at least in terms of their scale and iconic status: cafés, movie theaters, a gas station, a pharmacy, a shoe store, department stores, exposition pavilions, and retail blocks by Gropius, Mendelsohn, J. J. P. Oud, Erik Gunnar Asplund, and others.[56]

While it is difficult to determine the actual impact and influence of these various books and articles, of MoMA's Modern Architecture show, and of the Century of Progress International Exposition, there is no denying that, at the very least, they all served to popularize the International Style of European modernism, to equate it with a distinct set of formal characteristics, and to frame the debate about modern architecture in a new way, all of which would eventually come into play in the discourse of building modernization after 1934. This is not to imply that the International Style was the only, or even the most important, influence on store design in the 1930s. As demonstrated in chapter 4, industrial design, and streamlining in particular, exerted a tremendous influence on the storefront. But in sorting out the complications of modern architectural style as it was understood in the United States in the 1930s, and in attempting to track the diverse sources that contributed to storefront design, the influence of the International Style of European modernism—as architects encountered it in journals, books, and exhibitions—cannot be ignored.

Even a cursory glance at the hundreds of storefronts illustrated in articles and advertisements in *Architectural Record, Architectural Forum,* and *American Architect* reveals the influence of the European examples. This is equally evident in the winning entries of LOF's Modernize Main Street Competition. In particular, those in the drugstore category most dynamically embodied an architectural syntax derived from the International Style. Since drugstores represented "the last word in up-to-date retailing," at least according to LOF's competition jury, these designs employed deliberately of-the moment visual effects.[57] Asymmetrical and unornamented facades, planar and curving forms, ribbon-like windows, and boldly simplified graphics were key features of winning and mentioned drugstore schemes (fig. 5.8). With their careful arrangements of storefront elements and accenting colors rendered in new materials, these schemes were striking graphic compositions that recalled Oud's Café de Unie and Kiefhoek shops, Hans Borkowsky's Dapolin filling station, and even Joost Schmidt's posters for the Weimar Bauhaus (here just barely translated into three dimensions). When the jury described M. Righton Swicegood's first-prize scheme as "entirely modern" and "original without being bizarre," it indicated the degree to which precedents and standards had already been established.[58] Ultimately, the jury concluded that

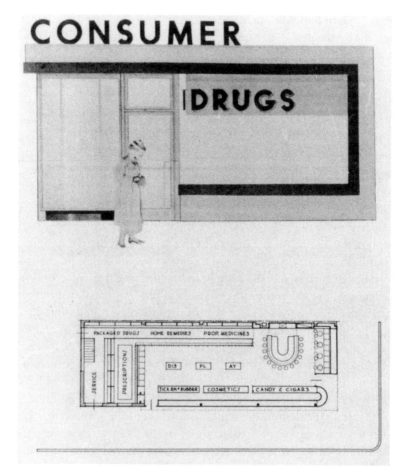

Figure 5.8 LOF Modernize Main Street Competition winner (Honorable Mention): Morrison Broun, Drug Store. The planar facade, asymmetrical composition, and simplified graphic treatment reveal the influence of European modernism on this storefront design. (*Architectural Record* 78 [October 1935]: 215. Courtesy of the Avery Architectural and Fine Arts Library, Columbia University, and Libbey-Owens-Ford Glass Company Records, MSS-066, the Ward M. Canaday Center for Special Collections, The University of Toledo.)

this modernism would soon become widespread with "the gospel of good design and good taste permeating through the thousands of Main Streets all over the country."[59]

In the coming years, this permeation was such that the term "drug store modern" entered the architectural lexicon, though not always as a term of aesthetic approval, especially when used by Henry-Russell Hitchcock in his 1951 essay "The International Style Twenty Years After."[60]

This reappraisal, which appeared in *Architectural Record*, makes clear what was already evident in the 1930s. While the International Style's underlying architectural principles of volume and regularity—so insistently propounded by Hitchcock and Philip Johnson, as curators of the MoMA exhibition, and evident in canonical buildings by Corbusier, Mies, and Gropius—remained inscrutable to the American public at large, its more accessible, or at least more conspicuous, formal elements soon appeared on Main Street itself. Asymmetry, planarity, and simplicity were taken up by architects who were either unconcerned with—or even unaware of—Hitchcock and Johnson's critical admonitions against appropriating only the surface features of the International Style (Mumford's "slogans and catchwords") or were unable to embrace anything but its surface features given the facade orientation of so many modernization commissions (fig. 5.9).

In a 1932 editorial in *Architectural Forum*, written on the occasion of the MoMA exhibition, Kenneth K. Stowell expressed his concern that the International Style would become "the happy hunting ground of copyist charlatans." Three years later, however, this hardly seemed to trouble him, as he noted how American architects were beginning to "assimilate the philosophy of the early and radical modernists and interpret it through their own individuality." Viewing this as a positive trend, Stowell came out in support of "this modern or international style" in his influential book *Modernizing Buildings for Profit*. With the approval of this store re/design expert, it was all but certain that "plain surfaces, geometric forms, and colorful simplicity" would proliferate on the nation's Main Streets as "public taste tends more and more to the new architecture." Assuming "the present trend toward modernism in store design" continued unabated, the new architecture would shortly be codified into a reductive storefront formula.[61]

On Main Street this formula invariably involved covering the existing building with modern veneers used in the manner of the International Style or industrial design streamlining, depending on one's point of view. The emphasized surface of the typical storefront appeared unbroken across the architectural volume like "a tight skin" or "a stretched textile," as Hitchcock and Johnson would have it.[62] Though white stucco had been used most often to create the precise machine-like surfaces they preferred, Hitchcock and Johnson were confident that other materials more durable, regular, and endowed with color that was "technically and psychologically permanent" would soon become available. In a remarkable coincidence, this description corresponds closely to the properties

Figure 5.9 Chapin's Open Kitchen, Cleveland, Ohio, designed by Wilbur Henry Adams in 1939. Adams's scheme demonstrates how architects borrowed the most obvious surface features of European modernism and used them to startling effect in their modernization work. (*Architectural Record* 87 [January 1940]: 88. Courtesy of the Avery Architectural and Fine Arts Library, Columbia University.)

of structural glass, which, at the time of their writing, the marketing departments of LOF and PPG were transforming into their very ideal of a modernist surface material: a "plate covering" available in nearly thirty colors made permanent during the manufacturing process by the fusion of oxides and silica; laid or installed with minimal joining (cement, cork tape, or felt) to become a smooth "sheathing" with "similarity in texture and scale to the glass planes of the windows," finally forming with the window glass a seamless continuity of surface, "reducing the contrast between the transparent and the opaque sections of the bounding wall."[63] In the modernized storefront, the transition between the transparent and the opaque was seductively orchestrated, the juxtaposed window and sheathing sharing not only a highly polished finish but a vitreous substantiality, as plate glass met structural glass mediated only by the attenuated profile of an extruded metal frame.

If modernism fetishized plate glass into a totem of transparency, modernization fetishized structural glass into its opposite—totem of opacity. Light-trapping and densely, impenetrably colored, structural glass purposefully obscured that which lay beneath its surface—a brick wall, a rusting bulkhead, an obsolete architectural detail. This opacity also served to obscure the economic expedients that lay beneath the surface of modernization as recovery—a troubling reliance on consumer credit, a false promise of guaranteed profits, a disturbing incitement of cutthroat competition. To stress the darkness and the murkiness of this opaque surface is, however, to deny its sensual impact on Main Street during the Depression (fig. 5.10). For the modernized storefront did not merely adhere to the modernist principle of surface; it celebrated that principle with glass that curved around bulkheads, slid over transoms, and slipped across facades, transforming the old-fashioned building beneath into a stylishly modern one. Purists like Hitchcock and Johnson denigrated such colorful facadism as a "tawdry" and "half-modern" parody, even though they acknowledged that in Europe in the 1920s "use of bright color had value in attracting attention to the new style."[64] In America in the 1930s, that was the point of modernism on Main Street, to attract attention to the *new style* of the modernized storefront through a publicity-seeking, self-celebrating, even crassly commercial architecture. But in the midst of this modernist marketing hype, this architecture was also giddily optimistic, emerging as it did out of national trauma and local despair in the unlikely form of the modernist, modernized storefront.

A Modern Vernacular

Ultimately, the critical assessments of MoMA polemicists are beside the point, and seventy years after the fact it hardly matters how well the architecture of modernization measured up to the formal prescriptions of the International Style. And yet, at the time, there were those who sought to defend the storefront against accusations of modernist failure and stylistic opportunism, none more so than the editors of *Architectural*

Figure 5.10 Uniqué ice cream parlor and soda fountain in Niagara Falls, New York, designed by C. T. Macheras of Buffalo in 1938. With their sleek forms and bright colors, modernized storefronts provided a vivid contrast to the social and economic realities of the Depression. (*Sweet's Catalogue File* [1940]: sec. 18, cat. 2. LOF *1940 Advertising Scrapbook*. Libbey-Owens-Ford Glass Company Records, MSS-066, Ward M. Canaday Center for Special Collections, The University of Toledo.)

Forum, who argued that American commercial design—retail shops in particular—represented a "progressive" architectural development regardless of its lack of commitment to the International Style as officially promulgated. In 1938 they made this position clear:

> Today's modern is a reality. If the term "International Style" is not broad enough to include it, this is the fault of the term; not the reality. And if streamlined storefronts are not precisely what the purist expected, let him closely check his arguments: extruded aluminum is clearly more a machine age product than the handicraft which went into most of his much-beloved Central European models. The question we must answer today is not "What is Modern?" but "Where is modern now?"[65]

The question begs answering. With respect to the storefront, modern was everywhere. By the late 1930s, the modernized storefront had proliferated sufficiently for Lewis Mumford to concede that it marked the emergence of "a modern vernacular."[66] At first, this term seems little more than a critical bon mot, a throwaway line. But Mumford was too astute a critic of American culture to have not been fully aware that his blithe conflation of these two apparently oppositional architectural categories was, in fact, charged with meaning. The author of such acclaimed architectural studies as *Sticks & Stones* and *The Brown Decades*, and curator of the housing section of the MoMA's International Style show, Mumford was well qualified to address both the modern and the vernacular in the architecture of the United States. Indeed, his critical project had long been concerned with revealing their nexus in the twentieth century:

> Just as the bridge summed up what was best in early industrialism, so the modern subway station, the modern lunch room, the modern factory, and . . . the modern school, have often been cast in molds which would make them [our] conspicuous aesthetic achievements.[67]

This passage from *Sticks & Stones* appeared in a chapter that was originally to have been called "The New Vernacular of the Machine." Mumford's argument here, like Le Corbusier's in the contemporaneous *Vers une Architecture*, was basically that the mechanical products of this mid-industrial culture—its ocean liners, airplanes, and automobiles—had much to teach architecture, both in "the scientific spirit in which they have been conceived . . . and in the aesthetic values they betrayed": their "clean surfaces, hard lines, and calibrated perfections."[68] For Mumford, any architecture that absorbed these lessons was worthy of the name *modern*. As for the vernacular, this was the architecture servicing "the direct aims and practices of everyday life."[69] And just as the settlement patterns of the New England village gave rise to the seventeenth-century vernacular in what would become the United States, so would the processes and products of the machine give rise to the twentieth-century vernacular in the contemporary nation. In 1924, when *Sticks & Stones* first appeared, the shape of that vernacular was as yet indistinct.

A decade later he had witnessed its emergence in the modernized storefront, not merely as a localized phenomenon, but as a nationwide movement. These storefronts were virtually mass produced, consisting of prefabricated ensembles ordered directly from manufacturers' catalogs or standardized parts assembled into individual architect designs. They were relatively inexpensive and quickly and easily installed. Most importantly, they were immediately recognizable with their sleek modern facades. Existing somewhere between full-fledged architecture and industrially designed consumer products, and functioning as billboards or advertisements as much as a physical shopping spaces, these modernized storefronts were a ubiquitous feature of the American commercial landscape, and by extension the American commercial culture.

In *Sticks & Stones*, Mumford predicted that the machine-age vernacular, when it arrived, would be "bound up with the course of civilization" and shaped by the "contingency and choice" of the American people—as perhaps all vernaculars are. But it would also be subject to a complement of "new factors" that Mumford believed could be "introduced at any moment [to] alter profoundly the economic and social life of the community."[70] In the United States, just as architecture was beginning to absorb the lessons of one new factor, machine production, another was introduced: the onset of the Depression after 1929, as well as the New Deal programs that attempted to reverse its effects. As Mumford predicted, this new factor further altered the economic and social life of the community, thus reshaping the architectural forms of everyday life that he would soon observe on the streets of New York. The Modernize Main Street program—as a product of government policy, corporate promotion, and local community support—gave form and substance to Mumford's modern vernacular.

But in this context, Mumford's term presents a paradox. How can a form of architecture predicated upon an imported high style (European modernism), promulgated by a state (the New Deal government and its corporate partners), and produced by highly industrialized methods (the prefabrication of building materials) be understood as a legitimate vernacular? When the modernized storefront is situated in the architectural and cultural climate that produced it, the answer is abundantly clear, as is the validity of the term with respect to the artifact at hand: *modern* designates the storefront's immediacy and temporality, as well as its stylistic basis; *vernacular* designates its widespread occurrence and everydayness, its hierarchical position at the low end of the architectural spectrum, and also its origins in particularized patterns of human behavior. But these designations, as embodied in the modernized storefront, cannot be separated so neatly, for it was in their very modernity that these storefronts became vernacular, born of the habits and customs that characterized American identity during the 1930s.

The specific nature of that identity (monolithically understood and accepted) had been intensely scrutinized and discussed by social commentators since at least the end of World War I. By the 1930s what was clear to intellectuals and ad men, politicians and sociologists, was that the American identity consisted of the deliberate linking of such supposedly authentic yeoman traits as rugged individualism and by-one's-own-bootstraps striving with such recently observed middle-class tendencies as therapeutic, self-improving, self-conscious consumption. As it was understood at the time, these merged into the contemporary American character, marked by progressiveness and modernity and turning toward commerce and business for ethical orientation. In other words, the American character was being gradually defined by consumerism—that morass of materialism endemic to advanced capitalism that even the most negative critics understood as the closest the United States had yet come to producing to an autochthonic culture. For some, this was reason enough to celebrate. Morris Lapidus believed that the consumerist, mass-production orientation of "Mr. and Mrs. Americas [*sic*]" presented "a chance for truly national architectural expression!"—one that had, in fact, already emerged as a modern vernacular in the commercial blocks of 1930s Main Street.[71]

Prior to the appearance of modern on Main Street, as recently as 1930 according to the editors of *House Beautiful*, to the man in the street "modern architecture mean[t] 'different architecture'—that is, architecture so unlike what he has been accustomed to that he feels strange in its presence and will have none of it."[72] By the end of the decade, while this assessment continued to hold sway in the domestic sphere, on Main Street's commercial corridors the opposite was true. As *Architectural Forum* observed in 1939: "There is no sentimental relationship between the owner and his store, which is one reason why today's shops are practically 100 per cent modern, while the house still breathes the spirit of 1776."[73] A restless and voracious consumer culture had assimilated modernism and given it a decidedly positive spin: what was strange and different was also eye-catching and sales-enhancing: "Today's shopkeeper regards modernization as an essential part of his merchandising technique and employs the dramatic attention-getting qualities of modern architecture as an extra salesman of prime importance."[74] If modernist modernizing became a useful sales strategy, it was because the corporate-government publicity machine had successfully identified it with native progress and optimism, interpreting in architectural terms the consuming public's long-cultivated desire "to be modern which means wrapping the past in moth balls . . . and realizing that we live in the year A.D. 1935."[75]

That this statement, produced by the FHA for radio publicity, has the rhetorical tone of advertising is, of course, not coincidental. Indeed, in the development of a modern architectural vernacular, it is absolutely crucial. By the 1930s advertising was recognized as a uniquely modern form of communication—a vernacular in its own right that served as the de facto language of the consumer culture. As such, it was a direct parallel to other forms of modern mass culture, including motion pictures and radio. As building modernization brought architecture into the embrace of consumerism, the priorities, values, and imagery of advertising were, to paraphrase Terry Smith, inserted so deeply into its productive process that architecture, as manifest in the modernized storefront, became its own form of mass communication—brash, slangy, and undeniably modern.[76] If this modern vernacular emerged too quickly for the evolutionary conventions of typical architectural vernaculars, this was a symptom of its modernity—it was keeping pace with the rapid tempo of modern life—a tempo whose beat was increasingly the same whether on Fifth Avenue or Main Street. This modern vernacular was neither nostalgic nor heroic. Rather it was a deliberate architectural response to the social and economic upheavals of the Depression that navigated an engaged middle path through the specificities of the Main Street condition and the generalities of the national discourse. Reinscribed with a political—though not radical—intent erased from the aestheticized International Style, this modern vernacular produced a storefront architecture fully charged with a progressive agenda, as it attempted, through the policies of the New Deal, to marshal the resources of the individualist capitalist economy for the collective public good of national recovery.

CHAPTER 6

Conclusion: A Main Street Modernized

December 1941 is often regarded as the symbolic end of the Great Depression, since the war mobilization that followed the attack on Pearl Harbor revived the economy more quickly and intensively, through the stimulation of industrial production and widespread building activity, than the New Deal ever had. As the war effort of the early 1940s gradually obviated the need for building modernization as an economic stimulus, the federal mechanism that made it possible, the Modernization Credit Plan (MCP), was retooled in response to the new national emergency. Specifically, in 1943, when defense housing priorities forced the exclusion of nonresidential (i.e., commercial) properties from the loan insurance program established through Title I of the 1934 National Housing Act, the FHA's effort to modernize Depression-era Main Streets officially came to an end. Technically, modernization was still allowable during the war because, as a building activity, it was classified as maintenance and repair rather than new construction. But the critical material restrictions the War Production Board put in place in 1942 had already made it difficult for architects to satisfy Main Street's modernizing impulses. Though structural glass was still available, the use of other key storefront materials—including metal for frames and trim, plate glass for display windows, and electrical fittings for signage and showcase illumination—was now strictly prohibited.[1]

In a 1942 *Architectural Record* article, "Store Modernizing without Metals," Morris Lapidus noted the difficulties these restrictions presented for storefront design. While Lapidus offered a few suggestions regarding effective wood and terrazzo facades, he recommended that modernization work now be directed toward store interiors, which could be replanned and redecorated "without interfering with the war effort." It is not insignificant that Lapidus, who had designed some of the boldest store exteriors of the 1930s, here emphasized "efficiency" in the arrangement of the selling floor rather than modernity in the appearance of the storefront.[2] Though material prohibitions obviously played a part, this shift in architectural emphasis indicates that the psychology of building modernization had also changed to reflect the new austerity of wartime frugality. As popular opinion and patriotic consumption shifted from depression to war and from a return to prosperity to victory in Europe and Japan, the exhibitionist architectural strategies of building modernization in the 1930s confronted an unsurprising marketing crisis: they became obsolete. Nonetheless, they had served their purpose well in the previous decade, creating an effective iconography of prosperity and a familiar everyday modernism that changed the face of Main Street America during the Great Depression.

Though supported by a massive public/private, national/local bureaucratic infrastructure and promoted with a grave, sometimes dire urgency, Main Street's modernization had not occurred overnight. Rather, in the years between 1934 and 1943, a gradual transformation had taken place, town by town, block by block, building by building. This transformation was neither complete nor final, but as each $2,000 transaction was financed, each minor architectural commission secured, and each glass and metal storefront designed, fabricated, and installed, Main Street's appearance did change. How could it have not changed? Enough money was ultimately spent on commercial modernization during this period—an estimated $4 to $6 billion in MCP loans and cash payments—to provide a new storefront for each of the 1.5 million retail establishments then operating in the United States.[3] If such figures are too abstract to comprehend modernization's actual impact in the 1930s, a survey of local conditions on a single Main Street will render them more concrete.

Reading, Pennsylvania, as Main Street, U.S.A.

In the 1930s Reading, Pennsylvania, was a medium-sized city of 111,000 inhabitants. As the seat of Berks County, Reading was the social, political, and economic focus for the predominantly agricultural communities that surrounded it. It was also a faultless embodiment of Main Street, U.S.A.—that iconic place *Architectural Forum* described as "big enough to have most of the features and most of the problems found on Main Streets the country over, small enough to retain the small-town atmosphere in which well over half the Nation's retail business is done."[4] Because of its proximity to Philadelphia and New York, both easily accessible by train, Reading was subject to big-city cultural influences that shaped its tastes and consumption habits. To this end, the local newspaper, the *Reading Eagle*, regularly reported on the art, culture, and lifestyles of both cities. Because of its political importance as the Berks County seat and its distinct historical heritage derived from its original Pennsylvania German settlers, Reading also possessed a deep-rooted local pride and a thriving middle-class booster culture that stressed its independence and self-sufficiency as "a city lacking nothing in the essentials of community life."[5] The town had a long tradition of civic organizing, from the City Beautiful to the Christian Temperance movements, and this localism continued through the Depression with, according to the Chamber of Commerce, "a purposeful community spirit that never falters in the face of difficult civic problems."[6] It is not surprising, then, that when the Democratic nominee for governor campaigned in Reading in 1934, he promised "a government by Main Street instead of Wall Street" to emphasize the town's autonomy and its belief in its ability to manage its own affairs.[7]

At its economic base, Reading was factory-dependent and, like many such towns in the 1930s, this "home of progressive industry" was hit hard by the Depression, experiencing labor unrest and widespread unemployment. While Reading possessed a variety of industries, including over forty hosiery and textile mills, its largest employers were allied with the building trades—manufacturers of hardware and fittings, nuts and bolts, terra-cotta, and bricks.[8] This meant that Reading would feel most keenly the building industry's post-1929 downward spiral, especially in the shrinking purchasing power and decreased spending of its under- and unemployed, be they factory workers, contractors, or architects. By 1932 some local unemployed men had built a large shantytown along the Schuylkill River with semipermanent shacks, garden plots, and rabbit hutches. Two years later this "Depressionville" was still in existence, with many of its occupants on federal relief.[9]

The Depression also left its mark on Reading's principal commercial corridor, densely built Penn Street, which stretched east to west for nearly a mile from the foot of Mount Penn to the banks of the Schuylkill River (fig. 6.1). Where Penn crossed Fifth Street, it became Penn Square, the anchor of the downtown core. Though it had been the site of the county courthouse in the eighteenth century, Penn Square had long since become the commercial crossroads of Reading and Berks County, serving a trading area with an eighteen-mile radius and a population of 300,000. In the 1930s it was experiencing the same fiscal and physical ills that plagued so many Main Streets at the time: a rotation of stores and other establishments into and out of business and a cycle of storefront and building occupancy and abandonment. In Reading the impact of the economic downturn was readily apparent by 1931 as signs announcing bankruptcies, expired leases, and merchandise reductions were gradually plastered over Penn Street shop fronts. Along the north side of the 600 block, seven out of fifteen stores had been forced out of business, including the well-established Victor Jewelry, whose "Pay Me Pay Day" sales slogan, spelled out on a two-story flashing marquee, must have seemed to Reading's jobless a bitter reminder of more prosperous times (fig. 6.2). Nearby, Keystone Meat announced that it would "redeem unemployment vouchers" presented by customers in lieu of cash payment, more accurately reflecting current conditions.[10]

Equally bitter to struggling Reading merchants must have been watching the national chains thrive, apparently at their expense, in what had become an all too familiar retail battle between insider and outsider. The depth of this conflict was apparent in the reopening of the locally owned B&J Saylor food store at Fourth and Penn streets after a disastrous fire in 1933. The building, which Saylor's had occupied since 1866, was a modest brick structure that had been gently modernized. Stripped of its decorative cornice and window surrounds, it created an appropriate stylistic balance for Reading's self-described "oldest and most modern food establishment." The advertisements Saylor's placed in the *Reading Eagle* to announce its reopening were anything but balanced, as the store deliberately set itself apart from its chain rivals, claiming that it was "a distinctly Reading Institution," which paid local taxes, supported local charities, employed local workers, and sold local products. But Saylor's went even further in explicitly rejecting the chains, which were described as "larger

Figure 6.1 Aerial view of Reading, Pennsylvania. In the 1930s Reading had a densely built downtown focused on the blocks surrounding Penn Square, at the intersection of Penn and Fifth streets. Penn Square served as the commercial center of the city and surrounding Berks County. (Photo from *The Passing Scene*, vol. 5 [1988], 15. Courtesy of Gloria Jean and George M. Meiser, IX, compilers of a series of histories of Berks County, PA.)

and more powerful business aggregations." It defended its traditional full-service approach to retail with unmistakable anti-chain rhetoric that would have likely resonated with Reading's citizens during the Depression: "Saylor's never approved of the self-service idea . . . the idea that labor should be eliminated from business as a matter of economy. If we are to live on automats, make this an all machine age and put everyone on doles, we better bust civilization or give it all to a few and be done with it."[11]

Though Saylor's successfully fought off chain competition, for most local merchants such efforts were largely fruitless in the face of chain expansion as the Depression wore on. In a single retail category, for example, chain five-and-dimes like Woolworth's, Kresge's, and McCrory's expanded their market share to a commanding 89 percent of all variety store business in Reading, with the five remaining independents attempting to stay open on the leftover 11 percent.[12] While this disproportion was due in part to the low prices the chains offered, it was also due to the ambitious store modernization programs the chains undertook, keeping their units up-to-date as a way of stimulating sales during the economic downturn. In Reading the W.T. Grant dime/department store completely

Figure 6.2 The 600 block of Penn Street, circa 1932. By the early 1930s, Penn Street was feeling the impact of the economic downturn, evident in the vacant storefronts and bankruptcy signs typical of the early years of the Depression. (Photo from *The Passing Scene*, vol. 6 [1988], 73. Courtesy of Gloria Jean and George M. Meiser, IX, compilers of a series of histories of Berks County, PA.)

remodeled its nineteenth-century commercial palazzo on Penn Square. The sole occupant of its building during the Depression, it demolished the top floor and faced the remaining stories in a streamlined veneer of two-tone porcelain enamel veneer that wrapped around the corner in a seamless curve emphasized by a stainless steel canopy above the storefronts.[13] Other chains seized the opportunity presented by Penn Street's apparent retail decline to seek out better locations, larger quarters, or more advantageous leasing terms, often moving in and modernizing after the failure of longtime local establishments. The Federal Furniture Store at 625 Penn had no sooner shut its doors than Thom McAn Shoes installed one of its 1932 "Model F" storefronts.[14] When the Sondheim's clothing store at 700 Penn finally went under, A.S. Beck Shoes took over the street level of this Victorian Gothic structure and modernized it, despite the chain's usual flamboyance, with a restrained design in porcelain enamel by New York architect Horace Ginsbern (fig. 6.3).[15]

As detrimental as the proliferation of the chains might have been to the stability of Penn Street's independent merchants during the Depression,

Figure 6.3 The corner of Penn and Seventh streets. As on so many Main Streets, chain retailers expanded aggressively on Penn Street in the 1930s. Here, A.S. Beck Shoes took over a prime corner location after a locally owned clothing store went out of business. (Photo from *The Passing Scene*, vol. 6 [1988], 75. Courtesy of Gloria Jean and George M. Meiser, IX, compilers of a series of histories of Berks County, PA.)

the high mortality rate of local stores could not be ascribed solely to the perceived incursion of anonymous corporate outsiders. As in other American cities, Reading's real estate industry and property owners had to share the blame, having produced an oversupply of business frontage and retail space. Though much of this seems to have occurred during the boom years of the 1920s, it continued into the Depression as landlords attempted to restore properties to profitability the easiest way they could—by creating retail space. In 1937 the Mansion House Hotel, where important visitors to Reading had stayed for nearly a century, was torn down and replaced by a streamlined taxpayer with three retail units, each occupied by a chain. When the stalwart Penn National Bank & Trust Company folded after nearly sixty years in business, its Georgian-style 1920s headquarters at Eighth and Penn were summarily modernized for retail leasing (fig. 6.4).[16] The banking hall was divided into two store spaces with deep vestibules, off-center curving displays, and glass-block panels illuminating the second floor. Though faced in structural glass to the height of the third-story stringcourse, the building's historical details were intact above—its balusters, oculus, and raking cornice contrasting sharply with the deliberate modernity of the facades below. By 1937 there was nothing remarkable about the storefronts of the former bank—similar ones could be found throughout the United States, and nearly identical ones were already in place on Penn Street itself (Sach's at 714, Gilman's at 660, Martin's at 658).

The New Deal on Penn Street

Throughout the 1930s Reading's retail shuffle was closely watched by a number of commercial organizations dedicated to promoting the city's business affairs. Chief among them were the Board of Trade, founded in 1881 with a mission of "fostering, protecting, and advancing the interests of the business community," and the Merchant's Bureau, committed to keeping retailers "working harmoniously" in the city's commercial interests.[17] Both organizations recognized the immediate impact that the Depression was having on the local economy through direct industrial downturns and trickle-down effects like the reduced purchasing power of consumers. In early October 1934, they joined with individual businesses to celebrate the opening of the Union National Bank (a new institution that emerged out of the Depression-induced failure of three local banks) and what it portended for Reading's future: "This new bank brings happiness to Reading . . . gives additional support to retail and industrial

Figure 6.4 The corner of Penn and Eighth streets in 1938. During the Depression, institutional failure frequently created retail opportunities. After the Penn National Bank & Trust Company folded in 1937, its building was divided and modernized. The storefronts featured structural glass, glass blocks, and extruded aluminum. (Photo from *The Passing Scene*, vol. 5 [1988], 161. Courtesy of Gloria Jean and George M. Meiser, IX, compilers of a series of histories of Berks County, PA.)

development already on the upgrade . . . the pulse of business will be quickened . . . improvements can be made." As the *Reading Eagle* noted, it was the first time since March 1933 that the city's financial institutions were in full operation with "no closed or restricted banks standing as a barrier to business."[18] By that fall the Reading business community had already been actively working to remove any other remaining barriers to business by embracing the diverse recovery programs of the New Deal. And just as the Union National Bank was preparing to open its doors to community lending, the blue eagle emblem of the National Recovery Administration, which the Chamber of Commerce had been distributing since July, was about to be supplanted by the black house logo of the Better Housing Program (BHP).[19]

In Reading, as in towns across the United States, the passage of the National Housing Act and the establishment of the Federal Housing Administration were front-page news in the summer of 1934, especially when FHA head James Moffett explained that the goal of the Modernization Credit Plan was to stimulate building activity in order to prime the pump for broader economic recovery.[20] Given the importance of the building industry, specifically building material manufacturing, to Reading's economic health, the community must have been closely following this particular recovery program. As early as July, local banks were already publicizing their commitment to extend credit to "worthy manufacturers and merchants" in order for "business to forge ahead in this community." Simultaneously, local department stores had already begun to promote "modernization" as a marketing catchword. Pomeroy's, at Sixth and Penn streets, even sponsored a contest for the best essay on the theme of "Why I like the modernized third floor," with the winner getting an all-expenses paid trip to the Century of Progress International Exposition in Chicago.[21] With such early support from the business community, it is not surprising that Reading was one of the first communities in Pennsylvania to organize a local BHP to promote building modernization.

The organization of the Reading and Berks County BHP committee began in October when regional FHA officials met with Reading mayor Heber Ermentrout, who soon announced that Frederick H. Dechant would serve as chairman of the Reading committee. Dechant was a civil engineer and a partner with his architect brother in a well-known Reading design firm founded by their father. In his initial comments to the press, Dechant echoed numerous FHA publicity statements, carefully explaining how the new program would help end five years of stagnant building activity, maintain and improve property values, provide local employment, and get money into circulation. Claiming that it was "very practical" and "prompted by nothing short of necessity," Dechant optimistically concluded that "everyone will welcome the campaign we are organizing locally."[22] He lost no time putting that campaign together along the lines recommended by the FHA: as assistant director, he named Carl Harbster, a sales manager in the wholesale lumber industry; as the head of specialized industry committees, he named Robert Millard, a building material and electrical appliances salesmen, and H. Raymond Hackman, an architect who was also superintendent of school buildings for the Reading district; as head of the women's committee, he named the wife of Allyn C. Taylor, manager of the Reading Gas Company and a former president of the Reading Rotary Club; to head the field campaign, he named Arthur Chafey, a former sales manager and field supervisor for the Atlantic Refining Company. With his team in place and the campaign headquarters prominently installed in the Ganster Building at Fifth and Walnut streets, just off Penn Square, Dechant launched the Reading modernization drive with an "electrical show" and a parade in late October.[23]

Even before Dechant's BHP committee began its work, the MCP was already having a local effect. City building inspector J. Earl Hickman found that the value of permits for repairs and alterations for August 1934 were more than double what they had been for the same period in 1933, jumping from $9,000 to $20,000.[24] Hoping to further encourage this trend, and as a sign of its cooperation with the federal effort, Reading announced that it would exempt building improvements from higher property tax assessments—a decision that the FHA had been actively promoting on the municipal level.[25] Also in anticipation of the modernization drive, city assessor Walter Ringler compiled a report from existing tax records on the number and types of buildings within Reading's corporate limits, including business, industrial, residential, and institutional structures. This report—which found 2,413 businesses occupying 2,173 buildings and 5,313 apartments occupying 1,827 buildings—was essential to the building-by-building canvass that took place in early November to determine the extent of building modernization required in Reading.[26] As the FHA repeatedly asserted in its promotional materials, the community canvass was to be the heart of the modernization campaign, and it was no different in Reading. Several weeks before it was scheduled to begin, Mayor Ermentrout requested that local residents cooperate fully since "what is to be done is in the line of a community welfare project." As the date of the survey drew near, he issued an official proclamation: "In this worthy and vital movement, made possible by the National Housing Act, we urge that every owner of real property act at once," declaring finally that "the opportunity and challenge are yours."[27]

The canvass began on the first Monday in November with one hundred workers covering the entire city, which had been divided into geographic field districts. These men and women were not volunteers but were paid from state and federal relief funds and drawn from local relief rolls by employment coordinator Paul Kintzer. They received several weeks of training at the local YMCA, including technical instructions and inspirational pep talks, with Chairman Dechant reminding them that only "prompt action will arrest the processes of obsolescence."[28] Once they were in the field, they canvassed all properties within a three-mile radius of Penn Square, including not only the city, but its inner suburbs as well. The canvassers' goal was to ascertain whether property owners were contemplating repairs and improvements, the nature and extent of contemplated repairs and improvements, and the possibility and/or necessity of additional repairs and improvements to the property. They also attempted to explain how property owners might prioritize the work, recommending which repairs and improvements could be undertaken at once with a minimum of preparation, thus getting Reading's building workers back on the job as quickly as possible.

Back at the campaign headquarters, Dechant and his staff "poured over statistics compiled by the first group of canvassers" and used the information collected to prepare cost estimates of modernization and repair work, and to provide leads for follow-up calls made by canvassers and contractors. Within one week the canvass had begun to show results, as sixteen repair permits were issued as a direct result of the BHP.[29] Dechant, meanwhile, was doing all he could to maintain high public interest in the campaign as the canvass continued. He released regular statements describing the value of building modernization, as, for example, in the case of an apartment building that was 30 percent occupied before modernization and 75 percent occupied after modernization or a vacant store building that was divided into two retail spaces and immediately leased.[30] Though Dechant was supposedly describing local examples, they tended to lack specifics—a strange omission in a city that frequently published exact addresses for which building permits had been issued—indicating that they were more likely taken from promotional materials prepared by the FHA Publicity Department. In any event, the strategy worked. By the spring of 1935, Reading's two leading financial institutions had extended over $62,000 worth of modernization credit representing nearly $350,000 of private capital unlocked and modernization work undertaken.

Assuming, as the FHA did, that only half this amount was spent on commercial modernization, store improvement expenditures in Reading may have potentially reached between $31,000 and $125,000.[31] With a modest storefront costing between $1,000 and $1,500 in the 1930s, more than a few Penn Street merchants were modernizing their establishments after 1935. And nowhere was this more apparent than with stores in and around Penn Square.

Competitive Modernization at Penn Square

These modernized storefronts, and the newness they embodied, had the same economic and architectural consequences in Reading as they did in towns across the United States: economic because they attracted the attention of customers and tenants; architectural because, as modernization advocates claimed, a single modernized store would force competing merchants to respond in kind, seeking through modernization to convince a skeptical public that their establishments were equally up-to-date. When A&P Supermarkets modernized an abandoned taxpayer at 806–10 Penn Street and opened a combination grocery with an in-house butcher, it posed a serious threat to the independent Keystone Meats just four doors away. This threat was obviously economic in nature, based on A&P's low prices and retail conveniences, which the company stressed in newspaper advertisements that were generally twice as large as those of its local competitors.[32] Keystone's response, however, was architectural. It modernized with a simple glass-and-aluminum facade reminiscent of A&P's own standardized front (fig. 6.5).

The pressure to modernize was not predicated solely on direct competition, however, since, as the FHA argued, the average Main Street merchant was "competing for the customers' dollars, not only with the other merchants in your line of business, but with all merchants in all lines of business."[33] In Reading businesses that had operated successfully for years felt compelled to modernize in the 1930s. At the commercial crossroads of Penn and Fifth streets, the Crystal Restaurant had occupied the same site since the 1890s and the same building with the same storefront since around 1905 (fig. 6.6). Nonetheless, in the late 1930s, though its only direct competition was a small lunch counter, the Crystal modernized, replacing its cast-iron and leaded-glass street-level facade with a sleek molded-steel front possessing an off-center entrance, rounded bulkheads, and neon signs, but given a distinctive note by its use of mirrored panels. When space became available two doors down, the Crystal expanded its

Figure 6.5 The 800 block of Penn Street circa 1935. After chain retailer A&P Supermarkets took over an abandoned taxpayer on Penn Street, local merchant Keystone Meats modernized its storefront, four doors away, as a means of keeping up with the competition. The A&P is visible at the far right of this image. (Photo from *The Passing Scene*, vol. 5 [1988], 159. Courtesy of Gloria Jean and George M. Meiser, IX, compilers of a series of histories of Berks County, PA.)

Figure 6.6 The 500 block of Penn Street circa 1930. The pressure to modernize was felt by many merchants in the 1930s, even when there was no direct retail competition occupying adjacent frontage. By the end of the decade, modernization would almost entirely transform this block at Reading's commercial crossroads. The Crystal Restaurant is at the far right; Tri-Plex Shoes occupies the storefront two doors to the left. (Photo from *The Passing Scene*, vol. 5 [1988], 29. Courtesy of Gloria Jean and George M. Meiser, IX, compilers of a series of histories of Berks County, PA.)

operations, opening a bar (after the 1933 repeal of Prohibition) with a glass-and-metal storefront notable for its gaping bull's-eye window (fig. 6.7). That space had been vacated by Tri-Plex Shoes, a longtime tenant who moved across the street into a building occupied until the Depression by the venerable dry goods store Kline, Eppihimer & Co, in business for over seventy years and regarded as one of the most "metropolitan [sic] establishments in Reading."[34] All traces of Kline, Eppihimer were erased from the street-level frontage by a flashy modernization that included banded letters and speed lines reminiscent of Raymond Hood's McGraw Hill Building (fig. 6.8). These motifs were increasingly familiar around Penn Square and on Main Streets across the United States as a small-scale modern vernacular became commonplace.

Despite similarities in form, materials, and recognizable motifs, each modernized storefront was unique, the product of a singular coordination of merchant, architect, contractor, and manufacturer operating under the auspices of the federal government with the assistance of the local chamber of commerce. One such successful coordination occurred in Reading

Figure 6.7 The 500 block of Penn Street modernized: the Crystal Restaurant and the Crystal Bar both have streamlined storefronts of the most up-to-date materials and forms. (Photo from *The Passing Scene*, vol. 7 [1991], 16. Courtesy of Gloria Jean and George M. Meiser, IX, compilers of a series of histories of Berks County, PA.)

when merchant Ferruccio A. Iacone, architect Elmer Adams, and contractors Paul and Jasper Kase of the J.M. Kase Glass Company modernized a men's clothing store at 519–21 Penn Street that occupied the street-level of a four-story nineteenth-century building. Iacone was an independent merchant who, in a reversal of retail expectations in the 1930s, took over the commercial lease of a space that was vacated by a chain shoe store. Adams was a Berks County native who had been in Reading since he graduated from the University of Pennsylvania in 1929. Though he spent several years as a draftsman in some of Reading's leading firms, including that of local BHP chairman Frederick Dechant, by 1932 he had entered into a partnership with a fellow Penn graduate. When his partner took a job with the U.S. Commerce Department in Washington in 1934, Adams set up as a solo practitioner. Like so many other young architects in the Depression, he seems to have dealt with the slowing of building activity by directing his skills into other channels, executing a series of watercolor renderings of Reading landmarks and scenes of local interest, presumably for sale.[35] Once the plans he prepared for Iacone were approved, Adams submitted them to J.M. Kase. Kase Glass was an art glass studio founded in 1888 that executed a number of important

Figure 6.8 The south side of the 500 block of Penn Street. A constant shuffle of retailers was commonplace in the 1930s. Here, the chain retailer Tri-Plex Shoes modernized the ground floor of the former Kline, Eppihimer & Co. dry goods store. Tri-Plex moved to this location from directly across the street. Note the McCrory's chain five-and-dime to the right. (Photo from *The Passing Scene*, vol. 5 [1988], 73. Courtesy of Gloria Jean and George M. Meiser, IX, compilers of a series of histories of Berks County, PA.)

commissions in and around Reading, notably the windows in the Council Chamber of the Reading City Hall, completed just before the stock market crash in 1929. As specialty stained-glass work fell off during the Depression, Kase increasingly turned to commercial and small-scale glass installations that were more factory-produced than studio-designed. Following Adams's material specifications, Kase placed an order with the Philadelphia Branch Sales Office of the Libbey-Owens-Ford Glass Company of Ohio for products from LOF's Complete Storefront line. Within a few weeks, Iacone's new storefront was installed on Penn Street (fig. 6.9).

Adams's distinctly modern design for the storefront featured a single continuous display area with tall show windows that were flush with the street. These gave way to a T-shaped vestibule that was wide, deep, and au courant for a double-frontage men's store in the 1930s. The vestibule allowed the compartmentalization of the window space into separate display areas for suits, haberdashery, and furnishings, and supposedly responded to the psychology of male consumers, who were thought to dislike street-side window-shopping.[36] Such arrangements were well publicized in the

Figure 6.9 F. A. Iacone men's clothing store at 519–21 Penn Street. The storefront, including the signage and vestibule display cases, was designed by Elmer Adams, a Reading architect, and installed by J.M. Kase Glass Company, a Reading art glass studio, with blue Vitrolite, tan Vitrolux, and Extrudalite trim manufactured by Libbey-Owens-Ford, 1938. (Libbey-Owens-Ford, *Vitrolite Album*. Libbey-Owens-Ford Glass Company Records, MSS-066, Ward M. Canaday Center for Special Collections, The University of Toledo.)

modernization articles, portfolios, and advertisements that appeared regularly in the decade's architecture journals as store re/design became increasingly important to American building culture. To complement this arrangement, Adams chose a rich but subdued color scheme of the type deemed appropriately masculine by retail experts, cladding his facade in Cadet Blue Vitrolite (structural glass) with Extrudalite (extruded aluminum) trim.[37] The signboard above the entrance had inset letters in Cadet Blue Vitrolite and was fabricated of back-lit Vitrolux (color-fused tempered plate glass) used here in Suntan. This cosmetic-like shade indicates the degree to which the marketing of building materials during the Depression had absorbed the lessons of a female-inflected consumer culture. Two smaller badgelike signs flanked the store's name, one with an Iacone "crest" and the other with the H. Kuppenheimer logo (a knight in chain mail)—a brand designation of high-quality menswear. Adams also specified Vitrolux for the top-lit ceiling panels of the vestibule and the display windows, which, like the signs above, glowed dramatically at night, giving the store what LOF would have called twenty-four-hour selling power. Though it was hardly a flamboyant composition, it would have been immediately noticeable to pedestrians leaving the numerous restaurants and movie theaters around Penn Square, especially because its modernism contrasted dramatically with the restrained stripped classicism of the Reading Trust Company building next door.

With its up-to-date styling, materials, and retail configuration, Iacone's shop now possessed a distinct, if momentary, advantage in downtown Reading: distinct, because Adams's design was notable for its modern, formal simplicity; momentary because the storefront's newness would be rapidly overshadowed by the subsequent modernization of other shops on Penn Square. Indeed, even when the store was brand-new, it was already competing with the flashing neon of the modernized stores directly across the street.[38] But such was the transitory nature of the commercial landscape in Reading, as the pressures of competitive modernization brought progressive visual change to Penn Street through seemingly endless iterations of the modern storefront. What was true of Penn Street was true of Main Streets across the United States. A relentless consumerism that grew more intense during the Great Depression produced these storefronts, and the federal government, concerned with stimulating the depressed building industry and the economy as a whole, underwrote them. Corporate manufacturers, desperate to maintain sales of their building materials, promoted them; and architects, anxiously seeking work and eagerly embracing modernism, designed them. Finally, as the observations of social commentators like Robert Lynd and Frederick Lewis Allen indicate, the American public received them, not merely as places to shop, but as a soothing visual panacea for a time of crisis. In other words, F. A. Iacone's storefront was ubiquitous, quotidian, and absolutely emblematic of American culture in the 1930s.

Postwar Penn Square: From Modernized to Marginal to Main Street

The building that once housed Ferruccio Iacone's men's clothing store still stands on the 500 block of Penn Street, but the Vitrolite-Vitrolux-Extrudalite storefront designed by Elmer Adams and installed by the J.M. Kase Glass Company is no longer extant. In its place is a nondescript facade of fake brick and wood siding, an alteration that may have resulted from maintenance necessities, from the vagaries of commercial design, or from a weak nod toward the historic character of the building. The store itself is occupied by a combination pawn shop and check-cashing store, the sort of retail tenant that the Reading BHP in the 1930s would have considered a harbinger of commercial blight, especially in as prominent a location as Penn Square. Today 519 Penn Street—the storefront and the tenant—stands as an indicator of the changes that Reading's commercial district has undergone in the decades since the New Deal effort to modernize Main Street came to a close at the start of World War II. If Reading was emblematic of Main Street, U.S.A., before the war, it remained so after the war. In 1939 the Chamber of Commerce declared proudly that "Reading can surely invite comparison with any city of its size or class in this country."[39] For better or worse, Reading's recent history has borne out this statement.

The war effort that finally brought increased production and employment back to Reading's factories and mills was undoubtedly a boon for downtown merchants. However, once the peacetime economy was in full swing in the years after 1945, Reading's workers were no longer spending their paychecks exclusively in Penn Square. The decentralization that began before the war only intensified with the suburbanization of the postwar period in the form of interstates, subdivisions, shopping centers, and malls. As these spread across the United States, the predominance of the historic center gradually eroded in the 1950s and 1960s. In many cases, Main Street merchants—chains and independents alike—even facilitated the outward movement, hoping to profit from the suburbs in the same way they had once profited from downtown. Solomon Boscov was one such retailer, having opened his first "economy" dry goods store in Reading in 1917, at Ninth and Pike streets on the northern edge of downtown. By the 1930s it had expanded across three storefronts and was regarded as Reading's leading discount department store. Though Boscov modernized this location in 1954, by the early 1960s the company had expanded beyond Reading's commercial core, first to its inner suburbs and then to the rapidly developing townships beyond Berks County. When fire destroyed the original Ninth Street location in 1967, the company did not rebuild, and it abandoned downtown Reading for good.[40]

At this time, it wasn't only the retailers and householders who were decentralizing; industry was as well, with consequences just as debilitating for Main Street merchants and for downtowns as a whole. In Reading manufacturers who had been the city's economic mainstay for decades, including the Reading Hardware & Butt Works and the Berkshire Knitting Mills, began to relocate or to shut down entirely, leaving Penn Square further drained of potential customers and surrounded by underutilized factories.[41] As it had in the 1930s, the federal government once again offered downtown assistance. Now, instead of "modernization," it was "urban renewal" that was put forth as the cure-all of the moment, especially after the introduction of the Model Cities Program in 1966.[42] In many downtowns, however, urban renewal looked more like suburban imitation, and Reading was no exception. Six blocks northeast of Penn Square were slated for demolition, to be replaced by an enclosed shopping mall.[43] Though the project never came to fruition, many buildings in the area were razed anyway, replaced by parking lots that did little to assist struggling merchants. In the early 1970s, the city tried a more modest suburban-style intervention, building an open-air pedestrian mall along the length of Penn Square (fig. 6.10). Featuring enlarged sidewalks, benches, lighting, brick pavers, concrete bollards, planted medians, and limited vehicular traffic, the Penn Square Mall was intended to function like an open-air shopping center, encouraging window-shopping and downtown strolling. But, like many pedestrianization schemes built in this period, the Penn Square Mall never produced the desired Gruen effect, and it was removed in 1993 to allow the reintroduction of buses on the Penn Street corridor.[44]

By that time, Main Street's increasingly dire predicament was once again a subject of intense debates at national and local levels as American cities and towns came to grips with the devastating dual legacies of suburbanization and urban renewal. Communities were forced to acknowledge that the golden era of Main Street had ended, and that it would never again be the nexus of social, civic, and commercial life that it was before World War II. But even as Main Street was confronting this reality, a new attitude emerged. Robert Venturi famously asked: "Is not Main Street almost alright?" and a generation of designers and developers eventually followed his lead. Critics of modern urban planning, such as Jane Jacobs and Kevin Lynch, championed the vitality of the street and the streetscape, proposing that commonplace activities and commonplace buildings all contributed to a unique definition of place that should be celebrated rather than bulldozed.[45] This helped refocus attention on the traditional commercial core, spotlighting precisely those things that made Main Street so successful in its heyday: a concentration and diversity of everyday uses and an eclectic mix of building types and styles. Enhancing these characteristics became a critical part of the downtown revitalization strategies that emerged in the late twentieth century and that are still ongoing at the start of the twenty-first.

In Reading the city's first historic district, listed on the National Register in 1980, centered on the blocks in and around Penn Square,

Figure 6.10 The 400 block of Penn Street circa 1975. To counteract Penn Street's post–World War II decline, Reading tried numerous redevelopment schemes. The Penn Square Mall was a failed attempt to pedestrianize the area through sidewalk amenities and limited vehicular traffic. It was removed in 1993. The abandoned building on the corner is the former B&J Saylor food store, 401 Penn Street; the adjacent State Store is a postwar modernization. (Library of Congress, Prints & Photographs Division, HABS-HAER [HABS PA-5148-1].)

including some that had been threatened with demolition only a few years before. Now, however, Penn Square was lauded for its nearly intact fabric of typical commercial buildings featuring styles "from federal to art moderne"—all reflecting the city's "historic regional strength in retailing."[46] A decade later merchants and property owners formed a Downtown Improvement District (DID) to stimulate commercial activity in Penn Square. With funding from special assessments, the Reading DID sponsors beautification programs (including painting murals, installing holiday lights, and upgrading street furniture); organizes street festivals, parades, and special shopping days; and trains "district ambassadors," who provide information about downtown to locals and visitors alike. The DID also assists property owners in securing facade improvement grants through the Reading Community Development Department.[47] None of these activities would have been out of place on Penn Street during the Great Depression.

In fact, what is so striking about efforts to *revitalize* Main Street today is how closely they resemble efforts to *modernize* Main Street in the 1930s. The buzzword may have changed, but the determination to fight commercial decline through architectural design, local boosterism, community organizing, and economic development is largely the same. These areas of engagement are the basis of the so-called Main Street approach currently advocated by the National Trust for Historic Preservation. Though the trust is a nonprofit organization (albeit one chartered by Congress), it plays a sponsorship and promotional role analogous to that of the Federal Housing Administration during the New Deal. Through its Main Street Center, founded in 1980 after a series of demonstration projects in the late 1970s, the trust provides technical assistance and support to over 1,200 member communities.[48] While this number hardly rivals the 8,000-plus towns that participated in the FHA's program, the trust's sphere of influence is still considerable, since hundreds of additional communities subscribe to its general precepts through various public-private partnerships, as in Reading. In many respects, the National Trust's goals for Main Street today are almost identical to the FHA's in the Depression: that Main Street, however diminished, should retain its economic and cultural importance as a center of employment, as a contributor to the tax base, and as a locus of community pride.

If the two Main Street programs share similar goals and means, there is at least one crucial difference between them. In the midst of the social and economic crisis of the Depression, the FHA promoted the short-term, high-impact solution of building modernization, which utilized the most striking visual hallmarks of contemporary design. The National Trust, by contrast, favors incremental, long-term strategies within the context of historic preservation, which utilize the subtle design tactics of restoration and rehabilitation. In the trust's view, Main Street's successful revitalization is to be based on a vision of the past as embodied in its "traditional" commercial architecture. In the FHA's view, Main Street's successful modernization was to be based on a vision of the future as embodied in its "modern" commercial architecture. In both cases, the storefront is made to represent the aspirations of the district as a whole, with traditional forms embodying what the National Trust perceives as Main Street's pre-WWII heyday and modern forms embodying what the FHA hoped would be Main Street's post-Depression glory days. Of course, *traditional* and *modern* are relative terms, especially within the ephemeral landscape of American commerce, and sometime between 1943 when the FHA program ended and 1977 when the National Trust program began, Main Street's future started to look an awful lot like its past.

Today there are federally approved standards and guidelines for preserving the *historic* modernized storefronts of the 1930s. They have apparently "gained significance over time," though they were never intended to endure much beyond the Great Depression—as virtual architectural consumables, it was understood that they would become obsolete as storefront trends changed.[49] But at a critical moment during the Depression, these storefronts provided an optimistic glimpse of a prosperous tomorrow, one seemingly guaranteed by the machine-age luster of chrome, neon, and glass. Encountering these modernized storefronts seven decades later, we realize that the machine age has ended, that the luster has dulled, and that a prosperous tomorrow is far from certain. But in the preservation of these storefronts, we may also realize something else, something that architects, merchants, consumers, and New Dealers all understood in the 1930s: that Main Street is more significant than just a place to shop.

While this book relies extensively on the editorial and advertising content of architectural trade journals of the 1930s, especially *Architectural Record* and *Architectural Forum*, archival materials were also critical to my research. The most important are the records of the federal government during the 1930s, which are housed at the United States National Archives in Washington, D.C., including the Records of the Federal Housing Administration (National Archives Record Groups 31 and 287) and the Records of the Housing and Home Finance Agencies (National Archives Record Group 207). These record groups contain published reports, pamphlets, and other documents, as well as internal and confidential memos and reports. The Libbey-Owens-Ford Collection in the Ward M. Canaday Center of the University of Toledo contains valuable advertising scrapbooks, annual reports, and in-house corporate publications that reveal LOF's marketing strategies throughout the 1930s. The Special Collections Research Center at the Syracuse University Library houses the papers of several designers who were involved in building modernization in the 1930s, including those of Egmont Arens (Egmont Arens Industrial Design Records Client and Project File, MSS 7), Walter Dorwin Teague (Walter Dorwin Teague Papers, NXSV1044-A), and Morris

Lapidus (Morris Lapidus Papers). Papers and drawings of two important 1930s store designers are housed in the Department of Drawings and Archives of the Avery Architectural and Fine Arts Library at Columbia University: Horace Ginsbern Architectural Records and Papers Collection and Morris Lapidus Photograph Collection.

Introduction

1. Mervyn LeRoy, director, *Gold Diggers of 1933* (Warner Brothers, 1933). Lyrics by Al Dubin and Harry Warren.

2. Franklin Delano Roosevelt, "First Inaugural Address," March 4, 1933, http://www.yale.edu/lawweb/avalon/presiden/inaug/inaug.htm.

3. Quoted in Frederick Lewis Allen, *Since Yesterday* (1939; repr., New York: Harper & Row, 1965), 21.

4. See Sarah Elvins, *Sales and Celebrations: Retailing and Regional Identity in Western New York State, 1920–1940* (Athens: Ohio University Press, 2004).

5. See Alastair Duncan, *American Art Deco* (New York: Harry N. Abrams, 1986); Richard Guy Wilson et al., *The Machine Age in America* (New York: Harry N. Abrams, 1986); Rosemarie Haag Bletter, "The World of Tomorrow: The Future with a Past," in *High Styles: Twentieth-Century American Design* (New York: Whitney Museum, 1985); Justin De Syllas, "Streamform," *Architectural Association Quarterly* 1 (April 1969): 32–41; David Gebhard, "The Moderne in the U.S., 1920–1941," *Architectural Association Quarterly* 2 (January 1970): 4–20; Donald J. Bush, *The Streamlined Decade* (New York: George Braziller, 1975); Claude Lichtenstein and Franz Engler, *Streamlined: A Metaphor for Progress* (Zurich: Lars Müller, [1993]); Martin Greif, *Depression Modern: The Thirties Style in America* (New York: Universe Books, 1975); J. Stewart Johnson, *American Modern* (New York: Abrams, 2000); Barbara Capitman, *Deco Delights* (New York: Dutton, 1988); Robert A. M. Stern et al., *New York 1930* (New York: Rizzoli, 1987); and Richard Striner, "Art Deco: Polemics and Synthesis," *Winterthur Portfolio* 25 (Spring 1990): 21–34.

6. See Jeffrey Meikle, *Twentieth Century Limited* (Philadelphia: Temple University Press, 1979).

7. See Richard Mattson, "Store Front Remodeling on Main Street," *Journal of Cultural Geography* 32 (Spring/Summer 1983): 41–55; Thomas C. Jester, ed., *Twentieth-Century Building Materials* (New York: McGraw-Hill and National Park Service, 1995); Douglas A. Yorke Jr., "Materials Conservation for the Twentieth-Century: The Case for Structural Glass," *Bulletin of the Association for Preservation Technology* 13, no. 3 (1981): 18–29; H. Ward Jandl, "Rehabilitating Historic Storefronts," *Preservation Briefs*, no. 11 (Washington, DC: U.S. Department of the Interior, 1984); "The Preservation of Historic Pigmented Structural Glass," *Preservation Briefs*, no. 12 (Washington, DC: U.S. Department of the Interior, 1984); and Rita Caviglia, "Architecture and Storefronts of the 1930s" (M.A. thesis, Columbia University, 1981).

8. See Kristina Wilson, *Livable Modernism: Interior Decorating and Design During the Great Depression* (New Haven, CT: Yale University Press, 2004); Chester H. Liebs, *Main Street to Miracle Mile: American Roadside Architecture* (1985; repr. Baltimore: Johns Hopkins University Press, 1995); M. Jeffrey Hardwick, *Mall Maker: Victor Gruen, Architect of an American Dream* (Philadelphia: University of Pennsylvania Press, 2004); Richard Longstreth, *The Drive-in, the Supermarket, and the Transformation of Commercial Space in Los Angeles, 1914–1941* (Cambridge, MA: MIT Press, 1999); Bernice L. Thomas, *America's 5 & 10 Cent Stores: The Kress Legacy* (New York: John Wiley and the National Building Museum, 1997); John A. Jakle and Keith A. Sculle, *Fast Food: Roadside Restaurants in the Automobile Age* (Baltimore: Johns Hopkins University Press, 1999); Chuihua Judy Chung, Jeffrey Inaba, Rem Koolhaas et al., *Harvard Design School Guide to Shopping Project on the City 2* (Köln: Taschen and Harvard University, 2001); Catherine Gudis, *Buyways: Billboards, Automobiles, and the American Landscape* (New York: Routledge, 2004); Sharon Zukin, *Point of Purchase: How Shopping Changed American Culture* (New York: Routledge, 2004); Mark Gottdiener, *The Theming of America: Dreams, Visions, and Commercial Spaces* (Boulder, CO: Westview Press, 1997); and Lizabeth Cohen, *A Consumer's Republic: The Politics of Mass Consumption in Postwar America* (New York: Knopf, 2003).

9. See Richard V. Francaviglia, *Main Street Revisited: Time, Space and Image Building in Small-Town America* (Iowa City: University of Iowa Press, 1996); John A. Jakle, *The American Small Town: Twentieth-Century Place Images* (Hamden, CT: Shoestring Press, 1980); and Robert M. Fogelson, *Downtown: Its Rise and Fall, 1880–1950* (New Haven, CT: Yale University Press, 2001).

10. See Max Page, *The Creative Destruction of Manhattan, 1900–1940* (Chicago: University of Chicago Press, 1999); and Daniel Abramson, "Obsolescence: Notes Towards a History," *Praxis* 5 (2003): 106–12.

11. Alison Isenberg, *Downtown America: A History of the Place and the People Who Made It* (Chicago: University of Chicago Press), esp. chap. 4, "Main Street's Interior Frontier," 143–52.

12. See ibid., 368n45.

13. See Richard Pommer, "The Architecture of Urban Housing in the United States During the Early 1930s," *Journal of the Society of Architectural Historians* 37 (December 1978): 235–64; Joseph Arnold, *The New Deal in the Suburbs: A History of the Greenbelt Town Program* (Columbus: Ohio University Press, 1971); Phoebe Cutler, *The Public Landscape of the New Deal* (New Haven, CT: Yale University Press, 1985); Diane Ghirardo, *Building New Communities: New Deal America and Fascist Italy* (Princeton, NJ:

Princeton Architectural Press, 1989); Lisa B. Reitzes, "Moderately Modern: Interpreting the Architecture of the Public Works Administration" (Ph.D. diss., University of Delaware, 1989); and Robert D. Leighninger, "Cultural Infrastructure: The Legacy of New Deal Public Space," *Journal of Architectural Education* 49 (May 1996): 226–36.

14. See Gwendolyn Wright, *Building the Dream: A Social History of Housing in America* (Cambridge, MA: MIT Press, 1981); Andrew Shanken, "Architectural Competitions and Bureaucracy, 1934–1945," *Architectural Research Quarterly* 3, no. 1 (1999): 43–55; and Keller Easterling, *Organization Space: Landscapes, Highways, and Houses in America* (Cambridge, MA: MIT Press, 1999).

Chapter 1

1. Franklin Delano Roosevelt, quoted in Charles W. Hurd, "Roosevelt Lauds Gainesville Spirit in Storm Problem," *New York Times*, April 10, 1936, 1, 3.

2. Earnest Elmo Calkins, "Give Your Town a Personality," *Rotarian*, March 1935, 11, 53–54. The article was reprinted in condensed form in *Reader's Digest*, June 1935, 45–46. See also Calkins, "Beauty the New Business Tool," *Atlantic Monthly*, August 1927, 150–56. Calkins, the creative force behind the Madison Avenue firm Calkins & Holden, had long promoted the reform of American design. Though in private Calkins was apparently an elitist who derided middlebrow taste, in public he was a democratizing booster who claimed a keen social responsibility to bring art and beauty to the masses. Thus, the *Rotarian* was an ideal outlet for Calkins's populist aesthetic agenda since its readers were precisely those members of the middle class whose taste, in his opinion, needed uplifting and whose Depression-blighted communities needed improving. For an analysis of Calkins's role in American advertising, see Michele H. Bogart, *Artists, Advertising, and the Borders of Art* (Chicago: University of Chicago Press, 1995), 207–12; and Jackson Lears, *Fables of Abundance* (New York: Basic Books, 1994), 308–16.

3. John Gunther, *Inside U.S.A.* (New York: Harper & Brothers, 1946), 315.

4. Sinclair Lewis, *Main Street* (New York: F. Collier & Son, 1920), 33–34; Lewis, *Babbitt* (New York: Harcourt Brace Jovanovich, 1922), 61.

5. Lewis, *Main Street*, 268, 417, 5, 131.

6. Lewis, *Babbitt*, 142, 222.

7. Ibid., 222.

8. Frederick Lewis Allen, *Only Yesterday* (1931; repr., New York: Harper & Row, 1964), 146; Robert S. Lynd, "The People as Consumers," in *Recent Social Trends in the U.S.: Report of the President's Research Committee on Social Trends* (New York: McGraw-Hill, 1934), 878–80; Robert S. Lynd and Helen Merrell Lynd, *Middletown in Transition: A Study in Cultural Conflicts* (New York: Harcourt, Brace & World, 1937), 379.

9. Jesse Rainsford Sprague, "New York Is Where the Money Is!" *Saturday Evening Post*, September 14, 1935, 31.

10. Paul Bonner, "Style and the Salesman," *Talk No. 7* (April 1931), Industrial Institute of the Art Center, 8.

11. "Main Street, U.S.A," *Architectural Forum* 70 (February 1939): 74. Bridgeport, Connecticut (population 149,000), was the representative town in the *Forum*'s study.

12. Ilya Ilf and Evgeny Petrov, *Ilf and Petrov's American Road Trip*, ed. Erika Wolf (New York: Cabinet Books and Princeton Architectural Press, 2007), 128.

13. My thanks to an anonymous reviewer of the manuscript for comments that helped clarify this point.

14. This description is derived from the work of cultural geographers and historians of commercial architecture. See especially Richard V. Francaviglia, *Main Street Revisited: Time, Space and Image Building in Small-Town America* (Iowa City: University of Iowa Press, 1996); and Richard Longstreth, *The Buildings of Main Street: A Guide to American Commercial Architecture* (Washington, D.C.: National Trust for Historic Preservation, 1987).

15. See Chester H. Liebs, *Main Street to Miracle Mile: American Roadside Architecture* (1985; repr., Baltimore: Johns Hopkins University Press, 1995); and John A. Jakle, *The American Small Town: Twentieth-Century Place Images* (Hamden, CT: Shoestring Press, 1980).

16. The actual count of stores was 1,543,158. Significantly, in terms of the marginal existence of many small retailers, the "under $12,000 per year" merchants were placed in the "$75,000 or less sales volume" category. See *Annual Supplement of the Survey of Current Business* 10 (1930), 230. See also "Number and Importance of Small Retail Stores Shown in Government Survey," *Real Estate Record*, March 4, 1939, 20–21.

17. See Liebs, *Main Street to Miracle Mile*, 10–16.

18. "Taxpayer" is a real estate term for an inexpensive and temporary structure erected solely to produce rental income to pay taxes on a given piece of land. See Central Housing Committee, *A Glossary of Housing Terms* (Washington, DC: GPO, 1937), 77.

19. Liebs, *Main Street to Miracle Mile*, 10.

20. See Richard Longstreth, "The Neighborhood Shopping Center in Washington, D.C., 1930–1941," *Journal of the Society of Architectural Historians* 51 (March 1992): 5–34; and Longstreth, "The Diffusion of the Community Shopping Center Concept During the Inter-War Decades," *Journal of the Society of Architectural Historians* 36 (September 1997): 268–91. Longstreth distinguished between "neighborhood" and "community" shopping centers according to the extent of the populations they served and the number and kind of stores they accommodated. Longstreth has studied the impact of these new retail areas in detail in his exhaustive examinations of Los Angeles. See Longstreth, *City Center to Regional Mall* (Cambridge, MA: MIT Press, 1997); and Longstreth, *The Drive-in, the Supermarket, and the Transformation of Commercial Space in Los Angeles, 1914–41* (Cambridge, MA: MIT Press, 1999). Park and Shop was designed by Arthur B. Heaton, a District of Columbia architect who directed the Commerce Department's 1933 "Renovize Washington Campaign" and was chair of the Modernization and Planning Committee of the Washington Better Housing Program (BHP) during 1934 and 1935. See chapter 2.

21. Dorothy Ducas, "Is Your Daily Shopping Work?" *House Beautiful* 88 (August 1946): 39.

22. These improvements are detailed in Warren M. Creamer, *Report of a Preliminary Study for the Construction of a Relief Highway to Alleviate Congestion on U.S. Route 1* (Hartford, CT: State Highway Department, 1923), 60–68. See also New England Regional Planning Commission, *The Problem of the Roadside*, Publication No. 56 (Boston: National Resources Committee, 1939).

23. Clarence S. Stein and Catherine Bauer, "Store Buildings and Neighborhood Shopping Centers," pamphlet reprinted with addenda from *Architectural Record* 77 (February

1934): 1–13. Best known for their work on modern housing, Bauer and Stein embraced a broad planning perspective that placed public facilities, transportation, and commercial services on par with housing as crucial elements of a vital community.

24. Ibid., 3, 1, 8, 13.

25. Ibid., 15. Although the over-zoning in L.A. did create a business property surplus, this assertion (credited to Carol Aronovici) is a gross exaggeration. According to Marc Weiss, the six hundred miles of business frontage would have actually served 14 million people at a time when L.A.'s population was 1.2 million and the population of the United States was approximately 120 million. See Marc A. Weiss, *The Rise of the Community Builders* (New York: Columbia University Press, 1987), 96.

26. Stein and Bauer, "Store Buildings," 14–15.

27. Godfrey M. Lebhar, "As We See It," *Chain Store Age*, July 1934, 84.

28. This was the average store volume in the Commerce Department's "under $12,000" category. See note 16 above.

29. Stein and Bauer, "Store Buildings," 1–2. The Census of Distribution was a retail survey of eleven representative cities undertaken in 1926–29 as a joint public/private venture supervised by Herbert Hoover's Commerce Department and funded by the U.S. Chamber of Commerce. Also known as the Consumption Census, the survey provided business with market research and statistics on the sale and distribution of consumer goods during the final years of prosperity. During the Depression, the census was used to forecast trends on recovery through consumption. The Federal Housing Administration's Division of Economics used census data to track buying power and markets for modernization.

30. See *Survey of Current Business* 15 (January 1935): 16–17.

31. See Lebhar, "As We See It," July 1934, 17. Only in 1933 with the commencement of the American Business Census did the Commerce Department begin collecting new data on independent stores. Even then the accuracy of the store mortality rate was uncertain because it was calculated by comparing yearly totals for all independent stores in operation, which did not indicate the degree to which store closures were offset by store openings. See Edward L. Lloyd, "Development of Retail Sales Indexes," *Survey of Current Business* 16 (February 1936): 16–18.

32. Lebhar, As We See It," July 1934, 84. Darrow was head of the National Recovery Review Board.

33. Lynd and Lynd, *Middletown in Transition*, 9, 11–12.

34. For a history of chains, see Godfrey M. Lebhar, *Chain Stores in America, 1859–1962* (New York: CS Publishing, 1962). See also Alan R. Raucher, "Dime Store Chains: The Making of Organization Men," *Business History Review* 65 (Spring 1995): 130–63. For one chain's architectural history, see Bernice L. Thomas, *America's 5 & 10 Cent Stores: The Kress Legacy* (New York: John Wiley, 1997).

35. So they were described in 1924 by retail expert Walter Hayward, cited in Raucher, "Dime Store Chains," 131.

36. Lewis, *Main Street*, 213.

37. John Dos Passos, *Manhattan Transfer* (1925; repr., Boston: Houghton Mifflin, 1976), 369.

38. John Kenneth Galbraith, *The Great Crash, 1929* (1954; repr., Boston: Houghton Mifflin, 1988), 45.

39. Harry W. Schacter, "War on the Chain Store," *Nation* 130 (May 7, 1930): 544. Louisville was one of eleven cities included in the Census of Distribution.

40. "Chain" was defined by single ownership of four or more store units. The grocery field accounted for 20 percent of all retail sales in the country. See "Chain Store Growth Analyzed in Trade Commission Report," *Chain Store Age*, July 1932, 426–27.

41. "The A&P from A to Z," *Business Week*, November 30, 1932, 9. A&P was the world's largest grocer in the 1920s and 1930s.

42. See "The A&P in Fairfield, Conn.," *Fortune*, July 1930, 41–45. For a general analysis of combination supermarkets, see Liebs, *Main Street to Miracle Mile*, 117–30.

43. Allen, *Only Yesterday*, 138.

44. "The A&P in Fairfield, Conn.," 43.

45. Stein and Bauer, "Store Buildings," 5–6. See also Godfrey M. Lebhar, "As We See It: Lower Selling Price," *Chain Store Age*, February 1935, 107.

46. Don Mowry, "How National Chain Benefits the Community," *Chain Store Age*, August 1932, 5. Mowry was a field executive with Sears. See also "The A&P Company as a Whole," *Fortune*, July 1930, 45.

47. So the Lynds characterized the situation of local independents in *Middletown in Transition*, 12.

48. Some chain store executives claimed they had never stopped expanding even during the "three lean years" following the Crash. See "Chain Store Expansion and Construction," appearing monthly in *Chain Store Age*. These listings are not comprehensive since they were submitted by the chains themselves.

49. Nate S. Shapero, "Full Speed Ahead! Is Our Slogan," *Chain Store Age*, January 1933, 71. Shapero was president of Cunningham-Economical Drug Stores, a Detroit-based regional chain with over one hundred stores in Michigan. For more on chains and high rents, see Raucher, "Dime Store Chains," 154–55.

50. R. V. Rasmussen, "We've Profited by the Times," *Chain Store Age*, November 1932, 644, 698.

51. "Chains Spend $37,000,000," *Chain Store Age*, November 1934, 128.

52. "Chain Store Modernization Active, Survey Reveals," *Chain Store Age*, November 1932, 635, 667.

53. Lebhar even sent a telegram to President Roosevelt to this effect, attempting to dispel notions that the chains were self-interested, non-community-minded corporations by demonstrating their patriotism, manifest in their willingness to fight the Depression. Lebhar, "As We See It," *Chain Store Age*, November 1933, 65, 76; Lebhar, "Why This Special Issue?" *Chain Store Age*, November 1932, 633.

54. Frank E. Landau, "Keeping Melville Stores Up-to-Date Is Standard Practice," *Chain Store Age*, November 1932, 654–55; "Melville Remodels 100 Stores," *Chain Store Age*, November 1934, 97–98.

55. Landau, "Keeping Melville Stores," 655, 654. As an executive with the G.C. Murphy variety chain put it, "Our stores must be modern; if not, we make them so." E. M. Mack, "Our Store Must Be Modern; If Not, We Make Them So," *Chain Store Age*, November 1932, 639.

56. "The Way to More Profit," *Chain Store Age*, November 1932, 634.

57. "How Beck Alters Store Fronts to Dominate Districts," *Chain Store Age*, October 1932, 599–600.

58. On the Fifth Avenue store, see "The A.S. Beck Shoe Store," *Architectural Record* 65 (June 1929): 543–53. On the Fulton Street store, see "Store Modernized for the A.S. Beck Shoe Corporation, Fulton Street, Brooklyn, New York," *Architectural Forum* 58 (January 1933): 70–71.

59. "How Beck Alters Store Fronts," 606.

60. "Chains Spend $37,000,000," 128. As building modernization became increasingly popular at mid-decade, distinctions between chain store improvement and chain store expansion were rarely observed. As long as the opening of the new unit involved the renovation of an *existing* building (at least its first floor) and not the construction of a *new* building, it was considered a store modernization regardless of its former occupancy.

61. Shapero, "Full Speed Ahead!" 72; Rasmussen, "We've Profited," 644; "Grand Union Spends $300,000 on New Equipment," *Chain Store Age*, November 1932, 652.

62. Mack, "Our Store," 639.

63. S. J. Besthoff, "Making the New Store Fit Its Location," *Chain Store Age*, January 1932, 31; Schacter, "War on the Chain Store," 544.

64. "We Can Be Thankful," *Chain Store Age*, November 1932, 698.

65. Lebhar, "Why This Special Issue?" 633; "Chains Spend $70,000,000 on Store Modernization," *Chain Store Age*, November 1935, 143.

66. Morris Lapidus, *Too Much Is Never Enough* (New York: Rizzoli, 1996), 94.

67. See Federal Trade Commission, Growth and Development of Chain Stores, Report to the U.S. Senate, 73rd Congress, 2nd Session (Washington, DC: GPO, December 14, 1934).

68. "Chain Store Probe Ends," *Chain Store Age*, July 1934, 84. The independents, not surprisingly, took an oppositional stance. As far as *they* were concerned, the FTC's findings were immaterial and largely inconsequential, and they remained convinced that the chains were actively preying on them in an attempt to drive them out of business.

69. Lebhar, "As We See It," November 1933, 76.

70. Quoted in C. Joseph Pusateri, "Radio Industry," in *The Encyclopedia of Southern Culture*, ed. Charles Regan Wilson and William Ferris (Chapel Hill: University of North Carolina Press, 1989), 938. See also Carl Ryan, "The South and the Movement against the Chain Stores," *Journal of Southern History* 39 (May 1973): 207–22.

71. "The A&P Company as a Whole," 45.

72. Quoted in "Chain Stores Are an Asset," *Chain Store Age*, December 1936, 114. This article describes anti-chain campaigns launched in New England and the Pacific Northwest.

73. William Z. Ripley, *Main Street and Wall Street* (1929; repr., New York: Arno Press, 1973), iv–v, 16.

74. Lynd and Lynd, *Middletown in Transition*, 12, 14, 20, 244. Though Middletown's independents did succeed in engendering animus toward the chains, they were unable to forestall the arrival of additional units of chain grocers, filling stations, and especially women's clothiers between 1932 and 1934. More recent studies of local conditions during the Depression have validated the Lynds' contemporary observations. See Catherine McNicol Stock, *Main Street in Crisis: The Great Depression and the Old Middle Class on the Northern Plains* (Chapel Hill: University of North Carolina Press, 1992); and Sarah Elvins, *Sales and Celebrations: Retailing and Regional Identity in Western New York State, 1920–1940* (Athens: Ohio University Press, 2004).

75. Godfrey Lebhar, "How to Meet Unfair Charges against Chain Stores—1," *Chain Store Age*, November 1935, 106, 142; Lebhar, "How to Meet Unfair Charges against Chain Stores—4," *Chain Store Age*, February 1936, 122, 148. The language employed here reflects a Wilsonian/Brandeisian tradition of an ideal economy driven by small units.

76. Lebhar, "How to Meet . . . —1," 106.

77. Quoted in "Number and Importance of Small Retail Stores Shown in Government Survey," 21. The article quotes William H. Mersole's report on retail sales using data collected between 1929 and 1933.

78. Lynd and Lynd, *Middletown in Transition*, 23.

79. Marquis W. Childs, "Main Street Ten Years After," *New Republic*, January 18, 1933, 264.

80. *Fortune* observed this contradictory consumer position in Fairfield, Connecticut, as early as 1930. While grocery customers were concerned that profits and salaries of their A&P did not remain local, they continued to shop there because of the savings it afforded. "The A&P in Fairfield, Conn.," 42.

81. "Looking Ahead with the Chains," *Chain Store Age*, January 1933, 76.

82. Mansel G. Blackford, "Small Business in America: A Historiographic Survey," *Business History Review* 65 (Spring 1995): 8.

83. Sinclair Lewis, *It Can't Happen Here* (New York: Doubleday, Doran & Company, 1935). Lewis turned the novel into a play for the Federal Theater Project that became one of the FTP's most successful productions. See Barbara Melosh, *Engendering Culture* (Washington, DC: Smithsonian Institution Press, 1991), chap. 1.

84. Quoted in William Leuchtenburg, *Franklin Roosevelt and the New Deal* (New York: Harper, 1962), 148.

85. Raymond Moley, *After Seven Years* (New York: Harper & Brothers, 1939), 24.

86. Ironically, this form of manufacturer-based price control had previously been enacted by the industrial codes of the NRA. Additional fair-pricing legislation was passed in the Miller-Tydings Act of 1937. See Richard Posner, *The Robinson-Patman Act: Federal Regulation of Price Differences* (Washington, DC: American Enterprise Institute, 1976).

87. Stein and Bauer, "Store Buildings," 2.

88. "FHA Modernization Loans," *Real Estate Record*, October 19, 1935, 8.

89. Frederick Lewis Allen, *Since Yesterday* (1939; repr., New York: Harper & Row, 1965), 46.

90. Lynd and Lynd, *Middletown in Transition*, 18.

91. On advertising's denial of the Depression, see Lears, *Fables of Abundance*, 236–38.

92. Arthur C. Holden, "Stabilized Modernization," *American Architect* 147 (September 1935): 37–38. Holden was a New York architect affiliated with the Regional Plan Association. Principally a designer of high-rise apartment buildings, he also collaborated with Lescaze and Shreve on the Williamsburg Houses (1937) and proposed slum clearance projects throughout the 1930s.

93. Bureau of Foreign and Domestic Commerce, *Real Property Inventory 1934, Cleveland, OH* (Washington, DC: GPO, 1934).The selection of the sixty-four representative cities was determined by population, geographical extent, and level of economic development. Inventoried cities ranged from Santa Fe, New Mexico, with 11,000 inhabitants, to metropolitan Cleveland, Ohio, with 1.2 million. The majority, including Atlanta, Seattle, San Diego, and Syracuse, had populations over 50,000 and under 300,000. The largest

cities were excluded from the initial survey because their size rendered them unrepresentative of the nation's typical urban areas. These were surveyed as part of separate, locally initiated, government-funded inventories, the data of which was incorporated into the national statistics. Between 1934 and 1936, data was collected on 203 locales through door-to-door canvassing and direct-mailed landlord surveys. According to the data, housing accounted for over 90 percent of the estimated 30 million structures in the United States. As the RPI saw it, though the standard Main Street type was "principally a store building," it almost always had "flats above or behind."

94. Inventory data was both structural and financial and also included information on the number, type, and age of buildings and their duration of current occupancy and vacancy rates; levels of rents and property values; and their market fluctuations since 1929. Data was divided into structural and financial classifications for purposes of analysis and, in fact, was collected in two separate but fully coordinated inventories. See BFDC, *Financial Survey of Urban Housing* (Washington, DC: GPO, 1937).

95. See "Definition of Terms" in Peyton Stapp, *Urban Housing: A Summary of the Real Property Inventories Conducted as Work Projects, 1934–1936* (Washington, DC: GPO, 1938), 315–17. This summary report was prepared by the WPA's Division of Social Research.

96. FHA, *Second Annual Report* (Washington, DC: GPO, 1936), 40–41. See also FHA, *Housing Fact Series No. 2* (Washington, DC: GPO, 1935); FHA, *Analysis of the Real Property Inventory and Financial Survey for Peoria, Illinois* (Washington, DC: GPO, 1935); FHA, "Markets for Modernization," in *Construction and Real Estate Data* (vol. c, sec. 1), February 9, 1935; and FHA, *Structure and Growth of Residential Neighborhoods in American Cities* (Washington, DC: GPO, 1939).

97. FHA, *Structure and Growth of Residential Neighborhoods*, 108–9.

98. FHA, Analysis of the Real Property Inventory, 103.

99. FHA, *Structure and Growth of Residential Neighborhoods*, 108.

100. "Survey Shows Many Stores in Need of Repairs," *FHA Clip Sheet* 11 (no. 1). "Store Modernization Survey of Department of Commerce Brings Interesting Conclusions," *Building and Modernization*, November 1936, 10–11.

101. These figures are cited in FHA, "Markets for Modernization."

102. The National Retail Dry Goods Association's widely circulated figure was based on an extremely small sample and had a far greater margin of error than the government's figure. The *Forum*'s figure appeared to be taken from BFDC statistics. See "Modernize Main Street," *Architectural Forum* 63 (July 1935): 51.

Chapter 2

1. Quoted in "Text of President's Speech at Gainesville," *New York Times*, March 24, 1938, 6.

2. "Tornado Over Gainesville," *Architectural Forum* 66 (February 1937): 154, 157.

3. "Gainesville Left in Ruins," *New York Times*, April 7, 1936, 1.

4. FHA, *Modernize for Profit* (Washington, DC: GPO, 1935), 2, inside back cover.

5. FHA, untitled typescript statement, stamp-dated April 15, 1936, 4 [NA RG 287, box y739].

6. Perkins is quoted in congressional testimony. See U.S. House of Representatives, 73rd Congress, 2nd Session, *National Housing Act: Hearings before the Committee on*

Banking and Currency (Washington, DC: GPO, 1934), 66 (hereafter *1934 House Hearings*).

7. This included $300 million in residential building and $100 million in commercial building. See U.S. Department of Labor, Bureau of Labor Statistics, "Value of Building Construction as Indicated by Building Permits, 1925–1941," reprinted in Broadus Mitchell, *Depression Decade*, vol. 9 of Economic History of the United States (New York: Holt, Rinehart and Winston, 1947), 447. Estimates of building activity vary widely. Some period sources used an activity "aggregate"; the FHA used building permits as the basis for its estimations.

8. For a discussion of how unemployment affected the architecture profession in particular, see my "The Odd-Job Alleyway of Building," *Journal of Architectural Education* 58 (May 2005): 24–40.

9. Cited in U.S. Senate, 73rd Congress, 2nd Session, *National Housing Act: Hearings before the Committee on Banking and Currency* (Washington, DC: GPO, 1934), 168 (hereafter *1934 Senate Hearings*). Colin Gordon cites the figure of 2.5 million workers in the building trades throughout the 1920s. See Gordon, *New Deals: Business, Labor, and Politics in America, 1920–1935* (Cambridge: Cambridge University Press, 1994), 117. Estimates of total unemployment released by government agencies, policy institutes, trade associations, and labor unions ranged from 12 to 17 million for 1933 and 1934. See Mitchell, *Depression Decade*, 453. Perkins put the range between 8 and 17.5 million, accepting 13 million as a fairly accurate count.

10. *1934 Senate Hearings*, 168–69. The latter figure was cited in the *Senate Hearings* and by the NRA's Durable Goods Industries Committee, 286–87.

11. *Congressional Record* 78 (part 9, May 14, 1934), 8739.

12. This included the work of the Federal Emergency Relief Administration (FERA), the Civil Works Administration (CWA), and the National Recovery Administration (NRA).

13. *Congressional Record* 78 (part 9, May 14, 1934), 8740. Many businessmen believed that direct relief was undermining the American work ethic. Roosevelt felt that it was too much of a financial burden on the nation. See William Leuchtenburg, *Franklin Roosevelt and the New Deal* (New York: Harper, 1962), 90–92.

14. The NEC was essentially a cabinet committee whose membership included Labor Secretary Perkins, the NRA's Hugh Johnson, and Home Owners' Loan Corporation (HOLC) chairman John H. Fahey. The executive director was Frank C. Walker, a longtime political ally of Roosevelt and treasurer of the Democratic National Committee.

15. "Home-Loan Groups Plan Building Aid," *New York Times*, January 30, 1934, 33. This NEC meeting is described in Marriner S. Eccles, *Beckoning Frontiers: Public and Personal Recollections* (New York: Knopf, 1951), 145.

16. These included the Johns-Manville Million-Dollar Fund, begun in 1931, which encouraged home owners to repair and modernize using Johns-Manville's asbestos building materials, purchased on installment with added interest. The company claimed the fund was fulfilling a civic need since "in many communities there is a lack of credit facilities to finance needed home repairs and improvements." The fund is described in *101 Practical Suggestions on Home Improvement* (New York: Johns-Manville, 1934), 2. See also *1934 House Hearings*, 329–46; and *1934 Senate Hearings*, 293–94. The for-profit Rehabilitation Corporation—organized by Johns-Manville, Westinghouse, and U.S. Rubber—offered credit financing for modernization to owners of "obsolete" income-producing

buildings. The corporation's stated goal was "improving the depressed real estate situation"; to receive financing, building owners had to use the products of participating manufacturers. See "Big Companies Join in Rehabilitation," *New York Times*, October 2, 1932, sec. IV, 8. Herbert Hoover's National Committee on Reconditioning, Remodeling, and Modernizing, established in 1932, involved no government money and was essentially a promotional campaign organized by the U.S. Chamber of Commerce and the National Association of Real Estate Boards (NAREB). The committee's function was "to cooperate with every community interested in promoting repairs and improvements of commercial, home, and industrial structures for the purpose of energizing industry and relieving unemployment." See "National Drive Is Pressed for Repair Work to Produce $3.5 Million Wages," *New York Times*, August 17, 1932, 19.

17. See, for example, Randolph Williams Sexton, *American Commercial Buildings of Today* (New York: Architectural Book Publishing, 1928), 154.

18. "Remodeling, Modernization, Repair . . . ," *American Architect* 146 (April 1935): 10. Figures are from "Value of Building Construction as Indicated by Building Permits," reprinted in Mitchell, *Depression Decade*, 447.

19. The other members of the subcommittee were Winfield Riefler, a Federal Reserve economist; James Daigler, a housing expert; and Frank Watson, a RFC lawyer. Eccles would shortly be appointed a governor of the Federal Reserve Board. Deane was in Washington as a special assistant to Averell Harriman of the NRA.

20. Eccles, *Beckoning Frontiers*, 148, 142–43. See also Arthur H. Schlesinger Jr., *The Age of Roosevelt: The Politics of Upheaval* (Boston: Houghton Mifflin, 1960), 237–41.

21. In practice, this meant that lenders would be reimbursed for 100 percent of their losses on bad loans as long as the amount of total losses did not exceed 20 percent of total modernization funds that lenders advanced. Statistical research showed that the loss ratio on similar loans was around 3 percent. See FHA, *Modernization Credit Plan, Bulletin No. 1* (Washington, DC: GPO, 1934).

22. Eccles, *Beckoning Frontiers*, 149, 151; "Roosevelt Acts to Speed Building Trades Recovery," *New York Times*, May 15, 1934, 1. Eccles credited Winfield Riefler with the co-invention of the loan insurance mechanism.

23. A related goal was to raise the amount of the average loan from $400 to $10,000. "50,000 Modernization Loan Bill Signed by President," *Building Modernization*, June 1935, 15; FHA, *National Housing Act as Amended and Provisions of Other Laws Pertaining to the FHA* (Washington, DC: GPO, 1935), 2.

24. Following FHA usage, "residential" is narrowly defined in this chapter. Multiple-family residential buildings like tenements and apartment houses were excluded from this definition because they were income producing and/or had commercial establishments occupying their first or second floors. See Central Housing Committee, *A Glossary of Housing Terms* (Washington, DC: GPO, 1937).

25. *1934 House Hearings*, 174; *1934 Senate Hearings*, 159. The witnesses appearing in congressional hearings reiterated the objective of generating as much lending and building activity as possible to counteract the severity of the building industry depression and its tremendous impact on national recovery. The witness roster included New Deal officials, building and banking professionals, and representatives of trade and professional organizations related to construction, architecture, and manufacturing.

26. The figure is cited in FHA, *First Annual Report* (Washington, DC: GPO, 1935), 1. After the passage of the National Housing Act, state banking regulations were liberalized

to allow banks to make this type of noncollateral loan. See "Correspondence between State Governors and President Roosevelt Concerning FHA Legislation, 1934–35" [NA RG 31, FHA Records, entry #11].

27. In congressional hearings, B&L directors and trustees were characterized as "small tradesmen in their communities, who know the properties and a good deal about these homes in their immediate neighborhood." See *1934 House Hearings*, 215. Allowing these diverse credit agencies to make character loans required changes to banking regulations, including allowing B&Ls to receive depositor insurance similar to that extended by the Federal Deposit Insurance Corporation, which guaranteed bank deposits of up to $5,000.

28. The loan applicant was required to provide the particulars of the property to be modernized, including building location, value, rent or mortgage payment amounts, and building type. In addition, the borrower was required to itemize the modernization work he or she wished to undertake, having already secured estimates for materials and labor. The financial institution then checked the proposed modernization work against the FHA's lists of eligible equipment and alterations. See FHA, *Modernization Credit Plan*, 23–24. See also FHA, *Eligible Improvements to Property Financed Under Title I, National Housing Act Amendments of 1938* (Washington, DC: GPO, 1938). Proper use of this loan relied on the good faith of the borrower since there was no regulated follow-up except in the case of payment default.

29. FHA, *Modernization Credit Plan*, 4–5. The FHA encouraged commercial banks in the larger cities to handle this type of "indirect" loan in order to increase their volume of Title I business and suggested that banks actively cultivate "working arrangements" with contractors, dealers, suppliers, department stores, utilities, architects, and real estate agents to whom the bank would offer volume discounts when purchasing the paper they held on modernization loans. Though "profitability" was the first reason given here for increasing Title I business, also included were goodwill, reemployment, and community improvement. See FHA Circular, "How Banks Can Increase Their Title I Business," August 31, 1936. [NA RG 287, box y740].

30. "Speech of Roger Steffan before the Convention of the Ohio Building Association League, Cincinnati," FHA press release no. 73, October 3, 1934, 1.

31. *1934 House Hearings*, 71.

32. Arthur Gross, an expert on personal credit, quoted in *1934 Senate Hearings*, 185, and *1934 House Hearings*, 345–47.

33. After World War II, the MCP was reinstated to assist in the transition to a peacetime economy, but in 1948 all nonresidential and commercial buildings were excluded from loan insurance as Title I finally became a true housing program.

34. *1934 Senate Hearings*, 24–25.

35. Though the FHA promoted both Title I (modernization credit) and Title II (mortgage finance) through the Better Housing Program, for the period June 1934–December 1935 the BHP promoted Title I almost exclusively. Throughout this chapter, "BHP" refers to efforts related to the modernization program.

36. In practice, modernization did not always provide an economic boost to the tax base since many state and local governments exempted property improvements from assessment in order to stimulate modernization. This meant that improved properties were not assessed at higher values; as a result, a property owner's tax bill remained static, at least for the year in which the improvements were made and possibly for an extended

period depending on the jurisdiction. By January 1935 modernization tax exemptions were on the books in nearly twenty states.

37. "City 'Housing Month' Declared by Mayor," *New York Times*, November 20, 1934, 12.

38. Robert S. Lynd and Helen Merrell Lynd, *Middletown: A Study in Modern American Culture* (1929; repr., New York: Harcourt, Brace & World, 1956), 490–91.

39. "Modernization Drive Sweeps Nation," *Better Housing*, October 15, 1934, 1. According to the 1930 census, there were 1,841 towns in the United States with a population over 5,000. Only Delaware, Idaho, Nevada, and Wyoming had towns with a population under 5,000 among their ten largest cities. See FHA, Division of Research and Statistics, *General Economic Data, Volume A*, 1934–35 [NA RG 207, Records of Housing and Home Finance Agencies, vol. 1].

40. The FHA acknowledged the Liberty Loan Drives as a model for its campaign in its *First Annual Report*, 4.

41. See "Wide Housing Plan Awaits Approval," *New York Times*, March 30, 1934, 23.

42. As a business organization, the FHA claimed it was run not by politicians or bureaucrats, but by businessmen, including Albert Deane, MCP co-creator now on long-term leave from General Motors, as deputy administrator in charge of Title I, and Roger Steffan, a vice president of the National City Bank of New York and a personal loan specialist, as director of the Division of Modernization Credits. See FHA, "Proceeds of National Conference of American Bankers Association Liaison Officers," Washington, DC, August 14, 1934, 12, 5, 3 [NA RG 287, box 737].

43. "Speech by Ward Canaday at Home Furnishing Industries' Dinner, Chicago," FHA press release no. 168 (January 10, 1935), 15 [NA RG 287, box y748]; FHA, "Proceeds of National Conference," 12, 5, 3.

44. FHA, "Proceeds of National Conference," 12–13, 6. Canaday was advertising director for the Willys-Overland Motor Company until he started his own ad agency in the 1920s. Concurrently, he organized a car finance corporation and lobbied for the passage of the NHA. In the late 1930s, he returned to Willys-Overland, overseeing the development of the Jeep for the military during WWII.

45. FHA, *First Annual Report*, 12; "Gets 60,000 Booklets," *Better Housing*, September 20, 1934, 3. See also "Order Form for Publicity Materials" and "Suggested Maximum Quantities of Publicity Material," in FHA, *Portfolio of Publicity for Use of Community Campaign Committees* (Washington, DC: GPO, 1934), 103–4. For calculating order quantities, the FHA dividing the nation's cities into ten size ranges and assigned each range with a minimum and a maximum.

46. The FHA promoted the *Clip Sheet* nationally through a direct-mail campaign to the nation's newspaper editors, encouraging its use in special Modernization and Better Housing pull-out sections that were similar to the automobile sections developed after WWI to increase advertising and sales.

47. "Modernized on Main Street," *Clip Sheet* 8, no. 7 (1936).

48. Newspapers are cited in "Confidential Supplement to FHA Press Digest #41," October 2, 1934 [NA RG 287, box y748]. The FHA monitored this usage through a private-sector clipping service that handled collection of national press, tie-in advertising, and newspaper usage. See Media Records, *Daily and Weekly Newspapers in Active Cooperation* and *Distribution of Newspaper Advertising*, 1935 [NA RG 287, box y742]. In-house press coverage was summarized in a daily *Press Digest* circulated throughout the agency.

Figures cited in FHA, *First Annual Report*, 1, and an FHA broadside stamped January 18, 1936 [NA RG 287, box y742].

49. At the time the *News Flashes* were distributed, there were approximately fifteen thousand movie theaters in the country, all wired for sound projection. *Better Housing News Flashes, Nos. 1–9* (FHA and Pathé, 1935–38?) [NA RG 031, items 31.1–31.9]. Figures cited in FHA broadside stamped January 18, 1936 [NA RG 287, box y742].

50. FHA, "Supplement No. 3-A" and "Supplement No. 3-C" in *Radio Portfolio* (Washington, DC: GPO, 1936); "Radio Used Effectively in Chicago" and "Women's Division Activities at Station WCOP," *Better Housing*, May 13, 1936, 4; "Unique Radio Program Takes Housing Message to Nation," *Better Housing*, November 12, 1934, 6; "Radio Broadcast Schedule," stamped January 22, 1935 [NA RG 287, box y742].

51. Popular economist Stuart Chase observed at the end of the 1920s that the businessman had become "the dictator of our destinies" and the "final authority on the conduct of American society." This did not really change as prosperity became depression, notwithstanding the hopeful attitudes of liberal thinkers who predicted that the economic collapse would spell the end of business hegemony. If anything, the collapse valorized the privileged position of the American businessman since when the federal government came to his assistance via the Reconstruction Finance Corporation, it was a straightforward bailout that preserved the business status quo and the capitalist democracy along with it. See Stuart Chase, "Prosperity—Believe It or Not," *Nation* 129 (October 23, 1929): 460–62. See also Frederick Lewis Allen, *Only Yesterday* (1931; repr., New York: Harper & Row, 1964), 133. For more on this interpretation of the RFC, see James Stuart Olson, *Saving Capitalism: The Reconstruction Finance Corporation and the New Deal, 1933–1940* (Princeton, NJ: Princeton University Press, 1988).

52. FHA, *Community Campaign: How Your City Can Get the Greatest Benefit from the National Housing Act* (Washington, DC: GPO, 1934), 3, 5. FHA, "Proceeds of National Conference," 11.

53. FHA, *Community Campaign*, 6. See Lynd and Lynd, *Middletown*, 285–309. See also Robert S. Lynd and Helen Merrell Lynd, *Middletown in Transition: A Study in Cultural Conflicts* (New York: Harcourt, Brace & World, 1937), 402–86.

54. See "Local Chairmen of Better Housing Program Committees, Released 2 November 1934" [NA RG 287, box y749]. See also "Group to Aid Housing Program, Borough President Levy Head Committee," *New York Times*, September 10, 1934, 32.

55. "Los Angeles' $100,000,000," *Architectural Forum* 65 (September 1936): 244. Senator McAdoo, a Democrat and early supporter of the MCP, served on the Senate Banking and Currency Committee, which oversaw the creation of the National Housing Act. So impressive was this advisory group that administrator James Moffett addressed their first meeting in January 1935. See FHA press release no. 192 (January 31, 1935), 1–7 [NA RG 287, box y748].

56. "Chicago Launches Spirited Campaign," *Better Housing*, September 27, 1934, 1; "Campaign to Spur FHA Program Here," *New York Times*, October 17, 1934, 25.

57. The American Legion was especially supportive of the MCP's reemployment aspect, since so many WWI veterans were out of work—a situation that gave rise to the 1932 Bonus Army encampment on the Anacostia Flats. After congressional approval of payment of the veterans' bonus in the spring of 1936, the FHA secured the cooperation of the American Legion to encourage vets to invest bonuses in modernization or new construction. See FHA, "Dear Veteran" direct mail piece (undated) [NA RG 287, box y741] and "New Program for Veterans Is Launched," *Better Housing*, May 13, 1936, 1.

58. Contribution amounts were determined by the number of firms in the community and the potential volume of business those firms could expect to receive from the modernization drive.

59. FHA, *Community Campaign*, 11; "Women and Youth Contribute to Success of Housing Drive," *Better Housing*, December, 1934, 4; "Women Organize Housing Drives," *Better Housing*, October 22, 1934, 8. See also FHA, *Ways for Women to Participate in the BHP* (Washington, DC: GPO, 1935).

60. "Clubs, National Bodies Support Women's Division," *Women's Page Clip Sheet* 1 (July 1935).

61. See "Revised List of Accepted Institutions as of 24 August 1934" [NA RG 287, box y737]; "National Housing Act—Title I Financial Institutions as of 29 June 1935" [NA RG 287, box y740]; FHA, *Financial Institutions That Are Extending Modernization Credit, Form FHE 61* (Washington, DC: GPO, September 1935) [RG 287, box y 740].

62. "New Jersey Bank Opens Campaign," *Better Housing*, November 30, 1934, 9, 7.

63. FHA, *Seven More Banks Tell How and Why They Make Modernization Loans* (Washington, DC: GPO, 1934).

64. FHA, *Community Campaign*, 11, 19.

65. "Exhibit the Newest of the New," *Better Housing*, September 20, 1934, 2; "Exhibits A–C: Typical Better Housing Headquarters," *Report of the BHP Headquarters for the State of New Jersey* (1936); "Expositions," *Better Housing*, October 8, 1934, 4; "30 Cities Open Campaigns with Better Housing Shows," *Better Housing*, October 15, 1934, 1, 8.

66. FHA, *Press Digest*, August–October 1934 [NA RG 287, box y748]. See also "Planning the Newspaper Office," *Architectural Record* 82 (November 1937): 75.

67. "Theaters Conduct Exhibits," *Better Housing*, November 1, 1934, 4; FHA, "Dear Hospital Administrator" and "Dear Retailer," direct-mail pieces (no date, 1935?) [NA RG 287, box y740].

68. FHA, *Portfolio of Publicity*, 2; FHA, "Announce Plans for Staging City-Wide Modernization Campaign," *Portfolio of Publicity*, 43; FHA, *Portfolio of Publicity*, 15, 29. See also "Publicity Folio Extensively Used," *Better Housing*, September 27, 1934, 1.

69. "Unique Contest Brings Prospects," *Better Housing*, December 12, 1934, 8.

70. Cited in the following issues of *Better Housing*: October 8, 1934; October 2 and 22, 1934.

71. "House Organ," *Better Housing*, May 13, 1936, 1. Ideas published in the newsletter were intended to inspire other BHPs. See "Spread the News" and "What Is Your Best Idea?" *Better Housing*, September 20, 1934, 1–2.

72. This description is based on parades held in Passaic, New Jersey; Jackson, Mississippi; Lewiston, Idaho; Dickinston, North Dakota; and Oakland, California. FHA, *Community Campaign*, 17, 9.

73. For middle-class fears of communism and labor in the 1930s, see Lynd and Lynd, *Middletown in Transition*, 428–33.

74. On these 1920s commercial pageants, see William Leach, *Land of Desire: Merchants, Power, and the Rise of a New American Culture* (New York: Pantheon, 1993).

75. *Better Housing News Flashes*, 1934–35, 4; and FHA, *Community Campaign*, 5. The FHA claimed that during the first two weeks of the national drive nearly thirty modernization demonstrations had commenced, with dozens more in the planning stages. See

"This Picture Tells a Story," *Better Housing*, November 12, 1934, 8; "Goodwill Cottage," *Clip Sheet* 5, no. 10 (1935); "Modernized in 4 Hours," *Better Housing*, December 1, 1934; "Thousands Visit Seattle Exhibit," *Better Housing*, November 12, 1934, 2.

76. "Chicago Stages Building Exhibit," *Better Housing*, October 22, 1934, 4; "House Rebuilt in Six Hours before World's Fair Crowd," *Better Housing*, November 1, 1934, 1–2.

77. See "Ancient House Will Get New Dress at Fair" and "Big Aerial Show Thrills Crowds at World's Fair," *Chicago Daily Tribune*, October 24, 1934, 11.

78. FHA, *Second Annual Report* (Washington, DC: GPO, 1936), v.

79. Ibid., 46–47. This figure represents Title I expenses and the FHA's publicity budget, which at that point was spent almost exclusively on Title I. The operating expenses of the field offices totaled $6.5 million, a large percentage of which must also be assigned to Title I. There were considerable additional outlays made by the FHA's sixty-three field offices that are not included in this figure.

80. Marc A. Weiss, *The Rise of the Community Builders* (New York: Columbia University Press, 1987), 152–53.

81. FHA, *Architects, Contractors, Building Supply and Other Merchants . . .* (Washington, DC: GPO, 1934), 1, 3.

82. Sinclair Lewis, *Main Street* (New York: F. Collier & Son, 1920), 416; Sinclair Lewis, *Babbitt* (New York: Harcourt Brace Jovanovich, 1922), 12, 244; Allen, *Only Yesterday*, 189; Frederick Lewis Allen, *Since Yesterday* (1939; repr., New York: Harper & Row, 1965), 127.

83. Lynd and Lynd, *Middletown*, 222, 285–309.

84. Lynd and Lynd, *Middletown in Transition*, 3, 123, 402–86.

85. Dr. Francis Townsend's plan promoted a revolving pension fund designed to end mass unemployment and financed by a business tax. Senator Huey Long's Share-Our-Wealth promoted the liquidation of all personal fortune with the proceeds divided equally among the American populace.

86. Quoted in Studs Terkel, *Hard Times: An Oral History of the Great Depression* (1970; repr., New York: Pantheon, 1986), 250.

87. FHA, *Architects, Contractors*, 1.

88. Lynd and Lynd, *Middletown*, 492.

89. Lewis, *Babbitt*, 307, 258, 222.

90. FHA, *Architects, Contractors*, 9; FHA, *Community Campaign*, 21.

91. "Speech by Albert Deane to National Paint and Varnish Association," FHA press release no. 102 (November 1, 1934), 4; "Address of Ward M. Canaday before Rotary Club of Washington, DC," FHA press release no. 76 (October 3, 1934), 2; Ward M. Canaday, "Great Potential Sales Field Created by National Housing Act," transcript of speech to Sales Executives Club in New York City, September 27, 1934, 1.

92. FHA, *Community Campaign*, 22.

93. See Thorstein Veblen, *Absentee Ownership and the Business Enterprise in Recent Times* (1923; repr., New York: Augustus M. Kelley, 1964); and Alfred Kazin, "H. L. Mencken and the Great American Boob," *Menckeniana* (Fall 1986): 1–8.

94. Lewis, *Babbitt*, 171.

95. FHA, *Community Campaign*, 22–23. FHA, *Better Selling of Better Housing, Complete Program* (Washington, DC: GPO, 1935), 8. In Boston the campaign employed a

system in which every city block was numbered and considered a separate canvassing unit. In New Rochelle, less than fifteen square miles in area, ninety-seven districts were created. "Canvassing Method," *Better Housing*, November 19, 1934, 5; "Canvassers Reach All within Limits," *Better Housing*, November 30, 1934, 4.

96. "Rhode Island Active," *Better Housing*, October 22, 1934, 5.

97. "Jersey Town Wants to Get Dressed Up," *Better Housing*, October 22, 1934, 6. See also "Use Billboards," *Better Housing*, November 1, 1934, 2. The FHA supplied such billboards (FHA 211) to the BHPs free of charge and display-ready but for the place and date of the canvass.

98. "Cities in Georgia Set Fine Record," *Better Housing*, December 12, 1934, 2; "Calls on Tenants and Owners," *Better Housing*, December 21, 1934, 3. The Atlanta canvass included a door-to-door survey of African American property owners, identified as the first of its kind in the country by the city's black newspaper. See "Housing Act Is Boon to Atlantans," *Atlanta Daily World*, October 31, 1934, 1, 4; FHA, *San Diego Sells an Idea: Results in Graphic Form*, No. 1 (Washington, DC: GPO, 1935), 6; "From House to House," *Better Housing*, November 12, 1934, 3.

99. "Salesmen Include 'Better Housing' in Bag of Wares," *Better Housing*, October 15, 1934, 4.

100. See "Reduces Relief Rolls" and "Canvasser Uncovers Big Repair Project," *Better Housing*, November 30, 1934, 6, 8; and "Takes Men Off Relief," *Better Housing*, October 8, 1934, 2.

101. U.S. House of Representatives, 74th Congress, 2nd Session, *Extending Title I of the National Housing Act: Hearings before the Committee on Banking and Currency* (Washington, DC: GPO, 1936), 33–41 (hereafter *1936 House Hearings*). See also "New Life for FHA," *American Architect* 148 (April 1936): 4; and State of New Jersey BHP, "1936 Report of Better Housing Headquarters" (WPA Project #S 5059) [NA RG 287, box y741].

102. Worker attitudes toward relief in the 1930s are summarized in Leuchtenburg, *Franklin Roosevelt*, 118–20. See also Terkel, *Hard Times*, esp. 419–38.

103. "Campaign Teams Formed," *Better Housing*, October 22, 1934, 2; "Quota Plan Succeeds in Kansas Campaign," *Better Housing*, November 30, 1934, 1, 5. On factors determining quotas, see "Markets for Modernization," in FHA Division of Research and Statistics, *Construction and Real Estate Data*, vol. C, sec. I (FHA Activities), 1935; and "Modernization and Repair Notes Based on Quota," confidential report from L. R. Gignilliat Jr., FHA Field Division Director, to Regional, State, and District Directors, October 31, 1935.

104. Rankings are explained in "Sure of Success, Chairmen Report," *Better Housing*, November 30, 1934, 1. Rankings were reported in "News from the Front." See *Better Housing*, October 22, 1934, 7.

105. The leading sales publications were those of the Dartnell Corporation of Chicago, which had tens of thousands of business subscribers during this period. See Lynd and Lynd, *Middletown*, 237. In 1931 Frederick Lewis Allen observed that the high-pressure, hard-sell pitch, which quotas and rankings fomented, had become an accepted part of consumer culture in the 1920s. Allen concluded that "if you could get away with such exploits, it helped business, and good business helped prosperity, and prosperity was good for the country." In the 1930s the goal of helping business had not really changed. See Allen, *Only Yesterday*, 141–42.

106. FHA, *Architects, Contractors*, 3, 9.

107. "Speech of James Moffett to Los Angeles Better Housing Campaign Committee," FHA press release no. 192 (January 31, 1935), 7 [NA RG 287, box y749].

108. FHA, *Architects, Contractors*, 3, 10, 21–23.

109. Ibid., 9, 24; "Address of Ward M. Canaday," 2.

110. FHA, *Architects, Contractors*, 18; Lynd and Lynd, *Middletown*, 46; "Main Street Plan Pushed by Business: Jersey Groups Develop Survey-Sales System," *Better Housing*, May 13, 1936, 3.

111. FHA, *Architects, Contractors*, 3.

112. FHA, Better Selling of Better Housing, 1.

113. FHA, *First Annual Report*, 5, 10; FHA, *Better Selling of Better Housing*, 1.

114. Arthur Walsh, typescript of speech before National Industrial Advertisers Association Pittsburgh Conference, September 19, 1935 [NA RG 287, box y749].

115. FHA, *Better Selling of Better Housing*, 12–13, 17, 23.

116. Ibid., 23.

117. Ibid.

118. James Dusenberry, "The Architect and Housing—Today," *Octagon* 7 (May 1935): 3–4. On the general prohibition against architects' advertising their services, see Walter J. Greenleaf, *Careers: Architecture*, leaflet no. 10 (Washington, DC: Department of the Interior, 1931), 2. For a full analysis of selling and the architecture profession, see Esperdy, "The Odd-Job Alleyway of Building."

119. Dusenberry, "The Architect and Housing," 3–4.

120. FHA, *Better Selling of Better Housing*, 26.

121. Ibid., 25–26.

122. Ibid., 24–26.

123. FHA, *First Annual Report*, 1. The actual figures were 3,070,274 calls, $30,450,583 insured loans, $210,833,974 total modernization work. The employment figure was based on estimated average value of work with the assumption that 80 percent of the amount spent went to labor. The per person average was based on total FHA expenses for Title I implementation and administration.

124. FHA, *First Annual Report*, 5, 10; FHA, *Better Selling of Better Housing*, 1.

125. "Active Modernization Program Laid Down by Stores," *Stores*, July 1935, 77; George L. Plant, "How Retail Stores Are Modernizing," *Stores*, February 1935, 163.

126. FHA, *Second Annual Report*, 4–5. See also Central Housing Committee, "Activities of the Housing Agencies," January 2, 1937 [NA RG 207, box 1]. This internal memorandum provides breakdowns for commercial and residential loans up to July 1936.

127. U.S. Senate, 74th Congress, 1st Session, *National Housing Act: Hearings before the Committee on Banking and Currency* (Washington, DC: GPO, 1935), 63.

128. The agency stated that it was "particularly concerned with the stimulation of this type of modernization." See "Administration Urges Nationwide Modernize Main Street Campaign," FHA press release no. 203 (March 8, 1935), 1 [NA RG 287, box y748]. See also Thomas F. Conroy, "Retailers in Move to Improve Stores," *New York Times*, March 10, 1935, sec. 11, 19.

129. According to the FHA, the low figure of 75,000 stores was based on a 5 percent depreciation rate that was typical of normal, non-Depression, conditions and that normally yielded an equivalent repair and improvement rate. However, because the

Depression had caused the deferment of normal property repairs, the FHA conjectured that the depreciation rate itself was somewhat higher and that the improvement rate in this first year of the "Modernize Main Street" initiative would be as well. After the initial boost in repair work caused by the FHA's promotion of modernization and retailers' simultaneous need to regain and surpass a level of pre-Depression building maintenance, depreciation and improvement rates would return to normal.

130. The FHA was confident that actual per store modernization expenditures would exceed $1,000, predicting that stores would undertake more "thorough" modernizations extending to the interior and including the installation of new floors, lighting systems, display cases, and mechanical equipment, especially air-conditioning, which was projected to rival storefronts in total expenditures. "Store Repairs May Surpass Billion Mark," *Modernization Clip Sheet* 1, no. 12 (1934).

131. FHA, *Modernize for Profit*, 7.

132. Ibid.

133. "Administration Urges Nationwide Modernize Main Street Campaign," 2.

134. "Retail Merchants Urged to Renovize," *Better Housing*, March 5, 1935, 3.

135. FHA, *Modernize for Profit*, 2.

136. FHA, "To the Merchants of America" (Washington, DC: GPO, 1935); FHA, direct-mail piece to service stations and garages (Washington, DC: GPO, 1935); FHA, "To Mr. Retailer" (Washington, DC: GPO, 1936); FHA, "To Owners and Management of Income Property" (Washington, DC: GPO, 1935) [NA RG 287, box y743]. See also "Renewal of Effort Title I Urged," *Better Housing*, July 8, 1936, 1.

137. The checklist contained thirty-nine items for improvement, including facade changes, alterations to display windows, awnings, canopies, entrances, loading platforms, electric signs, vending equipment (gas pumps, jukeboxes), and so on. See FHA, "Checklist for Modernizing Stores and Shops" (Washington, DC: GPO, 1936).

138. "Main Street Plan Pushed by Business," 3; "Business Groups Launch Program in New Jersey," *Better Housing*, April 15, 1936, 1; *West Orange Review*, March 27, 1936, 1; State of New Jersey BHP, "1936 Report," 4. The other communities included Princeton, Elizabeth, Hackensack, and Atlantic City.

139. "Main Street Plan Tried in Missouri," *Better Housing*, September 9, 1936, 4.

140. Between October 1935 and May 1936 when the San Francisco Main Street campaign was in full swing, the FHA's San Francisco office reported insured loans in excess of $15 million. See L. R. Gignilliat Jr., "Modernization and Repair Notes Insured . . . to Close of Business 31 October 1935," confidential memo dated November 21, 1935 [NA RG 287, box y742]; "Modernize for Profit Council Opens Campaign," *Better Housing*, March 31, 1936, 3; and "Northern California, Arizona Lead Nation," *Better Housing*, May 31, 1936, 3. See also Talbot Hamlin, "Some Restaurants and Recent Shops," *Pencil Points* 20 (August 1939): 500. Owens-Illinois, *The New Story in Pictures: Owens-Illinois Insulux Glass Block* (Toledo, OH: Owens-Illinois, 1937); "Some Recent Portfolio of Current Modernization Work," *Architectural Forum* 70 (February 1939): 106; "Portfolio," *Architectural Record* 81 (January 1937): 35; and "From Red into Black," *Architectural Forum* 67 (July 1937): 216–17.

141. FHA, *Community Campaign*, 20.

142. FHA, *How Owners of Home and Business Property Can Secure the Benefits of the National Housing Act* (Washington, DC: GPO, 1934), 5.

143. "Minneapolis Business Men to Modernize Four Blocks," *Better Housing*, June 10, 1936, 2. Within each unit, uniformity was achieved by adjusting building heights, regularizing fenestration, and reconfiguring the elevations to reduce the apparent number of buildings per block. For visual coherence, extraneous architectural detailing was removed and precast stone cladding was installed across the facades. Signage was coordinated with freestanding block letters. To protect shoppers from Minneapolis's climatic extremes, continuous canopies were installed across the length of each block. The corridor was later redesigned as a pedestrian mall (Lawrence Halprin, 1967). A shopping mall took the place of the street in 1973 (Johnson/Burgee, IDS Center).

144. To further encourage group participation, especially in blighted or marginal districts, the FHA suggested informing property owners that lending institutions would look more favorably on joint modernization projects than on individual property improvements. See FHA, *Community Planning*, 8, 10.

145. "Cooperative Modernization Campaign Rebuilds Values in Downtown Oakland," *National Real Estate Journal*, March 1936, 50; Dudley W. Frost, "Today Vacancies Are Not a Problem," *American City*, August 1939, 77. As collective responses to commercial decline, BHP group modernization projects anticipated subsequent developments in American urban renewal, especially undertakings such as Business Improvement Districts and the National Trust's Main Street program.

146. "Modernization of Main Street Starts in Texas," *Better Housing*, April 29, 1936, 3. See also Virginia Mae Moffett, "Face Lifting the Old Home Town," *Nation's Business*, December 1936, 69–70; and "Two Business Blocks," *Architectural Forum* 66 (March 1937): 60.

147. "Main Street Has Air of Old Spain," *Better Housing*, September 29, 1936, 1.

148. For a typical Piggly Wiggly, see "Modernize Main Street," *Architectural Forum* 63 (July 1935): 61.

149. "Weslaco Firms Benefit from Expenditures," *Better Housing*, July 22, 1936.

150. FHA, untitled typescript statement, stamp-dated April 15, 1936, 4.

Chapter 3

1. See "The Growth of Voluntary Chains," *Chain Store Age*, June 1936, 110.

2. LOF, "Featured as a First Prize in IGA's Greatest Sales Contest!" and "The Winners," reprinted from *IGA Grocergram*, January–June 1938 in LOF, *1938 Advertising Yearbook* [LOF MSS-066]. LOF produced new IGA-approved storefront designs for several subsequent years, each one a slight variation on the 1938 model.

3. PPG advertisement, "New Customers . . . Better Satisfied Customers," *Chain Store Age*, November 1934, 103.

4. These recommendations are outlined in FHA, "What a Manufacturer Can Do to Further the Successful Operation of the Better Housing Program," broadside, FHA 128, 1934–35 [NA RG 287, box y742]. Much of this cooperation was secured by the FHA's Industrial Division, a special committee of "leading industrialists" who worked closely with the trade associations and major manufacturers of the building industries. See FHA, *Bulletin for Manufacturers, Advertising Agencies and Publishers* (Washington, DC: GPO, 1934), 8. I have been unable to locate any list of committee membership, but it seems likely that it included the heads of the first group of manufacturers to support the MCP.

5. "Industries Spur Housing Program," *New York Times*, September 26, 1934, 10.

6. "Speech by Ward Canaday before National Association of Manufacturers at Waldorf-Astoria, New York City," FHA press release no. 131 (December 5, 1934), 1 [NA RG 287, box y748].

7. "Industries Spur Housing Program," 10. See also FHA, *First Annual Report* (Washington, DC: GPO, 1935), 11. The FHA did not compile a list of cooperating manufacturers comparable to that of participating financial institutions.

8. Building material manufacturers represented 10 percent of all American manufacturers.

9. "$70,875,000 Outlay Set to Spur Trade," *New York Times*, November 6, 1932, 19; "Modernizing Work to Cost $105,266,429," *New York Times*, December 19, 1932, 2. On the Rehabilitation Corporation, see "Big Companies Join in Rehabilitation," *New York Times*, October 2, 1932, sec. IV, 8; Allie Freed of Paramount Motors quoted in "New Group Set Up to Help Recovery," *New York Times*, November 6, 1934, 8. The committee also included Bruce Barton of Batten, Barton, Durstine & Osborn and Chester McCall of U.S. Advertising Corporation.

10. FHA, *First Annual Report*, 10.

11. See Owens-Illinois advertisement, "They're Going Modern with Insulux Glass Block," *American Architect* 150 (January 1937): 120. This advertisement explained the launching of such editorial campaigns as prompted by the FHA. This type of editorial coverage was the functional equivalent of the manufacturer's promotional tie-in. See FHA, *Bulletin for Manufacturers, Advertising Agencies and Publishers*, especially "Publishers Cooperation," 17–18.

12. By the end of 1935, the FHA reported that journals with national circulation had increased their business by 60 percent on average as a result of the modernization program. "Building Journals See Improvement," *FHA Clip Sheet* 5, no. 2 (1935).

13. "Editorial: Our Bow," *Building Modernization*, September 1933, 5; John W. Harrington, "More Profit Store Fronts," *Building Modernization*, December 1933, 6–13; Harrington, "Sales Psychology in Store Modernization," *Building Modernization*, September 1934, 5–11.

14. "What a Manufacturer Can Do to Further the Successful Operation of the Better Housing Program." The FHA never recognized tie-ins as product endorsements. In its own publications, the agency adopted a non-endorsement policy and avoided "recommending, either directly or by implication, the use of any particular type of building material, equipment, or service to the disadvantage of any other type of material, equipment or service." FHA, *Modernize for Profit: A Manual for Merchants, Manufacturers, and All Owners of Business Properties* (Washington, DC: GPO, 1935), cover.

15. U.S. Steel advertisement, "There's Money in Remodeling Store Fronts," *American Architect* 148 (February 1936): 99; Revere Copper & Brass advertisement, "It Pays to Practice What You Preach," *Building Modernization*, July 1935, 33.

16. See, for example, *Modernizing Money* (New York: The Ruberoid Company, 1935); *The Kawneer Book of Storefronts* (Niles, MI: The Kawneer Company, 1936); and *Formica for Store Modernization* (Cincinnati, OH: Formica Insulation Company, 1935), which was a reissue of *Translucent Shatterproof Formica* (Cincinnati, OH: Formica Insulation Company, 1933).

17. FHA, *Second Annual Report* (Washington, DC: GPO, 1936), 3. See, for example, "Address by George D. Buckley at a Breakfast Meeting of the National Conference of

Business Paper Editors at the National Press Club," November 22, 1934, typescript, 3 [NA RG 287, box y748].

18. "Forum of Events: Promotion Pieces," *Architectural Forum* 66 (June 1937): 98.

19. Metropolitan Life Insurance Co. Policy Holders Service Bureau, *Merchandising and Advertising Practices in the Building Material and Equipment Field* (New York: Met Life, 1931), 8.

20. See *Building Supply News*, September 1934; *Building Material Merchandising Digest*, October 1934; and *Plumbing and Heating Trade Journal*, October 1934.

21. See U.S. Chamber of Commerce, "Press Release: Construction Industry Conference," October 10, 1937; and U.S. Chamber of Commerce, *Program: Construction Industry Conference*, October 20–21, 1938, and November 16–17, 1939 [NA RG 207, HHFA/CHC/Exec. Sec., box 5].

22. "Speech by H. Dorsey Newson before the Tenth Annual Convention of Major Market Newspapers," FHA press release no. 88 (October 16, 1934), 5 [NA RG 287, box y749].

23. FHA, "The Building Industry Can Profit," in *Bulletin for Manufacturers, Advertising Agencies and Publishers*, 11.

24. *Building Modernization*, September 1935, 2. On advertising clichés of the period, see Roland Marchand, *Advertising the American Dream* (Berkeley: University of California Press, 1985).

25. See, for example, General Electric, "Electrical Convenience," *Building Modernization*, March 1935. On the Main Street initiative and GE air-conditioning, see "Air Conditioning Gaining," *New York Times*, March 10, 1935, sec. II, 19; and GE advertisement, "For Remodeling or New Construction," *Architectural Forum* 61 (August 1937): 14. In addition to its modernization print ads, GE sponsored numerous promotional activities, including radio programs and design competitions, related to the National Housing Act but publicizing the use of GE products in home modernization and Title II home construction. On General Electric's competitions, see Andrew Shanken, "Architectural Competitions and Bureaucracy, 1935–1945," *Architectural Research Quarterly* 3, no. 1 (1999): 43–55. See also Ronald C. Tobey, *Technology as Freedom: The New Deal and the Electrical Modernization of the American Home* (Berkeley: University of California Press, 1996).

26. See FHA, *Group II Lenders: Financial Institutions That Are Extending Modernization Credit, Form FHE 61* (Washington, DC: GPO, 1935) [NA RG 287, box Y 740]. All credit finance subsidiaries were approved for government insurance provided they offered government rates. Becoming a modernization lender was a promotional tool that involved no regulatory or institutional change.

27. The FHA put Johns-Manville on the front page of the October 22, 1934, edition of *Better Housing* with a signed letter from J-M president Lewis Brown attesting to the positive results of the two-month-old FHA program. J-M's Lewis Brown was "gratified by a substantial increase in volume of business," which he "attributed in a major degree to the program of the FHA." See "Program Bring Results," *Better Housing*, October 22, 1934, 1.

28. "Modernizing the Building Industry," *Atlantic Monthly*, October 1935; cited in FHA Division of Public Relations, "FHA Press Digest and Confidential Supplements" [typescripts], August–October 1934.

29. See "James Moffett over Johns-Manville Nation-Wide Hookup," FHA press release, September 15, 1934; and "Stewart McDonald at Building Industry Forum," FHA press release, January 1936 [NA RG 287, box y749].

30. Johns-Manville advertisement, "Johns-Manville Modernizes a Main Street Shop," *Chain Store Age*, November 1935, 96.

31. "Speech by George Lapointe before Building Industry Forum," typescript, January 13, 1936, 1 [NA RG 287, box y 748]. Lapointe was president of the National Retail Lumber Dealers Association, which supported the modernization movement as a temporary expedient to sustain the building industry until new construction was fully revived.

32. Plastic laminates included Formica and Micarta; porcelain enamels included Veribrite and Porceliron; extruded metals included Zouri and Brasco.

33. Structural glass should not be confused with other glass products used in storefront installations and having apparent "structural" uses, including prismatic glass (brand name Luxfer Prism) and glass blocks.

34. On the early history of structural glass, see PPG, *Glass: History, Manufacture and Its Universal Application* (Pittsburgh: PPG Company, 1923), 158–69. For recent preservation-oriented studies, see Carol J. Dyson, "Structural Glass," in *Twentieth-Century Building Materials*, ed. Thomas C. Jester (New York: McGraw-Hill and National Park Service, 1995), 200–205; and "The Preservation of Historic Pigmented Structural Glass," *Preservation Briefs*, no. 12 (Washington, DC: U.S. Department of the Interior, 1984).

35. Figures cited in W. E. S. Turner, "The North American Glass Industry in 1938," *Journal of the Society of Glass Technology* 24 (1940): 8; and U.S. Tariff Commission, *Flat Glass and Related Glass Products*, report no. 123, 2nd series (Washington, DC: GPO, 1937), 137; J. W. Wiley, "Structural Glass Has Arrived," *Glass Industry* 13 (September 1932): 148–49. Wiley was an employee of the Vitrolite Company.

36. Paul Frankl, *Form and Re-Form* (New York: Harper & Co., 1930), 163; Walter Dorwin Teague, "Structural and Decorative Trends in Glass," *American Architect* 141 (May 1932): 112.

37. Total flat-glass production fell from a 1929 high of 150 million feet to a 1932 low of 52 million feet. Production climbed back to 86 million in 1933, due to the continued demand for auto glass. See Turner, "The North American Glass Industry," 8.

38. PPG was cooperating with the National Committee on Industrial Rehabilitation and the Committee on Reconditioning, Remodeling, and Modernizing.

39. See "Advertising News," *New York Times*, December 25, 1936, 29. The figure is also cited in FHA press release no. 88, 6.

40. "Manufacture of Structural Glass: Works No. 6 of the Pittsburgh Plate Glass Company," *Glass Industry*, 20 (June 1939): 215. Carrara was manufactured at this factory.

41. In this context, structural glass served as a kind of curtain wall, existing independent of the structure of the building. Unlike a true curtain wall (as the term is commonly understood), structural glass required the presence of the actual wall surface beneath, to which the glass sheets were attached with mastic.

42. Teague, "Structural and Decorative Trends," 112; Harrington, "More Profit Store Fronts," 10.

43. Quoted in *Sweet's Architectural Catalogue* (1933), B2486, B2471. See also PPG advertisement, "Our Organization Is Particularly Well Qualified," *Chain Store Age*, November 1932, 661.

44. Committee on Reconditioning, "Tentative Operating Manual for Conducting a Local Modernizing Campaign," cited in "Modernization Field Offers Many Business Tips to the Industry," *Ceramic Industry* 20 (March 1933): 145.

45. "Equipment and Construction Directory, Section 1, Store Fronts," *Chain Store Age*, November 1933, 109. PPG's marketing of Carrara was unchanged from nearly a decade before. See PPG, *Glass*, 97.

46. "Equipment and Construction Directory," *Chain Store Age*, November 1934, D3, D7; *Sweet's Catalogue File* (1934), C222–23.

47. See *Sweet's Catalogue File* (1936), sec. 17, cat. 19; and *Sweet's Catalogue File* (1937), sec. 19, cat. 25.

48. Fabrication and installation for structural glass were the same for interior and exterior use. Costing between $.50 and $.70 per square foot, it was far less expensive than marble or granite. While brick and glazed terra-cotta were cheaper to purchase than structural glass, they were more expensive to install, requiring both a higher skill level of labor and more man-hours. By contrast, an entire storefront of structural glass could be very nearly "glued" to an existing facade in a matter of hours.

49. PPG advertisement, "Why Does a Pittco Store Front Make Your Chain Store Individual?" *Chain Store Age*, November 1936, 121.

50. In 1935 plate glass cost approximately $.30 per square foot.

51. PPG introduced EasySet Metal in 1908. In 1910 Kawneer brought a patent infringement suit against the company. It was settled out of court, and PPG became a distributor for Kawneer's reclaimed storefront setting system.

52. The new line of extruded metal settings included sashes, sills, moldings, jambs, thresholds, and other vertical and horizontal members. See "Products and Practices: Metal Store Front Construction," *Architectural Forum* 62 (March 1935): 38.

53. "Pittco" was used first to identify only PPG's new metal settings, but it was eventually adopted as the unifying label for all PPG storefront products. H. S. Wherrett is quoted in "Retailers in Move to Improve Stores," *New York Times*, March 10, 1935, sec. 11, p. 19. If 1 million merchants each spent $1,000 on modernization, it would generate $1 billion of business.

54. PPG advertisement, "For Perfect Execution of the Store Fronts You Design," *American Architect* 148 (March 1936): 15.

55. PPG advertisement, "When Designing New Fronts for Old Stores Under NHA," *Architectural Forum* 62 (April 1935): 65; PPG advertisement, "It Pays to Modernize Main Street," *Chain Store Age*, June 1935, 73.

56. FHA, Architects, Contractors, Building Supply and Other Merchants (Washington, DC: GPO, 1934), 23.

57. Though PPG's version of the MCP required a 20 percent down payment, it offered credit at FHA rates, enabling merchants to pay for storefront remodeling and related expenses in monthly installments.

58. See, for example, PPG, "It Pays to Modernize Main Street," *Chain Store Age*, June 1935, 73.

59. On the use of missionary men, see *Merchandising and Advertising Practices*, 7–8; and PPG advertisement, "We Offer Architects the Services of Our Staff of Store Front Specialists," *Architectural Forum* 63 (July 1935): 45.

60. PPG, *How Modern Store Fronts Work Profit Magic* (Pittsburgh: PPG Company, 1934). Nearly every advertisement from 1934 and 1935 promoted the booklet. See, for

example, PPG advertisement, "Send for Free Book," *Chain Store Age*, December 1935, 73. PPG promoted this booklet until 1937, when it introduced *Producing Bigger Profits with Pittco Store Fronts*, which was followed in 1938 with *How to Get More Business with Pittco Store Fronts*.

61. PPG advertisement, "10 New Detail Drawings of Pittco Store Front Metal Applications," *Architectural Record* 84 (November 1938): 39. See also *Sweet's Catalogue File* (1939), sec. 19, cat. 5. The *Folders* were updated regularly as part of PPG's Glass Data Service, whenever the company brought out a new sash to keep abreast of storefront design trends. In 1938 PPG released a portfolio of ten "up-to-date" Pittco Metal details that abandoned molding profiles reproducing the classical orders in favor of more abstracted forms that the company described as "clean, sharp profiles" with "simplicity of line."

62. For *Design of the Month* promotion, see PPG, "For the Perfect Execution of the Store Fronts You Design," *American Architect* 148 (March 1936): 15. For a discussion of this type of repetitive merchandising, see *Merchandising and Advertising Practices*, 12.

63. *Sweet's Catalogue File* (1936), sec. 17, cat. 19. For a complete list of the PPG designs, see Walter Dorwin Teague Associates Invoice for Pittsburgh Plate Glass Company, Job No. P-100, Store Front Construction, Shipments #2 & #8, Walter Dorwin Teague Collection, George Arents Research Library for Special Collections, Syracuse University [NXSV1044-A]. See also Jeffrey Meikle, *Twentieth Century Limited* (Philadelphia: Temple University Press, 1979), 117–21.

64. "Model Store Fronts Exhibited," *New York Times*, September 9, 1936, 38. The text of this article, which seems to be from a PPG press release, appears verbatim in several other publications. In New York the designs were displayed at the Architects Sample Corporation. All of PPG's seventy-four distribution warehouses were located east of the Rockies.

65. "Store Front Designs in the Modern Mode," *Building and Modernization*, November 1936, 12.

66. The models also included a gift shop, haberdasher, dress shop, jeweler, luggage store, and fabric store. All of the models are lost, as are most of Teague's designs (only four original drawings survive). To date, I have located images of seven.

67. The *Architectural Forum* found them "superlative in craftsmanship and extremely interesting in design." See "Store Front Caravan," *Architectural Forum* 65 (November 1936): 42.

68. "Model Windows," *FHA Clip Sheet* 11, no. 4 (December 29, 1936). See also "Three Store Front Modernization Suggestions," *Real Estate Record*, September 19, 1936, 14. "Store Front Caravan Starts Tour to Show New Arrangements," *Economist*, September 12, 1936, 6.

69. "Trade Announcements: Pittsburgh Plate Glass Company," *Architectural Record* 78 (December 1935): 34. Though the industry announcement was not made until December, Teague had been working for PPG since the summer.

70. PPG and Westinghouse produced four short films (ten minutes each) for distribution to local groups (BHPs, chambers of commerce, Rotary clubs, etc.) interested in lighting and modernization. See "News of the Field: Films on Store Modernization," *Architectural Record* 78 (July 1935): 8. I have been unable to locate these films.

71. Figures cited in "Profits Report: Pittsburgh Plate Glass," *New York Times*, March 14, 1935, 33; "The Month in Building: Modernization," *Architectural Forum* 63 (July 1935): 5; *Flat Glass and Related Glass Products*, 137.

72. Harold M. Alexander, "Creating Glass Business," *The Batch*, March 1939, 2. Alexander was head of the New Uses Department. *The Batch* was LOF's monthly house organ.

73. LOF was affected by a combination of declining prices and sales, but it still managed to stay marginally in the black that year.

74. LOF, *18th Annual Report for Year Ending 31 December 1934* (Toledo: Libbey-Owens-Ford, 1935), 5–6.

75. It is likely that Canaday and Biggers knew each other: both men were active in the Toledo Chamber of Commerce and appeared together at numerous local business and social events during the 1930s. LOF supplied auto safety glass for Willys-Overland cars, of which Canaday was chairman of the board. In addition, the United States Advertising Corporation, an agency founded by Canaday before he went to Willys-Overland, had the LOF account throughout the decade. It seems likely that Canaday, through his PR Division, would have made certain that Biggers, through LOF's government liaison in Washington, was informed of FHA developments relevant to the glassmaker, such as congressional passage of the $50,000 amendment to Title I. See Clipping File and Chronological List of Events and Articles in *Toledo Blade* and *New York Times*, Ward M. Canaday Collection, Ward M. Canaday Center, University of Toledo [Collection No. 072, folders 8–10].

76. Quoted in LOF, *19th Annual Report for Year Ending 31 December 1935* (Toledo: Libbey-Owens-Ford Glass Company, 1936), 5.

77. *Sweet's Architectural Catalogue* (1932), B2479; "Equipment and Construction Directory," *Chain Store Age*, November 1934, D7. See also *Sweet's Catalogue File* (1934), C131.

78. The early history of Vitrolite is described in Earl Aiken, "LOF at Parkersburg," *The Batch*, October 1939, 12. In the 1920s a variety of American manufacturers recognized the usefulness of color as a distinctive merchandising strategy. See Marchand, *Advertising the American Dream*, 120–27.

79. Vitrolite Company advertisement, "Find Out How Little It Costs to Beautify with Vitrolite," *American Architect* 146 (June 1935): 97.

80. See Contract of Sale, dated May 22, 1935 [LOF MSS-066]. LOF purchased the Vitrolite Company for $470,000.

81. Letter from Stewart McDonald to John D. Biggers, reprinted in "Retail Store Planning," *Architectural Record* 78 (July 1935): 72. So obvious a program tie-in as LOF's Modernize Main Street Competition could hardly have escaped FHA notice and, given the close relationship between Canaday and Biggers, it may even have been planned with FHA input.

82. Kenneth K. Stowell, "The Editor's Forum: The National Housing Act," *Architectural Forum* 60 (June 1934): 25. On how architects responded to building modernization practice as a result of the profession's changed circumstances during the Depression, see my "The Odd-Job Alleyway of Building," *Journal of Architectural Education* 58 (May 2005): 24–40.

83. "The Architectural Forum Remodeling Competitions," *Architectural Forum* 61 (October 1934): 9. Stowell hoped these competitions would supply much-needed "illustrative material" on modernization to serve as "good precedent" in publications and exhibitions.

84. See Kenneth K. Stowell, *Modernizing Buildings for Profit* (New York: Prentice-Hall, 1935).

85. Kenneth K. Stowell, "Modernize Main Street Competition Program," *Architectural Record* 78 (July 1935): supplement, 2.

86. All entrants were required to submit an outline sheet detailing their design's storefront materials. This sheet contained twenty-one specifications for glass—including show windows, bulkheads, exterior facings, signboards, and doors—all of which could be fabricated of products manufactured by LOF. The program assured designers that material specifications would not be a factor in jury decisions. Rather, they were used to augment publication of the winning designs by LOF, which owned all the designs once they were submitted. See Stowell, "Modernize Main Street Competition Program," 7–8.

87. LOF, "'Modernize Main Street' Competition," announcement, *Architectural Forum* 62 (June 1935): 29.

88. See Stowell, *Modernizing Buildings for Profit*, 164.

89. Stowell, "Modernize Main Street Competition Program," 4–6, 2. To a certain extent, this also meant that the submitted schemes would not be *modernizations* in any real sense, since they did not have to deal with the exigencies of an existing building—with an oddly placed structural column or an inconvenient entrance to an upper story. In the auto service station problem, it was even permissible for competitors to tear down the existing building in order to use the lot most efficiently. Thus, in a sense, the submitted schemes were *new* store designs fitted to standard lots, identified as modernizations because it was politically and promotionally expedient to do so.

90. Ibid., 1–2. In addition, the schemes were required to meet the special merchandising needs and facilitate the particular selling activities of each store type, with drugstore soda fountains and lunch counters, gas station service bays, apparel shop changing rooms, and so on.

91. Ibid., 2.

92. J. André Fouilhoux et al., "Jury Report for Modernize Main Street Competition," *Architectural Record* 78 (October 1935): 209. The full text of the report appears in LOF, *52 Designs to Modernize Main Street with Glass* (Toledo: Libbey-Owens-Ford, 1935), 2–6.

93. Records of the exact number of entries do not exist, and the original drawings are not preserved in LOF's corporate archives.

94. See, for example, Kenneth C. Welch, "The Apparel Store," *Architectural Record* 78 (July 1935): 62–64.

95. Fouilhoux, "Jury Report," 209.

96. The winning designers represented a cross section of young architects in the United States in the mid-1930s and included a considerable number of ethnic professionals. The majority had completed their architectural training after 1929. This meant that the path to conventional practice would be circuitous at best due to the building slowdown. While a number of these young architects were working for firms such as Shreve, Lamb & Harmon, others found employment in advertising and merchandising. Still others were participating in New Deal–sponsored public works. Not all of the winners were novices: Royal Barry Wills partnered with a young Hugh Stubbins to earn an Honorable Mention for a Food Store design. Alfred Clauss, who took first prize in the Automotive Service Station category, had already passed through the offices of Mies van der Rohe and Howe & Lescaze. In addition, he had codesigned a gas station prototype for the Standard Oil Company of Ohio that Hitchcock and Johnson selected for the International Style Show at the Museum of Modern Art in 1932. See "Prize Winners," *Architectural Record* 78 (October 1935): 210.

97. Fouilhoux, "Jury Report," in LOF, *52 Designs*, 2. The comments of the jury were largely confined to the storefronts since this was the principal vehicle for fulfilling the program mandate to "attract the public," the chief means of promoting LOF products, and the store feature most likely to be modernized.

98. Fouilhoux, "Jury Report," 209.

99. See, for example, "Modernizing Main Street: Selected Designs," *Pencil Points* 16 (October 1935): 501–19; and "Forum of Events: Winners in Modernize Main Street Competition," *Architectural Forum* 63 (October 1935): 78, 81.

100. "Modernizing Main Street: A Few Designs and Comments," *Building Modernization*, October 1935, 9–15.

101. "Boom," *Tide*, October 1935; cited in FHA, "FHA Press Digest."

102. LOF advertisement, "To Keep in Step with Competition," *Chain Store Age*, December 1935, 79; LOF advertisement, *Chain Store Age*, November 1935, 95; "52 Prize-Winning Designs," *Building Modernization*, November 1935, 3; LOF advertisement, "Glass Dominates Designs for Modernization," *Architectural Forum* 63 (December 1935): 50.

103. See "Marvels in Glass," dated March 1939 [LOF MSS-066]. The competition designs that appear are Orlo Heller's apparel shop and Charles du Bose's service station.

104. LOF, "Glass Dominates Designs for Modernization," *Architectural Forum* 63 (December 1935): 50.

105. See, for example, the competition sponsored by the American Terra Cotta Company and conducted by the Chicago Architectural Club. "Terra Cotta Wall Block Competition," *Pencil Points* 16 (November 1935): 10; and "Prize Winning Designs: Terra Cotta Wall Block Competition," *Pencil Points* 17 (January 1936): 49–52.

106. "2nd Competition for Insulux Glass Block, a Group of Three Stores," *Architectural Forum* 70 (May 1939): 23.

107. "4 Competitions for Insulux Glass Block," *Architectural Forum* 70 (April 1939): 31.

108. "Prize-Winning Designs in the Insulux Glass Block Competition No. 2," *Architectural Forum* 71 (November 1939): 19. The jury was based on the West Coast and included San Franciscans William Wurster and Timothy Plfueger and Los Angelenos Donald Parkinson and Stiles O. Clements.

109. Quoted in LOF, *20th Annual Report for the Year Ending 31 December 1936* (Toledo: Libbey-Owens-Ford, 1937), 6.

110. The promotional battle in which the two companies engaged over storefront modernization in the 1930s was made more intense by the fact that they were simultaneously involved in litigation over licensing disagreements and patent infringements concerning the manufacture of safety glass. See Biggers & Wherrett Correspondence in Miscellaneous Company Documents [LOF MSS-066].

111. These activities are described in "Creating Glass Business" and "Your Company's Sales Department," *The Batch*, February 1939, 1. See also "Vitrolite Albums," in Sales and Promotion Files [LOF MSS-066].

112. Originally an architect in Chicago, Sohn had been with the Vitrolite Company for over a decade before it was acquired by LOF. In LOF's account of Vitrolite's development at the factory in Parkersburg, West Virginia, the product's history is divided into pre-1922 and post-1922 to denote the arrival of Sohn and color. See Aiken, "LOF at Parkersburg," 12.

113. LOF cautioned architects against using mirror-finish Vitrolite for facing structural members since it apparently imparted "an effect of empty space and unreality." See "Vitrolite," in *Sweet's Catalogue File* (1936), sec. 17, cat. 2. To compare Vitrolite and Carrara, see "Carrara Structural Glass," *Sweet's Catalogue File* (1936), sec. 17, cat. 1.

114. "Vitrolite for Store Fronts" and "Put on a New Front. It Pays!" in *1936 Advertising Scrapbook* [LOF MSS-066].

115. Notable differences included Sohn's exaggerated use of agate Vitrolite and his presentation of the storefronts within a visible streetscape.

116. It was possible to achieve a nearly curved, but still faceted, profile by setting narrow vertical strips of Vitrolite on a curved substructure; this procedure involved greater expense in cutting, beveling, and, ultimately, installing small units and also held greater potential for damage and breakage. It also produced an unsatisfying appearance especially in conjunction with the streamlined profile of extruded metal trim—none of which was likely to appeal to merchants and their architects.

117. See LOF, *20th Annual Report*, 7; LOF, *21st Annual Report for the Year Ending 31 December 1937* (Toledo: Libbey-Owens-Ford, 1938), 7. On the agreement with the Invisible Glass Company, see LOF, *19th Annual Report*, 6.

118. See also Owens-Illinois advertisement, "Merchandising by Day and by Night," *Architectural Forum* 67 (July 1937): 33. With the increased interest in luminosity in storefront design, the day-and-night photographic pairs became as important in modernization advertising as before-and-after images.

119. PPG and the Corning Glass Works entered a joint venture in 1937 to develop a glass block to compete with Insulux. PC-Block, introduced in 1938, was not marketed as part of the Pittco line. See "The Pittsburgh Corning Corporation," *Pittsburgh Plate Products* 47 (March–April 1938): 3–4.

120. This was a matter of no small concern because there were an increasing number of luminous materials from which to choose, including several traditional materials updated for modernization and storefront use. The Vermont Marble Company, for example, introduced Lumar, a thin marble facing, available in six shades with varying degrees of translucency, that could be used for illuminated storefront installations. See "Lumar: A New Marble Product," *Architectural Record* 79 (March 1936): 234–36.

121. "Vitrolux Color Fused Tempered Plate Glass," *Sweet's Catalogue File* (1938), sec. 18, cat. 3, p. 9. Unlike Vitrolite, Vitrolux had a promising future as a postwar building material: in the 1950s LOF began marketing it as "spandrel glass" suitable for curtain-wall construction and used in such iconic buildings of the period as the Lever House.

122. LOF, *19th Annual Report*, 6.

123. Though LOF claimed that entire storefronts could be fitted with Vitrolux, the time and expense of installing lighting units on bulkheads, side panels, and upper facades generally prohibited such extensive usage, especially in projects where budgetary concerns were paramount.

124. LOF advertisement, "Storefronts That Have Maximum Display Both Night and Day," *Architectural Record* 84 (September 1938): 9; LOF advertisement, "Night Is Brighter than Day," *American Architect* 151 (July 1937): 28.

125. "New LOF Plan Helps Utilities Sell More Luminous Storefronts," *Electrical World*, July 30, 1938; reprinted in LOF, *1938 Advertising Yearbook* [LOF MSS-066].

126. "Dean Lowry Ties Up a Package," *The Batch*, July 1940, 3.

127. "Libbey-Owens-Ford Announces Extrudalite," *Sweet's Catalogue File* (1938), sec. 19, cat. 8.

128. LOF, *21st Annual Report*, 7. The downturn of 1937 did not hit LOF's books until 1938, when the company recorded a 63 percent drop in profits and net profits were almost as low as they had been in 1934. See LOF, *22nd Annual Report for Year Ending 31 December 1938* (Toledo: Libbey-Owens-Ford, 1939), 1.

129. Lobbying for Title I's reinstatement began in October: Roosevelt called for reinstatement in November, and congressional debates were held in December. Title I was then back in operation on February 3, 1938.

130. With the start of this promotional program, LOF adopted the compound noun "storefront" for use in its advertisements and literature.

131. "LOF Colorful Storefronts Are an Invitation to Stop and Shop" [LOF MSS-066]. This promotional piece was probably distributed at the Modern Shopping Center display; it includes material specifications for each of the five storefronts.

132. Bruce Miller, "Show 'Em . . . Sell 'Em," *The Batch*, May 1941, 11. Breaking down the resistance of prospects was also the motivation for LOF's 1938 modernization of its Chicago showroom: architect Bruce Goff redesigned the conference room and information booth as Complete Storefronts, using all the products in LOF's line. See "The Showroom as a Design Problem," *Architectural Record* 84 (July 1938): 75–76.

133. See "LOF Storefronts of Metal and Glass," in *American Architect, Architectural Record, Pencil Points, Architectural Forum* (February 1938), reprinted in LOF, *1938 Advertising Yearbook*; Advertisement No. 4425, in *New York Society of Architects Handbook* and *Illinois Society of Architects Handbook*, reprinted in LOF, *1938 Advertising Yearbook*.

134. See LOF, *1938 Advertising Yearbook* for reprints of the advertisements that appeared in these magazines.

135. The folder also included several stores in Canada. "Why a New LOF Storefront Is a Business Asset," 1938 [LOF MSS-066].

136. Cited in Job No. 5238 and Job No. 5356, appearing in *Glass Digest*, March and September 1938, reprinted in LOF, *1938 Advertising Yearbook*.

137. "Visual Fronts by the LOF Glass Company" (1943), 5; and "Today's Main Street Is Open for Business" (1956), 2 [LOF MSS-066].

138. Johnson Service Company advertisement, "When Johnson Controls . . . ," and Westinghouse advertisement, "2 New Luminaires," *Architectural Forum* 70 (February 1939): 34–35.

139. Owens-Illinois advertisement, "An Appreciation of Architecture Long Overdue," *Architectural Record* 85 (April 1939): 125; "Modernity—Here Today . . . It May Be Gone Tomorrow," *Architectural Forum* 61 (September 1934): 157.

Chapter 4

1. "Winning Entries, Pittsburgh Glass Institute Competition," *Architectural Forum* 67 (August 1937): 103. See also "Portfolio of Commercial Work," *Architectural Forum* 64 (May 1936): 426–28.

2. Emrich Nicholson, *Contemporary Shops in the United States* (New York: Architectural Book Publishing, 1945), 12–13.

3. Ibid., 12.

4. For an in-depth history of streamlining in industrial design as it emerged during the Depression, see Jeffrey Meikle, *Twentieth Century Limited* (Philadelphia: Temple University Press, 1979).

5. Nicholson, *Contemporary Shops*, 12–13.

6. See Joseph D. Weiss, "Store Design Practice," *New Pencil Points* 24 (February 1943): 43.

7. Quoted in Meikle, *Twentieth Century Limited*, 164–65.

8. As the term *streamlining* gained popularity for product restyling, it came into general usage having the same basic meaning as *modernizing* with only shades of difference between them. Both implied improved efficiency and appearance, but *streamlining* also implied speed while *modernized* implied newness. For a full discussion see ibid., 168.

9. Egmont Arens, "Report to the Industries Sales Committee," November 23, 1934 [Special Collections Research Center, Syracuse University Library, MSS Egmont Arens Industrial Design Records Client and Project File, MSS 7, box 19].

10. Egmont Arens, telegraph to Franklin Roosevelt [Special Collections Research Center, Syracuse University Library, MSS Egmont Arens Industrial Design Records Client and Project File, MSS 7, box 27]; also cited in Meikle, *Twentieth Century Limited*, 164.

11. Marc Weiss has similarly argued for an understanding of "the production of homes as a manufacturing and merchandising process of high social significance." See Marc A. Weiss, *The Rise of the Community Builders* (New York: Columbia University Press, 1987), 147.

12. Lewis Mumford, *Sticks and Stones: A Study of American Architecture and Civilization* (1924; repr., New York: Dover, 1955), 100–101.

13. In this cultural definition of consumer goods, I am not denying the degree to which consumption habits were created or cultivated by corporate advertising, but—following the arguments of Jackson Lears, Roland Marchand, Richard Wightman Fox, and others—I believe that consumers made (and make) conscious choices as much as they were (are) exploited or manipulated.

14. Both of these operations were marked by what historian Terry Smith described, in an analysis of industrial design, as "the insertion of the priorities, values, and imagery of advertising deep into the productive process." Terry Smith, *Making the Modern* (Chicago: University of Chicago Press, 1993), 357.

15. Robert S. Lynd and Helen Merrell Lynd, *Middletown in Transition* (New York: Harcourt, Brace & World, 1937), 46.

16. By the early 1930s, such a view of consumption was sufficiently widespread for Aldous Huxley to viciously satire it in *Brave New World*, his dystopian novel of 1932 in which Fordism and hyper-consumption have become the new religion. See also Jackson Lears, "From Salvation to Self-Realization: Advertising and the Therapeutic Roots of the Consumer Culture, 1880–1930," in *The Culture of Consumption: Critical Essays in American History, 1880–1980*, ed. Richard Wightman Fox and T. J. Jackson Lears (New York: Pantheon Books, 1983), 18.

17. Robert S. Lynd, "The People as Consumers," in *Recent Social Trends in the U.S.: Report of the President's Research Committee on Social Trends* (New York: McGraw-Hill, 1934), 867–68.

18. FHA, *Selling Better Housing* (Washington, DC: GPO, 1935), 6.

19. This was how the Lynds characterized the effect of installment buying. Robert S. Lynd and Helen Merrell Lynd, *Middletown: A Study in Modern American Culture* (1929; repr., New York: Harcourt, Brace & World, 1956), 46.

20. See Ward Canaday, "Speech at Furnishing Industries Dinner," FHA press release no. 168, January 10, 1935, 1 [NA RG 287, box y749]; FHA, *Selling Better Housing*, 14; *FHA Promotion Pointers* 1, no. 9 (1935); "Modernizing Main Street," *Building Modernization*, October 1935, 15.

21. FHA, *Selling Better Housing*, 15. On popular attitudes toward consumer credit, see Christine Frederick, *Selling Mrs. Consumer* (New York: The Business Bourse, 1928), 282, 285. See also Lynd, "The People as Consumers," 861–64.

22. Ilya Ilf and Evgeny Petrov, *Ilf and Petrov's American Road Trip*, ed. Erika Wolf (New York: Cabinet Books and Princeton Architectural Press, 2007), 101.

23. "Modern Store Fronts Merit Cash Outlays," *FHA Clip Sheet* 7, no. 8 (1936); FHA, *How Owners of Homes and Business Property Can Secure the Benefits of the National Housing Act* (Washington, DC: GPO, 1934), 19.

24. Shepard Vogelgesang, "Architecture and Trade Marks," *Architectural Forum* 50 (June 1929): 897. Vogelgesang observed this trend in stores in New York City, especially on Fifth Avenue, discussing Joseph Urban's redesigned facade for the Bedell Store at length. The changes implicit in the form and meaning of the *advertising front* parallel changes to advertising in the 1920s as ads shifted from the subtle to the sensational, from simply presenting product information to consciously attracting attention. See Lears, "From Salvation to Self-Realization," 18.

25. Morris Lapidus defined the "billboard" type of the 1930s in "Store Design," *Architectural Record* 89 (February 1941): 124. See also the jury report (by Mies van der Rohe, Morris Ketchum, and others) for a 1943 competition sponsored by Kawneer in anticipation of postwar construction. "Store Fronts of Tomorrow," *New Pencil Points* 24 (February 1943): 32. According to J. R. Von Sternberg, "The store front is a three-dimensional advertisement." See Von Sternberg, "Unit Planning No. VI: The Store," *American Architect* 150 (June 1937): 100.

26. E. M. Frankel, "Peggie Hale Shop Shows New Trend in Store Design," *Chain Store Age*, November 1934, 116; Warren F. Morgan, "Why Should I Modernize?" *Building Modernization*, September 1933, 8; John W. Harrington, "More Profit Store Fronts," *Building Modernization*, December 1933, 12.

27. See Lapidus, "Store Design," 119. See also Lapidus, *Too Much Is Never Enough* (New York: Rizzoli, 1996), 98.

28. PPG advertisement, "Turn Passers-by into Profitable Customers," *Chain Store Age*, May 1935, 93.

29. FHA, *Modernize for Profit* (Washington, DC: GPO, 1935), 2. Some of these buildings can be identified as structures modernized prior to 1935: the J.W. Robinson Department Store in Los Angeles, the Glenn Building in Cincinnati, the Medinah Temple in Chicago, and the Block & Kuhl Building in Decatur, Illinois.

30. Ernest M. Fisher, "The Research Program of the FHA, Address Delivered to Annual Meeting of National Association of Real Estate Boards," January 11, 1935 [NA RG 287, box y748].

31. FHA, *Modernization Credit Plan, Bulletin No. 1* (Washington, DC: GPO, 1934), 3.

32. Arthur C. Holden, "Modernization—Ballyhoo or Progress?" *Survey Graphic* 23 (July 1934): 335. The FHA may have actually borrowed some of its terminology from

Holden. His article appeared prior to the release of *Bulletin No. 1* and was included in the FHA's *Press Digest*. In addition, New Deal agencies often shared technical data with one another.

33. Lynd, "The People as Consumers," 864; see also 858.

34. Paul Bonner, "Style and the Salesman," *Talk No. 7* (April 1931), Industrial Institute of the Art Center; Lynd, "The People as Consumers," 877–79. See also Kenneth Stowell, *Modernizing Buildings for Profit* (New York: Prentice-Hall, 1935), iii; and "Modernity—Here Today . . . It May Be Gone Tomorrow," *Architectural Forum* 61 (September 1934): 157.

35. LOF, *Marvels in Glass*, 1939 [LOF MSS-066]. Loewy's charts appeared in Sheldon Cheney and Martha Cheney, *Art and the Machine* (New York: McGraw-Hill, 1936).

36. "Obsolete Appearance Detriment to Shop, Businessmen Claim," *FHA Clip Sheet* 10, no. 11 (1936).

37. FHA, *Selling Better Housing*, 25, 5.

38. Meikle, *Twentieth Century Limited*, 70–71. On the advertising schema employed here, see also Roland Marchand, *Advertising the American Dream* (Berkeley: University of California Press, 1985), 158.

39. They were right: artificial obsolescence did attempt to strip consumers of agency with regard to personal taste and purchase decisions, creating need and desire out of a void. See Stuart Chase and F. J. Schlink, *Your Money's Worth* (New York: The Business Bourse, 1927). See also Marchand, *Advertising the American Dream*, 314.

40. In the present context, some of those relationships bear repeating: Ward Canaday, head of public relations at the FHA, was the founder of the U.S. Advertising Agency, the firm that had the LOF account throughout the 1930s. Albert Deane, head of modernization credit at the FHA, was also head of consumer finance at General Motors, one of the first American manufacturers to successfully utilize style obsolescence to boost the sales of its cars and refrigerators. In his memoirs, GM chairman Alfred Sloan noted that GM's credit finance innovations were as important to the corporation's success as its model change/style program. See Alfred Sloan, *My Years at General Motors* (New York: McFadden Books, 1965), chaps. 15, 17.

41. Frederick, *Selling Mrs. Consumer*, 246–47. Frederick's ideology of progressive obsolescence is also analyzed in Marchand, *Advertising the American Dream*, 156–59.

42. Frederick, *Selling Mrs. Consumer*, 246–47, 250–55.

43. Morgan, "Why Should I Modernize?" 8.

44. FHA, "Talk for General Audience," *Portfolio of Radio Publicity* (Washington, DC: GPO, 1934), 2.

45. Christine Frederick, Frederick Lewis Allen, and Robert Lynd all used these phrases in this popular sense in their contemporary discussions of the emergent consumer culture. See Frederick, *Selling Mrs. Consumer*, 246; Frederick Lewis Allen, *Only Yesterday* (1931; repr., New York: Harper & Row, 1964), 92, 142; and Lynd, "The People as Consumers," 878.

46. FHA, "Rivalry Is Incentive," *Clip Sheet* 2, no. 1 (1935).

47. LOF advertisement, "Sell Your Store," *IGA Grocergram*, May 1940; reprinted in LOF, *1940 Advertising Yearbook* [LOF MSS-066].

48. Morgan, "Why Should I Modernize?" 8. Holabird and Root are quoted in Harrington, "More Profit," 12; LOF advertisement, "To Keep in Step with Competition," *Chain Store Age*, November 1935, 95.

49. R. V. Rasmussen, "We've Profited by the Times," *Chain Store Age*, November 1932, 644.

50. R. S. Sweeley, "Activities in Retail Store Design," *Architectural Record* 83 (February 1938): 102.

51. "Public Demands Up-to-Date," *FHA Clip Sheet* 11, no. 1 (1936); FHA, *Modernize for Profit*, 4.

52. FHA, *Modernize for Profit*, 12, 2.

53. FHA, "Talk for Merchants," *Portfolio of Radio Publicity*, 1.

54. History bears this out. As Richard Wightman Fox observed, "The Depression and the Second World War, far from undermining the consumer ethos, merely delayed for many the day of gratification. The ideal of fulfillment through consumption and leisure was if anything furthered by the experience of voluntary deprivation." Richard Wightman Fox, "Epitaph for Middletown: Robert S. Lynd and the Analysis of Consumer Culture," in *The Culture of Consumption*, ed. Fox and Lears, 103. See also "Depression Consumption" in Lynd, "The People as Consumers," 906–8.

55. Christine Frederick analyzed the typical/female consumer in *Selling Mrs. Consumer*, 11–18.

56. Ibid., 53, 245. See also Marchand, *Advertising the American Dream*, 131.

57. PPG advertisement, "Split Seconds," *Chain Store Age*, September 1936, 123; LOF advertisement, "The Newest Idea in Luminous Storefronts," *IGA Grocergram*, October 1938; reprinted in LOF, *1938 Advertising Yearbook* [LOF MSS-066]. The copy presented a detailed shopping scenario: "A potential chain store customer walks down the street. She's going to buy merchandise somewhere. She sees your store. And in a split second she decides whether she'll come in and patronize you or seek further for a more inviting store."

58. Ward Canaday, "Speech before the 24th Annual Convention of the National Retail Drygoods Association," FHA press release no. 173, January 16, 1935, 1 [NA RG 287, box y748].

59. Comprehending the logic of this influence in general terms, design historian Ellen Lupton observed that "although the built environment is designed largely by men, much of it is constructed with female consumers in mind." Ellen Lupton, *Mechanical Brides: Women and Machines from Home to Office* (New York: Princeton Architectural Press, 1993), 12.

60. This concept of a gendered architecture is influenced by Ann Douglas's notion of "feminization" to explain how American Victorian women (white and middle class) seized the reins of national culture—of the arts and literature—while having little impact on the larger industrial society. See Ann Douglas, *The Feminization of American Culture* (1977; repr., London: Papermac, 1997), esp. 1–13. My concept is also related to gender-based critiques that have explored the relationship between women and the production of architecture, especially Joan Ockman, "Mirror Images: Technology, Consumption, and the Representation of Gender in American Architecture Since World War II," in *The Sex of Architecture* (New York: Harry N. Abrams, 1996).

61. Canaday in FHA press release no. 173, 1. In searching for the specifically *female* imprint of this commercial architecture, and in making a link between female consumption and architectural production, I am aware of the degree to which the gendered imprint of the modernized building was informed by styles and ideals created and manipulated by modernization's producers and publicists—manufacturers, advertising agencies, and

government officials. While this certainly mitigates against female agency in shaping consumption choices and the consumption environment, it does not completely invalidate it since, at the time, consumer advocates like Christine Frederick viewed the manipulation as working both ways. This was especially true during the Depression: while fierce competition forced producers to intensify their efforts to shape consumption habits, it also forced them to be more responsive to consumers.

62. Stowell, *Modernizing Buildings*, 11.

63. Frederick, *Selling Mrs. Consumer*, 6. Frederick Lewis Allen also noted Ford's capitulation "to style and beauty." See Allen, *Only Yesterday*, 134.

64. Stowell, *Modernizing Buildings*, 11.

65. Frank E. Landau, "Keeping Melville Stores Up-to-Date Is Standard Practice," *Chain Store Age*, November 1932, 656.

66. FHA, *Bulletin for Manufacturers, Advertising Agencies and Publishers* (Washington, DC: GPO, 1934), 17.

67. LOF advertisement, "Salesmanship in Metal and Glass," *Motor Magazine*, September 1938; reprinted in LOF, *1938 Advertising Yearbook*. Fashion's implications for modernization are analyzed below.

68. Stowell, *Modernizing Buildings*, 26; "Undesirable Features May Be Removed," *FHA Clip Sheet* 10, no. 1 (1936); "Apply Brick Siding," *FHA Clip Sheet* 2, no. 2 (1934); "Survey Shows Many Stores in Need of Repairs," *FHA Clip Sheet* 11, no. 1 (1936); "Obsolete Appearance Detriment"; "Rescued from Obsolescence," *FHA Clip Sheet* 2, no. 6 (1935).

69. Stowell detailed the procedure: "Resurface all exterior walls . . . striking wall surfaces can be produced with the new types of non-corrosive metals, porcelain-enameled iron, colored opaque glass or sheet plastics." Stowell, *Modernizing Buildings*, 167.

70. Armco advertisement, "Modernized . . . and Modern," *Architectural Record* 83 (February 1938): 148.

71. See, for example, "Modern Theater Remodeling Institute," *Box Office*, August 1935, 10–15.

72. Veribrite advertisement, "Resplendent!" *Architectural Forum* 66 (March 1937): 61.

73. Stowell, *Modernizing Buildings*, 11, 3. The fact that a commercial establishment could remain open for business while an exterior alteration was under way was probably of equal importance. Stowell urged architects to demonstrate for their potential clients the extent to which a building's appearance could be modified without disturbing the structure, inhabitants, or business at all.

74. The FHA occasionally warned against exclusively exterior modernizations, cautioning merchants that although "the new storefront might attract customers and have excellent advertising value," it would become an "anticlimax" once customers realized that modernization "stopped at the front door," making the merchants themselves "guilty of false pretense." See "Obsolete Appearance Detriment."

75. Robert Venturi, Denise Scott Brown, and Steven Izenour, *Learning from Las Vegas* (1972; repr., Cambridge, MA: MIT Press, 1977), 8–9, 87–92.

76. Form also followed merchandising, as manufacturers and the government employed gendered marketing strategies to sell modernization. See the discussion of the ensemble below.

77. Randolph Williams Sexton, *American Commercial Buildings of Today* (New York: Architectural Book Publishing, 1928), 154–55; Ralph Richmond, "The Old Store Puts on a New Front," *Stores*, February 1935, 157.

78. FHA, *Modernize for Profit*, 7. "Modern Elevators Aid Progressive Store Owners," *FHA Clip Sheet* 6, no. 11 (1935); "Survey Shows Many Stores in Need of Repair."

79. Harold Van Doren, *Industrial Design: A Practical Guide* (New York: McGraw-Hill, 1940), 350. See also Meikle, *Twentieth Century Limited*, 116–19.

80. See Charles Dalton Olson, "Sign of the Star: Walter Dorwin Teague and the Texas Company, 1934–37" (master's thesis, Cornell University, 1987).

81. "The Architect Working in Commerce," *Architectural Record* 89 (March 1941): 58.

82. This was the Theresa Pharmacy in the Ansonia at 2109 Broadway. See Lapidus, *Too Much Is Never Enough*, 87; and Frederick, *Selling Mrs. Consumer*, 193–94.

83. "Portfolio of Commercial Work," *Architectural Forum* 65 (October 1936): 317.

84. Loewy seems to have borrowed this motif from his 1934 project for a model industrial designer's office from the Metropolitan Museum of Art's Contemporary American Industrial Arts Exposition. Against the white cladding of the facade, the semicircular ends, as well as the porthole windows of the entrance doors, appeared nautically modernist in the manner of André Lurcat and Rob Mallet-Stevens with whose work the Parisian-born Loewy was undoubtedly familiar. On Cushman's modernization program, see "How Chains Modernized in 1936," *Chain Store Age*, November 1936, 116. On Loewy's work for Cushman's, see "Portfolio," *American Architect* 150 (June 1937): 93–96. See also "Portfolio of Current Modernization Work," *Architectural Forum* 70 (February 1939): 105.

85. PPG advertisement, "New Freedom in Store Design," *American Architect* 149 (August 1936): 114. The Darkroom still stands today in slightly altered form as an Indian restaurant. In 1995 the Darkroom was reproduced in its original form by Catherine Wagner on *Hollywood Boulevard* at Disney-MGM Studios, Orlando, Florida.

86. *Skin job* also evokes Raymond Loewy's quip that Betty Grable's liver and kidney were "no doubt adorable," but he would rather have her "with skin than without." Cited in Richard Pommer, "Loewy and the Industrial Skin Game," *Art in America*, March/April 1976, 46.

87. From modernization publicity posters reprinted in "Sprucing Up Main Street," *Building Modernization*, September 1934, 14.

88. *Women's Page Clip Sheet* 1, no. 3 (1935). This campaign was organized by the trade publications *Beauty Shop News* and *Modern Beauty Shop* in conjunction with the Main Street initiative. See "Uncle Sam Will Help You Modernize Your Beauty Shop—Here's How," *Modern Beauty Shop*, July 1935.

89. Elizabeth Haiken, *Venus Envy: A History of Cosmetic Surgery* (Baltimore: Johns Hopkins University Press, 1997), 132.

90. Stowell, *Modernizing Buildings*, 1, 11.

91. "Stores Must Modernize," *Better Housing*, June 24, 1936; "Modern Elevators Aid Progressive Store Owner"; Modernize Sacramento Campaign Committee, *Let Inspiration House Show You the Way* (Sacramento, CA, 1934), 10.

92. Lynd and Lynd, *Middletown in Transition*, 120.

93. PPG advertisement, "A Pittco Store Front Says Come In," *Chain Store Age*, October 1935, 87; Republic Steel advertisement, "Modernize Main Street," *Architectural*

Forum 62 (June 1935): 45; Chase Brass & Copper advertisement, "The Penalty of 'Skin-Deep' Modernization," *Architectural Record* 63 (September 1935): 217.

94. Henry Churchill, "No Mere Facial Uplift Can Cure the Wrinkles of Our Cities," *American City*, June 1935, 56. Churchill was responding to the FHA's promotion of modernization as a method of large-scale urban revitalization. See FHA, *Community Planning* (Washington, DC: GPO, 1934).

95. Allen, *Only Yesterday*, 88.

96. LOF advertisement, "Vitrolite, the Colorful Structural Glass," *Chain Store Age*, September 1935, 119; "Beauty Always Pays!" *American Architect* 146 (June 1935): 97; "Beautify and Modernize for Permanence," *Architectural Record* 63 (October 1935).

97. Kathy Peiss, *Hope in a Jar: The Making of America's Beauty Culture* (New York: Henry Holt, 1998), 167–201. Christine Frederick also discussed the increased usage of cosmetics and the growth of the beauty culture. See Frederick, *Selling Mrs. Consumer*, 188–89, 191.

98. "Remodeled Beauty Salon," *Real Estate Record*, November 16, 1935, 19–21.

99. Peiss, *Hope in a Jar*, 151. On the signification of the made-up woman, see Peiss, *Hope in a Jar*, 133–58. See also Allen, *Only Yesterday*, 88–90.

100. Frederick Kiesler, *Contemporary Art Applied to the Store and Its Display* (New York: Brentano's, 1930), i. For Kiesler, "cosmetics" was not a favorable designation.

101. Peiss, *Hope in a Jar*, 150–51; Frederick, *Selling Mrs. Consumer*, 195, 193. See also Cutex Lipstick and Nail Polishes advertisement, "Smoky Shades for Summer!" *Chain Store Age*, June 1936, 59.

102. Frederick, *Selling Mrs. Consumer*, 192; Stowell, *Modernizing Buildings*, 11.

103. W. F. Bartels, "Better Practice: Store Fronts," *Architecture* 73 (March 1936): 159–61. See also Peiss, *Hope in a Jar*, 161–62.

104. Kiesler, *Contemporary Art Applied*, 81, 87.

105. PPG, "A Pittco Store Front Says Come In," 87.

106. US Steel advertisement, "Modern Architects Do Wonders," *American Architect* 150 (June 1937): 116.

107. LOF direct mail piece, "Red and White and Libbey-Owens-Ford Join Hands," 1937 [LOF MSS-066].

108. Frederick, *Selling Mrs. Consumer*, 206. See also Marchand, *Advertising the American Dream*, 132–40.

109. See "LOF Storefronts of Metal and Glass," in *American Architect, Architectural Record, Pencil Points, Architectural Forum* (February 1938), reprinted in *1938 Advertising Yearbook*; and advertisement no. 4425, in *New York Society of Architects Handbook* and *Illinois Society of Architects Handbook*, reprinted in *1938 Advertising Yearbook*.

110. Brasco advertisement, "Bring It to Life with Brasco," *Architectural Record* 85 (April 1939): 123.

111. PPG advertisement, "Make the Store Fronts You Design Better Looking," *American Architect* 146 (April 1935): 102.

112. Frederick, *Selling Mrs. Consumer*, 205.

113. PPG advertisement, "Now . . . Design Unified Store Fronts," *Architectural Forum* 67 (July 1937): 73.

114. Brasco advertisement, "In All Modern Metals and Finishes," *Architectural Forum* 66 (June 1937): 9.

115. Canaday, quoted in FHA press release no. 173, 2.

116. George D. Buckley, typescript of "Address at Breakfast Meeting of the National Conference of Business Paper Editors," National Press Club, November 22, 1934, 4 [NA RG 287, box y748]. Implicit in Buckley's statement was the notion that men did not think about their clothes as women did, being disinclined to deal with issues of fashion.

117. Deborah Fausch and Paulette Singley, eds., *Architecture: In Fashion* (New York: Princeton Architectural Press, 1996), 7.

118. James Moffett, "Speech to Los Angeles Better Housing Campaign Committee," FHA press release no. 192, January 31, 1935, 7 [NA RG 287, box y749]; James Moffett, "Speech at Radio City Music Hall," FHA press release no. 110, November 11, 1934, 1 [NA RG 287, box y749].

119. Val K. Warke, "'In' Architecture: Observing the Mechanisms of Fashion," in *Architecture: In Fashion*, ed. Fausch and Singley, 125–26.

120. J. Howard Ardrey, "Address before the National Association of Real Estate Boards," FHA press release no. 181, January 25, 1935, 1 [NA RG 287, box y749].

121. LOF advertisement, "The Wallflower of Main Street," *Architectural Record* 85 (April 1939): 17. The ad also appeared in *Architectural Forum* 70 (May 1939): 13.

122. This wallflower/belle scenario appeared frequently in films of the era. See, for example, MGM's *Follow the Fleet*, 1936.

123. This interest in surface color brings to mind the theory of the polychrome architecture that Le Corbusier and Fernand Léger developed in the 1920s. See Mark Wigley, *White Walls, Designer Dresses* (Cambridge, MA: MIT Press, 1995), 273–74.

124. Lapidus, *Too Much Is Never Enough*, 98–99; Lapidus, "Store Design," 118. Kiesler, *Contemporary Art Applied*, 79.

125. See, for example, Republic Steel advertisement, "From Fifth Avenue to Main Street Alloy Steels Have Changed the Driving Habits of America," *Fortune*, January 1936, 97. On another level, the Main Street/Fifth Avenue opposition exemplifies the "Democracy of Goods," identified by Roland Marchand as one of the most prevalent advertising parables of the 1920s and 1930s. In this parable, democratic social equality (and social stability) was achieved through equal access to consumer products. As related in advertisements, two extremes with an implied class distinction (Main Street and Fifth Avenue) were first contrasted, and then the gulf between them was bridged with the particular product being sold (LOF storefront materials). See Marchand, *Advertising the American Dream*, 217–22, 295.

126. It was for this reason that New York's storefronts were the best documented of the decade, appearing regularly in the architecture and retail trade journals in portfolios and advertisements.

127. "Some Fall Ideas in Store Fronts," *Chain Store Age*, November 1933, 72. This article was the first in a series of *Chain Store Age* features in which the trade journal showcased the latest fashions in modernized facades in multipage photographic spreads.

128. "Portfolio of Modernization," *Architectural Forum* 61 (August 1934): 116.

Chapter 5

1. Laurie Mercier, *Anaconda: Labor, Community, and Culture in Montana's Smelter City* (Champaign: University of Illinois Press, 2001), http://www.press.uillinois.edu/epub/books/mercier.html. See especially the introduction and chapters 1 and 2.

2. Mercier described these in detail in *Anaconda,* chap. 2.

3. Lewis Mumford, "The Sky Line: New Facades," *New Yorker,* November 20, 1937, 85. Mumford had been reviewing these small-scale architectural compositions almost from the moment he began writing for the *New Yorker* in 1931. See also Robert Wojtowicz, ed., *Sidewalk Critic: Lewis Mumford's Writings on New York* (New York: Princeton Architectural Press, 1998).

4. Morris Lapidus, "Store Design," *Architectural Record* 89 (February 1941): 113.

5. FHA, *How Owners of Home and Business Property Can Secure the Benefits of the National Housing Act* (Washington, DC: GPO, 1934), 19; FHA, "Talk for Merchants," *Portfolio of Radio Publicity* (Washington, DC: GPO, 1934), 2.

6. See Warren I. Susman, "'Personality' and the Making of Twentieth-Century Culture," in *Culture as History* (New York: Pantheon, 1984), 271–85.

7. Earnest Elmo Calkins, "Give Your Town a Personality," *Rotarian,* March 1935, 54. The article was reprinted in condensed form in *Reader's Digest,* June 1935, 45–46.

8. LOF, *52 Designs to Modernize Main Street with Glass* (Toledo: Libbey-Owens-Ford, 1935), 70.

9. See the following PPG advertisements: "When You Hire Employees," *Chain Store Age,* December 1935, 73; and "Good Chain Store Locations," *Chain Store Age,* March 1935, 105. See also PPG, "Store Front Metal," *Sweet's Catalogue File* (1936), sec. 17, cat. 19; and "Glass Is Modernizing Main Street," *Architectural Record* 88 (October 1940): 131. On personality's indeterminacy as a term, see Jackson Lears, "From Salvation to Self-Realization: Advertising and the Therapeutic Roots of the Consumer Culture, 1880–1930," in *The Culture of Consumption: Critical Essays in American History, 1880–1980,* ed. Richard Wightman Fox and T. J. Jackson Lears (New York: Pantheon Books, 1983), 21. Lears noted how personality, subject to overuse, has been "severed from any meaningful referent."

10. "Store Fronts and Show Windows," *American Architect* 147 (December 1935): 65. In some ways, the use of personality and character in the discourse of 1930s architecture was simply a revival and updating of eighteenth-century notions of *caractère.* If the rhetoric of Madison Avenue replaced the rhetoric of the Académie, it was because the building culture, at least in the United States, had moved away from the classical high tradition to assimilate the practices of modern popular, consumerist society.

11. Roland Marchand, *Advertising the American Dream: Making Way for Modernity, 1920–1940* (Berkeley: University of California Press, 1985), 208–10.

12. Ralph Richmond, "The Old Store Puts on a New Front," *Stores,* February 1935, 157.

13. LOF, *Put on a Good Front,* 1936 [LOF MSS-066].

14. LOF advertisement, "Dress Up for Bigger Business," reprinted in LOF, *1938 Advertising Scrapbook* [LOF MSS-066].

15. Calkins, "Give Your Town," 54.

16. *Promotion Pointers* 1, no. 6 (1935); Richmond, "The Old Store," 157.

17. The popularization of Adler's inferiority complex and its relationship to consumer culture (and cosmetic surgery) are discussed by Elizabeth Haiken in *Venus Envy: A History of Cosmetic Surgery* (Baltimore: Johns Hopkins University Press, 1997), 91–130. See also Susman, "'Personality,'" 279.

18. Susman, "'Personality,'" 280.

19. The effect of these anxieties on Main Street in particular are discussed in Lewis Atherton, *Main Street on the Middle Border* (1954; repr., Chicago: Quadrangle Books, 1966), 355–57.

20. FHA, *How Owners of Home and Business Property*, 5; "Administration Urges Nationwide Modernize Main Street Campaign," FHA press release no. 203 (March 8, 1935), 2 [NA RG 287, box y748].

21. "Main Street, U.S.A.," *Architectural Forum* 70 (February 1939): 86.

22. S. R. DeBoer, *Shopping Districts* (Washington, DC: American Planning and Civic Association, 1937): 44–45; Arthur C. Holden, "Stabilized Modernization," *American Architect* 147 (September 1935): 38.

23. Susman, "'Personality,'" 278.

24. PPG advertisement, "Make Chain Store Sales Grow," *Chain Store Age*, June 1936, 127; PPG advertisement, "For Individuality in Store Fronts," *Architectural Record* 85 (April 1939): 9.

25. "Store Building," *Architectural Forum* 64 (May 1936): 403.

26. Lawrence A. Schoen, "Keying Stores to Locations," *Chain Store Age*, January 1933, 72; "Chains Spend $70,000,000 on Store Modernization," *Chain Store Age*, November 1935, 143.

27. See Frank E. Landau, "Store Fronts: Chains Adapt Family Types to Suit Specific Locations," *Chain Store Age*, June 1936, 111; "Stores," *Architectural Forum* 65 (October 1936): 316; "Portfolio of Current Modernization Work," *Architectural Forum* 70 (February 1939): 94–95. On the changing character of Fifth Avenue, see Max Page, *The Creative Destruction of Manhattan, 1900–1940* (Chicago: University of Chicago Press, 1999), esp. chap. 2.

28. Frank E. Landau, "Childs Remodels 25 Units in Drive for Modernization," *Chain Store Age*, April 1935, 71–72; Lewis Mumford, "The Skyline: A Survivor of the Brown Decades," *New Yorker*, March 19, 1932, 71.

29. Landau, "Childs Remodels," 72.

30. Talbot Hamlin, "Some Restaurants and Recent Shops," *Pencil Points* 20 (August 1939): 485; Lewis Mumford, "The Skyline: Concerning Glass Houses," *New Yorker*, April 11, 1936, 58. Between 1937 and 1939, Sweet modernized two other Times Square Childs (Forty-ninth and Broadway, Forty-sixth and Broadway) as variations on the theme established here. See also Robert A. M. Stern et al., *New York 1930* (New York: Rizzoli, 1987), 275–79.

31. For the restaurant's projecting neon signs, Sweet utilized three different typefaces in three different colors: a French-inspired sans serif type in five-tube channel letters, the same type condensed in double-tube channels, and Childs' traditional script in a single tube (without channels).

32. Lyrics from the song "42nd Street" written by Al Dubin and Harry Warren, *42nd Street*, dir. Busby Berkeley, Warner Brothers, 1933.

33. Quoted in Landau, "Childs Remodels," 71.

34. George Nelson, foreword to Emrich Nicholson, *Contemporary Shops in the United States* (New York: Architectural Book Publishing, 1945), 5–9.

35. Lewis Mumford, "The Sky Line: Old and New," *New Yorker*, January 11, 1936, 42. On Ginsbern's work for Hanscom, see "Portfolio," *Architectural Forum* 61 (September 1934): 166–67; and "The Trend in Store Fronts," *Chain Store Age*, November 1934,

83–84. The original drawings are in the Horace Ginsbern Collection (1989.005), Avery Archives, Columbia University [numbers A101.09–10, A101.12–14, A102.15].

36. FHA, *Modernization Credit Plan, Bulletin No. 1* (Washington, DC: GPO, 1934), 3.

37. James Moffett, "Address Broadcast over NBC at Radio City," FHA press release no. 110, November 11, 1934, 1; Moffett, "Better Housing Campaign Rally in Los Angeles," FHA press release no. 192, January 31, 1935, 1 [NA RG 287, box y749].

38. Though the FSA photographers did train their lenses on the commercial landscapes of Main Street, buildings and storefronts usually served as a backdrop to the action on the street. See "America from the Great Depression to World War II," *Photographs from the FSA-OWI, 1939–1945,* American Memory/Library of Congress, http://memory.loc.gov/ammem/fsowhome.html.

39. John Tagg defined such a currency as "an objective social validity." See John Tagg, "The Currency of the Photograph," in *The Burden of Representation: Essays on Photographies and Histories* (Amherst: University of Massachusetts Press, 1988), 163.

40. Moffett, "Better Housing Campaign Rally in Los Angeles," 1.

41. Karal Ann Marling, *Wall-to-Wall America* (Minneapolis: University of Minnesota, 1982).

42. C. B. Louden, "Review of Alteration Trends," *Real Estate Record,* October 1935, 6.

43. *FHA Promotion Pointers* 1, no.13 (1935); "Real Money Getting Busy," *Better Housing,* September 20, 1934, 3.

44. Robert S. Lynd and Helen Merrell Lynd, *Middletown in Transition: A Study in Cultural Conflicts* (New York: Harcourt, Brace & World, 1937), 7, 120, 471.

45. Marshall Berman, *All That Is Solid Melts into Air* (1982; repr., New York: Penguin, 1988), 288.

46. Lynd and Lynd, *Middletown in Transition,* 296.

47. Terry Smith, *Making the Modern* (Chicago: University of Chicago Press, 1993), 311. See also Marchand, *Advertising the American Dream,* 261–62.

48. In *Only Yesterday* Frederick Lewis Allen observed a changed social outlook after 1929 that was reflected in all manner of fashion and style. More recently Kristina Wilson documented a similar attitude among designers and critics in the early 1930s, when they specifically rejected art deco for its earlier associations. See Frederick Lewis Allen, *Only Yesterday* (1931; repr., New York: Harper & Row, 1964); and Kristina Wilson, *Livable Modernism: Interior Decorating and Design During the Great Depression* (New Haven, CT: Yale University Press, 2004), 8.

49. Richard Guy Wilson, "International Style: The MoMA Exhibition," *Progressive Architecture* 63 (February 1982): 97; David Gebhard, "The Moderne in the U.S. 1920–1941," *Architectural Association Quarterly* 2 (January 1970): 5. On the ideological divisiveness that frequently accompanied these distinct modernisms, see Richard Striner, "Art Deco: Polemics and Synthesis," *Winterthur Portfolio* 25 (Spring 1990): 21–34.

50. George Howe, "What Is This Modern Architecture Trying to Express?" *American Architect* 137 (May 1930): 22–25, 106, 108.

51. Catherine Bauer, *Modern Housing* (Boston: Houghton Mifflin, 1934).

52. See Frederick Kiesler, *Contemporary Art Applied to the Store and Its Display* (New York: Brentano's, 1930); Adolf Schuhmacher, *Ladenbau* (Stuttgart: Julius Hoffman, 1934); and "Retail Store Planning," *Architectural Record* 78 (July 1935): 49–71.

53. Arthur F. Woltersdorf, "Carnival Architecture," *American Architect* 143 (July 1933): 10; R. L. Duffus, "The Fair: A World of Tomorrow," *New York Times Magazine*, May 28, 1933, 2.

54. Philip Johnson, "The Architectural Exhibition for the Museum of Modern Art in 1932: A Confidential Statement," dated February 10, 1931, 2–3. Registrar Exhibition Files, Exhibition #15, Philip Johnson Correspondence Files, Museum of Modern Art Archives.

55. "Itinerary Architectural Exhibition with Models" and "Itinerary Photography Exhibition of Modern Architecture." Program, Checklist, Model Information Folder, Registrar Exhibition Files, Exhibition #15, Philip Johnson Correspondence Files, Museum of Modern Art Archives.

56. "Exhibition Checklist," Program, Checklist, Model Information Folder, Registrar Exhibition Files, Exhibition #15, Philip Johnson Correspondence Files, Museum of Modern Art Archives.

57. J. André Fouilhoux et al., "Jury Report for Modernize Main Street Competition," in LOF, *52 Designs*, 2–6.

58. LOF, *52 Designs*, 8, 23.

59. Fouilhoux et al., "Jury Report," 2.

60. This, according to Henry-Russell Hitchcock in 1951, who credited William Wurster with the term's coinage. See Hitchcock, "The International Style Twenty Years After," in *Architecture Culture, 1943–1968*, ed. Joan Ockman (New York: Rizzoli, 1993), 139.

61. Kenneth K. Stowell, "The International Style," *Architectural Forum* 56 (March 1932): 253; Kenneth K. Stowell, *Modernizing Buildings for Profit* (New York: Prentice-Hall, 1935), 12; Republic Steel Corporation, "Store Fronts of Enduro," *Sweet's Catalogue File* (1937), sec. 16, cat. 10, p. 10.

62. This is not to imply that store designers were following Hitchcock and Johnson's specifications, but rather is an attempt to demonstrate the compelling similarities between their ideal and the Main Street reality.

63. Henry-Russell Hitchcock and Philip Johnson, *The International Style* (1932; repr., New York: Norton, 1966), 45, 76, 50–52.

64. Ibid., 65, 76.

65. "Where Is Modern Now?" *Architectural Forum* 68 (June 1938): 467.

66. Mumford, "The Sky Line: New Facades," 85.

67. Lewis Mumford, *Sticks & Stones: A Study of American Architecture and Civilization* (1924; repr., New York: Dover, 1955), 83.

68. Ibid., 83.

69. Ibid., 100.

70. Ibid., 92.

71. Lapidus, "Store Design, 113.

72. "Our Home Builders Service Designs a Modern House," *House Beautiful*, January 1930, 80; cited in Rosemarie Haag Bletter, "The World of Tomorrow: The Future with a Past," in *High Styles: Twentieth-Century American Design* (New York: Whitney Museum of Art, 1985), 87.

73. "Stores," *Architectural Forum* 71 (December 1939): 427.

74. "Main Street, U.S.A.," 86.

75. FHA, "Talk for General Audience," in *Portfolio of Radio Publicity*, 1.

76. Here I am paraphrasing Terry Smith's discussion of industrial design and advertising. See Smith, *Making the Modern*, 357.

Chapter 6

1. See "War Board's Building Conservation Order," *American Builder and Building Age*, May 1942, 39–41.

2. Morris Lapidus, "Store Modernizing without Metals," *Architectural Record* 92 (October 1942): 71.

3. By 1943 the government had insured $1.7 billion of modernization credit. According to the FHA, this base figure represented only a fraction of the total amount spent on modernization since it did not include work paid for in cash or financed by non-MCP means. According to the FHA's Division of Economics and Statistics (and corroborated by data of the F.W. Dodge Corporation), such work amounted to between four and seven times greater than the face value of the notes insured. This meant that cash and non-MCP modernization work stood somewhere between $6.8 and $11.9 billion by 1943, bringing the estimated total of *all* modernization work to between $8.5 and $13.6 billion. Of this figure, approximately half ($4.25–$6.8 billion) was spent on commercial building improvements. See FHA, *9th Annual Report* (Washington, DC: GPO, 1944), 1. Calculations on the amount of modernization work generated or "developed" by the MCP appear in most FHA annual reports. See FHA, *First Annual Report* (Washington, DC: GPO, 1935), 1; and FHA, *Third Annual Report* (Washington, DC: GPO, 1937), i.

4. "Main Street, U.S.A.," *Architectural Forum* 70 (February 1939): 75. In the 1930s Reading was Pennsylvania's fifth largest city. See 1930 Census data tabulated in FHA, Division of Research and Statistics, *General Economic Data, Volume A*, 1934–35 [NA RG 207, Records of Housing and Home Finance Agencies, vol. 1].

5. Chamber of Commerce, "Reading, PA," *Boyd's Reading City Directory* (New York: R. L. Polk, 1939), 10. Reading was founded in 1748 by sons of William Penn and settled by Pennsylvania Germans in the late eighteen and early nineteenth centuries.

6. Chamber of Commerce, "Reading, PA," 10. In 1908 Reading's leading citizens formed a civic improvement association that raised enough money through subscription ($3,300) to hire planner John Nolen to "come here and tell us what Reading needed and how it should be developed." Quoted in *Reading Old and New* (1909), reprinted in George M. Meiser and Gloria J. Meiser, *The Passing Scene*, vol. 7 (Reading, PA: Historical Society of Berks County, 1991), 113.

7. "Earle Pledges 'Main Street' Government," *Reading Eagle*, October 3, 1934, 10.

8. These firms included Reading Hardware Company, Penn Hardware Company, Reading Terra Cotta and Brick Works, and Keystone Iron Works. The hosiery mills suffered a notorious wildcat strike in 1931. See Colin Gordon, *New Deals: Business, Labor, and Politics in America, 1920–1935* (Cambridge: Cambridge University Press, 1994), 104. For statistics on Reading industries in the 1930s, see Chamber of Commerce, "Reading, PA," 9–11.

9. "Unemployed Ordered to Quit Depressionville," *Reading Eagle*, July 23, 1934, 11.

10. See Keystone Meat Market advertisement, *Reading Eagle*, July 6, 1934, 6.

11. B&J Saylor advertisement, *Reading Eagle*, September 5, 1934, 8.

12. Figures cited in "Where the Chains Stand," *Chain Store Age*, January 1932, 7. Woolworth's opened in 1883 at 530 Penn; Kresge's in 1920 at 648 Penn. By 1939 only

one independent five-and-dime remained open on Penn Street, that of George Neizel at number 542. See Chamber of Commerce, *Boyd's Reading City Directory*, 1059.

13. W.T. Grant's modernization program in Reading and across the country can be tracked by examining the "Chain Store Expansion and Construction" listing that appeared in every issue of *Chain Store Age* in the 1930s.

14. On Thom McAn's modernization program, see Frank E. Landau, "Keeping Melville Stores Up-to-Date Is Standard Practice," *Chain Store Age*, November 1932, 654–55; and "Melville Remodels 100 Stores," *Chain Store Age*, November 1934, 97–98.

15. This was one of six storefronts he executed for the Beck's shoe chain. See Horace Ginsbern Collection (1989.005), Avery Archives, Columbia University [numbers A101.11, A37A.03–05].

16. Though once heralded as "one of the staunchest and most important banking institutions in Reading," Penn National fell victim to Depression-induced insolvency. Quoted in *Reading Old and New*, 147.

17. Cited in George M. Meiser and Gloria J. Meiser, *The Passing Scene*, vol. 6 (Reading, PA: Historical Society of Berks County, 1988), 104; and Meiser and Meiser, *The Passing Scene*, vol. 7, 108.

18. See full-page advertisement in *Reading Eagle*, October 8, 1934, 15; and "City Joyous as Bank Opens," *Reading Eagle*, October 8, 1934, 1.

19. "NRA Code Eagles Received Here," *Reading Eagle*, July 24, 1932, 2.

20. "Housing Chief Outlines Aims," *Reading Eagle*, July 8, 1934, 1.

21. City Bank & Trust Company of Reading advertisement, *Reading Eagle*, July 14, 1934, 3; Pomeroy's Department Store advertisement, *Reading Eagle*, July 20, 1934, 5.

22. "Housing Drive Purposes Told," *Reading Eagle*, October 14, 1934, 8; "Housing Drive Planned," *Reading Eagle*, October 19, 1934, 20.

23. On the Reading BHP, see "News from the Front," *Better Housing*, November 30, 1934, 5.

24. "Permits Show Work Increase," *Reading Eagle*, September 2, 1934, 18; "Building Work Jumps $11,190," *Reading Eagle*, September 4, 1934, 7. The number of repair permits increased to sixty-two from thirty-nine for the same period in 1933.

25. "City to Cooperate in Housing Drive," *Reading Eagle*, October 19, 1934, 17.

26. "Survey Lists Apartments," *Reading Eagle*, September 2, 1934, 2.

27. "Consider Survey before Better Housing Campaign," *Reading Eagle*, September 10, 1934, 13; "Mayor Urges Housing Drive," *Reading Eagle*, November 2, 1934, 1.

28. "Housing Drive Purposes Told," 8.

29. "Housing Drive Survey Starts," *Reading Eagle*, November 6, 1934, 3; "Housing Drive Shows Results," *Reading Eagle*, November 9, 1934, 21.

30. "Dechant Shows Repair Values," *Reading Eagle*, November 7, 1934, 2.

31. These figures assume that FHA estimates concerning the eventual value of MCP pump-priming were correct. Loan totals are cited in entries #341 and #950, FHA, "Confidential Report: National Housing Act—Title I Financial Institutions Which Had Reported 25 or More Insured Modernization Loans or Notes Purchased as of 29 June 1935" [NA RG 287, box y740]. The two financial institutions were the Berks County Trust Company and the Reading Trust Company.

32. See, for example, A&P advertisement, *Reading Eagle*, July 6, 1934, 22.

33. FHA, "Talk for Merchants," *Portfolio of Radio Publicity* (Washington, DC: GPO, 1934).

34. See *Reading Old and New.*

35. See Meiser and Meiser, *The Passing Scene*, vol. 7, 256, 263.

36. On the psychology of vestibule design, see Morris Lapidus, "Basic Plans and Profiles of Store Front Construction," *Architectural Forum* 63 (July 1935): 53.

37. For specifications, see LOF, *Vitrolite Photo Album*, plate no. 1230 [LOF MSS-066].

38. Signs for Tri-Plex (520 Penn) and Lobel's (518 Penn) are visible as reflections in the night view of Iacone's store.

39. Chamber of Commerce, *Boyd's Reading City Directory*, 10.

40. The original Boscov store was called Economy Shoe and Dry Goods. See ibid., 195. See also "About Boscov's," Boscov's Department Store, 2000–2005, http://www.boscovs.com/static/about_boscov/history.html. Today Boscov's is the largest privately owned department store chain in the country, with stores across the Mid-Atlantic region.

41. Others stayed put, including Ludens, Inc., now a division of Hershey Foods, which has made candies and cough drops at a factory at Eighth and Walnut streets since 1900. Ironically, when the Vanity Fair factory closed, it also signaled a shift to the post-industrial economy. The VF Corporation, which began in Reading in 1899 as a manufacturer of gloves and mittens and soon became a leading producer of undergarments, relocated its factories and corporate headquarters to Tennessee in the late 1960s. But in 1970 it opened a factory outlet in one of its abandoned mill buildings just west of downtown Reading. Today Vanity Fair operates an outlet mall spread throughout its former manufacturing complex that has given a much-needed boost to Reading's economy, though it has not had much of an impact on merchants in the historic core at Penn Square.

42. On Lyndon Johnson's Model Cities program, see Robert Halpern, *Rebuilding the Inner City* (New York: Columbia University Press, 1995), 124.

43. John Graham was the architect of the Penn Mall; a rendering is reproduced in Meiser and Meiser, *The Passing Scene*, vol. 7, 17.

44. For a brief discussion of the pedestrian mall, see "About BARTA," Berks Area Reading Transportation Authority, http://www.bartabus.com/about.htm. On pedestrianization, see Kent A. Robertson, "Downtown Retail Revitalization: A Review of American Development Strategies," *Planning Perspectives* 12 (1997) 383–401. On the Gruen effect, see M. Jeff Hardwick, *Mall Maker: Victor Gruen, Architect of an American Dream* (Philadelphia: University of Pennsylvania Press, 2004), 2, 8.

45. Robert Venturi, *Complexity and Contradiction in Architecture* (New York: Museum of Modern Art, 1966), 104. See also Jane Jacobs, *The Death and Life of Great American Cities* (1961; repr., New York: Vintage Books, 1989).

46. Today the Callowhill Historic District, as it is known, is bounded by Fourth and Sixth streets and Buttonwood and Laurel streets and encompasses twenty-two city blocks. See "Pennsylvania at Risk 1995," Preservation Pennsylvania, 2005, http://www.preservationpa.org/files/publications/Risk95.htm.

47. The Downtown Improvement District was founded in 1995. See "History" and "DID Projects," Reading Downtown Improvement District, http://downtownreading.com. See also City of Reading, *Welcome to Reading: A Neighborhood Resource Guide*, 2005, 33–37.

48. The trust's involvement with Main Street began with a series of demonstration projects in the late 1970s. "The Main Street Four-Point Approach to Commercial District Revitalization," National Trust Main Street Center, National Trust for Historic Preservation, 2004, http://www.mainstreet.org.

49. The National Trust makes a distinction between storefronts of the 1930s and those modernized in the 1950s and 1960s. These later modernizations are described as well-meaning but ineffective since they did nothing to halt decline but only "covered over architectural features." See "History of the National Trust Main Street Center" and "America's Main Streets." National Trust Main Street Center, National Trust for Historic Preservation, 2004, http://www.mainstreet.org. On guidelines for preserving historic storefronts, see "Exterior Features: Storefronts," *The Secretary of the Interior's Standards for the Treatment of Historic Properties with Guidelines for Preserving, Rehabilitating, Restoring and Reconstructing Historic Buildings,* National Park Service, 2001, http://www.cr.nps.gov/hps/tps/standguide/credits.htm.